D0897676

THE GREAT DEMOGRAPHIC ILLUSION

The Great Demographic Illusion

Majority, Minority, and the Expanding American Mainstream

Richard Alba

PRINCETON UNIVERSITY PRESS
PRINCETON AND OXFORD

Copyright © 2020 by Princeton University Press

Requests for permission to reproduce material from this work
should be sent to permissions@press.princeton.edu

Published by Princeton University Press
41 William Street, Princeton, New Jersey 08540
6 Oxford Street, Woodstock, Oxfordshire OX20 1TR

press.princeton.edu

Epigraph is from "In Front of Your Nose." In *In Front of Your Nose,
1945–1950: The Collected Essays, Journalism and Letters of George Orwell*,
Volume 4, edited by Sonia Orwell and Ian Angus. Harcourt, 1971.
Reprinted by permission by Literary Executor for George Orwell.

The excerpt appearing in chapter 6 from Richard Alba and Jan Willem Duyvendak,
"What about the mainstream? Assimilation in super-diverse times," *Ethnic and
Racial Studies*, Jan. 2019, is reprinted by permission of Taylor and Francis Ltd.

All Rights Reserved

Library of Congress Cataloging-in-Publication Data

Names: Alba, Richard D., author.
Title: The great demographic illusion : majority, minority, and the
    expanding American mainstream / Richard Alba.
Description: Princeton : Princeton University Press, [2020] | Includes bibliographical
    references and index. | Summary: "A book that examines the growing population
    of mixed minority-white backgrounds and society"—Provided by publisher.
Identifiers: LCCN 2020012702 (print) | LCCN 2020012703 (ebook) | ISBN 9780691201634
    (hardcover ; alk. paper) | ISBN 9780691206219 (paperback) | ISBN 9780691202112 (ebook)
Subjects: LCSH: Ethnic groups—United States. | Racially mixed people—United States. |
    Minorities—United States. | Majorities. | United States—Population—History—21st century.
Classification: LCC E184.A1 .A453 2020 (print) | LCC E184.A1 (ebook) | DDC 305.800973—dc23
LC record available at https://lccn.loc.gov/2020012702
LC ebook record available at https://lccn.loc.gov/2020012703

British Library Cataloging-in-Publication Data is available

Editorial: Meagan Levinson and Jacqueline Delaney
Production Editorial: Leslie Grundfest
Jacket/Cover Design: Karl Spurzem
Production: Erin Suydam
Publicity: Kate Hensley
Copyeditor: Cynthia Buck

Jacket/Cover Credit: Zoonar GmbH/Alamy Stock Photo

This book has been composed in Adobe Text and Gotham

Printed on acid-free paper. ∞

Printed in the United States of America

10 9 8 7 6 5 4 3 2 1

To see what is in front of one's nose needs a constant struggle.

—GEORGE ORWELL, "IN FRONT OF YOUR NOSE" (1946)

Eppur si muove. (And yet it moves.)

—ATTRIBUTED TO GALILEO

For the next generations:
Sarah, Michael, and Jessica Alba,
Cyrus Alba,
and
Oscar and Marcus Ter Schure

And for my great love, Gwen

CONTENTS

ACKNOWLEDGMENTS

"No man is an island, entire of itself," wrote the great English meta-physical poet John Donne. Likewise, one could say that no author (of nonfiction, at least) writes alone, regardless of what the title page says.

Based on ideas I have pursued for decades, this book has been enriched by many exchanges and collaborations over the years with a community of other scholars, including Paul Attewell, Maurice Crul, Nancy Foner, Herb Gans, Phil Kasinitz, Frans Lelie, Douglas Massey, John Mollenkopf, Ann Morning, Dowell Myers, Victor Nee, Jeff Reitz, Roxane Silberman, Mary Waters, and now Van Tran, whom I can happily call a departmental colleague. Nancy, Phil, Jeff, and Van read the entire manuscript and provided numerous helpful suggestions. John and Mary read some key chapters and did the same.

Many other colleagues and friends read all or part of the book in a developmental stage. Jan Willem Duyvendak, Todd Gitlin, and Michael Olneck read the complete version, as did John Iceland and Dowell Myers on behalf of the Press. Tomás Jiménez and Victor Ray read portions. At the Census Bureau, Eric Jensen, Nicholas Jones, Kimberly Mehlman Orozco, and their colleagues in the Expert Group on Racial Diversity at the Population Division gave me a detailed set of comments on the chapters most concerned with demographic data issues. I am grateful for the many suggestions from all of these readers.

Paul Starr and Ken Prewitt played critical roles in the germination of the project. At an early stage, when my ideas were focused mainly on census data problems and their implications for the majority-minority conception of the future, Paul invited me after a talk at Princeton to write an article about the issues for *The American*

Prospect. He then solicited and published comments from several social scientists, among them Ken, a distinguished political scientist who is also a former Census Bureau director.

Ken and I subsequently formed a partnership to advance the discussion, and we organized a conference to that end. That conference was held in December 2016 at the Russell Sage Foundation, with its support, and resulted in an issue of the *Annals of the American Academy of Political and Social Science* entitled "What Census Data Miss about American Diversity" (May 2018). I am very grateful to Sheldon Danziger, the foundation's president, for this support, and to Aixa Cintrón-Vélez, program director, and Leana Chatrath, a senior program officer, for their efforts to bring the conference about. The participants in the conference included many prominent demographers and social scientists, who contributed numerous insights about improvements that could be made to our demographic data system; the Census Bureau professionals who attended, along with Katherine Wallman, then the chief statistician of the United States, enriched the conversation afterwards. Thomas Kecskemethy played a vital role in shepherding the conference papers into a first-rate volume, whose papers are repeatedly cited in this book.

I owe a special debt to the professionals of the Census Bureau. There is no way to make the argument of this book without confronting the flaws in our current demographic data system and the part they play in the distorted picture that Americans receive of ethnoracial change in the nation. Inevitably, and despite my best efforts to depict the constraints under which the Census Bureau operates, an account of these flaws reads as criticism of the bureau's practices. Yet I have consistently found the professionals there to be cordial, willing to listen, and helpful, and I have great respect for the work they do. Especially critical for the development of my thinking was a multiple-day visit to the bureau in 2018 as part of its "Summer at Census" program. Eric Jensen, Nicholas Jones, and Roberto Ramirez were important conversation partners at that time. During the visit, Larry Sink made me aware of the utility of birth certificate data, and he, along with Aliya Saperstein of Stanford University, steered me away from potential problems in using them. My talk to a bureau audience during my visit provided vital reassurance that I was on the right course.

Of the other talks I have given based on materials that appear in this book, the most memorable took place before a home audience, at the CUNY Institute for Demographic Research. There, some good friends, Deborah Balk and Ann Morning, engaged me in an intense conversation afterwards. They convinced me to reassess how I was presenting the role of the Census Bureau.

I consistently found colleagues willing to take extra steps to assist me as I assembled the evidence presented here. Nathaniel Kang of the Higher Education Research Institute of UCLA made the parental ethno-racial origin data from the 2001–2003 freshman survey available to me. Brian Duncan generated some data I requested from the Current Population Survey analysis he and Steve Trejo carried out (discussed in chapter 5). Lauren Medina of the Census Bureau found some early reports based on population projections. At the Pew Research Center, Mark Hugo Lopez ran some tables from the "Hispanic Identity" data, and Anna Brown generously made available the data to create the intermarriage trend graph that appears in chapter 4. I thank D'Vera Cohn for serving as a liaison to other Pew professionals. Joseph Pereira of the CUNY Center for Urban Research was a key resource for demographic data preparation at an early stage of the project. My cousin Stephen Sanacore was my informant for valuable insights about the Uniondale Volunteer Fire Department.

I've had lots of help from students as I prepared this book. Brenden Beck, Guillermo Yrizar Barbosa, and Duygu Basaran Sahin helped me with some of the data analyses that appear here. Michelle Cannon and Cristine Khan helped in the creation of the graphic presentations of data. I am grateful to Cristine for her willingness to tackle the challenge of learning Adobe Illustrator.

Finally, I am delighted to be publishing again with Princeton University Press. Meagan Levinson is the paragon of an academic editor. I owe a debt to my dear friend Mitch Duneier for bringing us together. It has been a pleasure to work with the other members of the PUP team for this book: Jacqueline Delaney; Leslie Grundfest and Karen Carter, production editors; and Cynthia Buck, the copyeditor.

THE GREAT DEMOGRAPHIC ILLUSION

1

Introduction

THE NARRATIVE OF THE MAJORITY-MINORITY SOCIETY

Many Americans believe that their society is on the precipice of a momentous transformation, brought about by the inevitable demographic slide of the white population into numerical minority status and the consequent ascent of a new majority made up of nonwhites. The large-scale immigration of the last half-century is a major driver of current demographic change, as is the aging of the white population. Should it occur, the transformation to what is often called a "majority-minority" society—one in which today's ethno-racial minorities (African Americans, Asians, Hispanics, and Native Americans)* together will constitute a majority of

---

*I generally use the term "ethno-racial" to refer to the distinctions that Americans commonly make among the big five origin categories: white (non-Hispanic presumed), Hispanic or Latine, African American or black, Asian, and American Indian (in order of size). I do so for two reasons. First, the Hispanic group, the second-largest ethno-racial population in the United States, is only partially identifiable on the basis of racial distinctiveness, and ethnic characteristics, such as names, language, and countries of origin, are required to complete its identification. Second, ethnicity and race are concepts on a spectrum, with a murky

the population—is presumed to entail profound and wide-ranging effects. These could range from its impact on the distribution of political power to a rising prominence of minority experiences in cultural domains like the movies.

For many whites, the current narrative about ineluctable demographic shift, ending in their minority status, congeals into a threatening vision about their place in America. At the extreme, their uneasiness about the future takes the form of what the *New York Times* columnist Charles Blow has described as "white extinction anxiety" and propels them into the embrace of white nationalism.[1] Political scientists who have analyzed the forces behind the startling and unanticipated 2016 election of Donald Trump as president argue that white "racial resentment," stoked in part by the anxiety over massive demographic change and its implications for whites, was the most consequential among them. For many minority Americans, the same perception engenders optimism about the future and a hope that they will see the mainstream better reflect their group and its experiences.

Demographic data are playing a remarkable role in these developments. It is in fact rare for demographic data to receive so much

---

boundary between them. What seems like a racial distinction at one historical moment can evolve into an ethnic one at another.

I also abbreviate the complexity of some of these categories for purposes of exposition. By the definitions that the Census Bureau is required to use, the white category includes individuals whose family origins trace back to the Middle East or North Africa as well as to Europe; the American Indian category includes the native peoples of Alaska; and there is a separate Native Hawaiian and Other Pacific Islander category, which I do not consider because of its small size (0.4 percent of the population). For clarification of these categories, see Office of Management and Budget 1997.

One other terminological note: I use "Hispanic" and "Latine" as equivalent ways of referring to the population of groups with origins in Latin America. I have selected the latter term as an acceptable way to avoid the masculine implication of the gendered term "Latino." This solution originates with a movement in Latin America to diminish gendered language, and it is therefore linguistically consistent with a Romance language. Moreover, it does not have the vocal and orthographic awkwardness of another solution, "Latinx," now common in North American academia.

public attention. Announcements by the Census Bureau, such as the 2015 press release reporting that the majority of children under the age of five are no longer white (according, I have to add, to the narrow definition of "white" employed by the census), receive wide publicity and are greeted with headlines such as "It's Official: The US Is Becoming a Minority-Majority Nation" (this one in *US News & World Report*).[2] When the Public Religion Research Institute conducted its annual American Values Survey in 2018, it asked a representative sample of Americans:

> As you may know, US Census projections show that by 2045, African Americans, Latinos, Asians, and other mixed racial and ethnic groups will together be a majority of the population. Do you think the likely impact of this coming demographic change will be mostly positive or mostly negative?

Only a small percentage of respondents (4 percent) were unable to respond. The vast majority, in other words, were familiar enough with the idea to have an opinion, which incidentally was positive in the majority (except among whites, who were evenly divided).[3]

Yet there are powerful reasons to be skeptical about this demographic imagining of the present and the near future: it assumes a rigidity to racial and ethnic boundaries that has not been characteristic of the American experience with immigration. As a nation, we have been here before. A century ago, when immigration from southern and eastern Europe was at its zenith, bringing masses of southern Italian and Polish Catholics and eastern European Jews to Ellis Island, there was a spasm of near-hysteria in the white Protestant elite about the superior racial characteristics of native white Americans being submerged by the numbers and fertility of these inferiors. Reflecting ideas about eugenics widely discussed at the time, the patrician New Yorker Madison Grant wrote *The Passing of the Great Race* (1916), decrying the pernicious racial impact of the new immigrants on what he viewed as America's native Nordic stock. The introduction of IQ testing shortly before World War I seemed to confirm the inferiority of the new immigrants, many of whom appeared to be intellectually deficient.[4] Yet the national decline anticipated from the immigration of newcomers, who were held to be racially unlike established white Americans, failed to materialize.

The rigidity of ethno-racial lines is already being challenged by a robust development that is largely unheralded: a surge in the number of young Americans who come from mixed majority-minority families and have one white parent and one nonwhite or Hispanic parent. Today more than 10 percent of all babies born in the United States are of such mixed parentage; this proportion is well above the number of Asian-only children and not far below the number of black-only infants. This surge is a by-product of a rapid rise in the extent of ethno-racial mixing in families. What makes this phenomenon new is the social recognition now accorded to mixed ethno-racial origins as an independent status, rather than one that must be amalgamated to one group or another.

The book uses the rise of mixed backgrounds that span the minority-white divide as a lens through which to scrutinize and challenge the idea of an inevitable majority-minority society, envisioned by many Americans as one cleaved into two distinct parts with opposing interests, experiences, and viewpoints. As a first step, I show the crucial significance of the mixed group for census data that appear to herald a minority status for whites. Census ethno-racial classifications do not deal appropriately with mixed minority-white backgrounds. There is an interesting story behind this failure, which the book will tell. But the bottom line is this: for the critical public presentations of data, the Census Bureau classifies individuals who are reported as having both white and nonwhite ancestries as *not* white; my analyses for the book show that the great majority of all mixed Americans are therefore added to the minority side of the ledger. This classification decision has a profound effect on public perceptions of demographic change, but it does not correspond with the social realities of the lives of most mixed individuals, who are integrated with whites at least as much as with minorities. The census data thus distort contemporary ethno-racial changes by accelerating the decline of the white population and presenting as certain something that is no more than speculative—a future situation when the summed counts of the American Indian, Asian, black, and Latine categories exceed the count of whites.

The reasons to be concerned about the widespread belief in a majority-minority future go far beyond demographic accuracy. The political impact has already been cited. Of broader significance is the role of the "majority-minority society" as a *narrative*: an account— often abbreviated in common understanding—about the ethno-racial changes taking place now and in the near future that shapes our perceptions of them and determines our fundamental understanding of American society and of its evolution in an era of large-scale immigration. The narrative most widely believed about the immigration past, overwhelmingly European in origin, is that the descendants of the immigrants were absorbed into the mainstream society, despite initial experiences of exclusion, discrimination, and denigration for alleged inferiority. This is an assimilation story. That narrative now collides with the perception, nourished by the majority-minority concept, of a stark and deep-seated cleavage between the currently dominant white majority and nonwhite minorities. That perception feeds a different narrative: that a contest along ethno-racial lines for social power (taking that term in its broadest sense) is intensifying. This collision of narratives in the public sphere is mirrored in academic debate—between the adherents of race theory (or critical race theory), currently the dominant perspective at American universities, and those who view ethnicity and race as more malleable and potentially reshaped by assimilatory processes.

The book addresses the conflict between these narratives. And by combining key ideas from apparently conflicting social-science theories, it seeks a more nuanced understanding of American society in the early twenty-first century. (The time span I have in mind extends to midcentury; past that point, too many unanticipated changes are likely to have taken place, clouding anyone's ability to envision their cumulative impact.) Race theory, which has been mostly tested on the African American experience and is most relevant to groups that have been incorporated into American society by conquest, colonization, or enslavement, is in fact applicable to the new forms of ethno-racial mixing: I show evidence that individuals with black and white parentage have a very different experience from other mixed persons and identify more strongly with the minority side of their backgrounds. However, many other mixed majority-minority Americans have everyday experiences, socioeconomic locations, social affiliations, and identities that do not resemble those of minorities. On the whole, these individuals occupy a liminal "in between," but their social mobility and social integration with whites are indicative of an assimilation trajectory into the societal mainstream. In arriving at this conclusion, the book synthesizes new data analyses, based on such data sources as the American Community Survey and public use files of birth certificates, with the research record, both qualitative and quantitative, concerning individuals with mixed ethno-racial origins.

To understand better the larger significance of the growing subpopulation with mixed minority-white backgrounds, the book revisits assimilation theory. Important for my argument is the twenty-first-century version of the theory, which envisions assimilation as a process of integrating into the mainstream society instead of joining the white group. This new version does not require erasure of all signs of ethno-racial origin.[5] The mainstream—which is constituted by institutions, social milieus, and cultural spheres where the dominant group, whites at this moment in history, feels "at home"—is not closed off against others. Just as the white Protestant mainstream that prevailed from colonial times until the middle of the twentieth century evolved through the mass assimilation of Catholic and Jewish ethnics after World War II, the racially defined mainstream of today is changing, at least in some parts of the country, as a result of the inclusion of many nonwhite and mixed Americans.

As this discussion suggests, the theoretical exposition of mainstream assimilation must be coupled with a close examination of the assimilation past, especially the period of mass assimilation following the end of World War II. The justification for this examination is not the mistaken belief that assimilation today will replicate the patterns of the past, but rather the need to correct ideas about assimilation that have become distorted by one-dimensional understandings of that period as well as by the rhetorical tropes of anti-assimilation theorizing. A deeper understanding reveals clues about what to look for in the present and what to expect in the near future.

The currently widespread understanding of white ethnic assimilation is racial in nature: the ethnics were assimilated when they were accepted as full-fledged whites.[6] This understanding depicts assimilation into the mainstream as a homogenizing process. However, it is more accurate, I argue, to view the white ethnics' assimilation as diversifying the mainstream because, before the middle of the last century, religion had been a basis for the exclusion of Catholic and Jewish ethnics from a white Protestant mainstream; mass assimilation was accompanied by the acceptance of Judaism (in its non-ultra-Orthodox forms) and Catholicism as mainstream religions alongside Protestantism. The post-1945 mainstream society redefined itself as Judeo-Christian. We should understand the assimilation of today therefore as neither inherently excluding the descendants of the newest immigrants because they cannot become white nor requiring them to present themselves as if they were white. Instead, the mainstream can expand to accept a visible degree of racial diversity, as long as the shared understandings between individuals with different ethno-racial backgrounds are sufficient to allow them to interact comfortably. In this way, increasing participation in the mainstream society is associated with "decategorization," in the sense that the relationships among individuals in the mainstream are not primarily determined by categorical differences in ethno-racial membership. In colloquial terms, they treat each other by and large as individuals rather than as members of distinct ethno-racial groups.

My argument is that, for the most part, the new, or twenty-first-century, phenomenon of mixed minority-majority backgrounds is a sign of growing integration into the mainstream by substantial portions of the new immigrant groups, especially individuals with Asian and Hispanic origins. The mainstream integration of mixed individuals is signaled by such indicators as their high rates of marriage to whites. But of course, it is not simply the children from mixed families who are integrating; many of the nonwhite parents are doing so as well, and as will be shown, they are often settling with their families in integrated neighborhoods, where many whites are also present. The mainstream does appear to be expanding and becoming more diverse, and the implications are potentially quite consequential. However, the impact of racism on Americans who are visibly of African descent is also consequential, and racism presumably also affects some portions of other groups, such as dark-skinned Hispanics. In addition, the expanding role of legal exclusions condemns unauthorized immigrants to the margins of the society and hinders their children.[7]

What will the growing diversity in the mainstream mean for its definitional character? In the recent past and even today, the mainstream has been equated with whiteness. One scenario, compatible with race theory, sees the mainstream expansion as essentially a whitening process that will ultimately leave the mainstream defined as it is now. More plausible in my view is that the mainstream in the more diverse regions of the country will come to be—or maybe already has been—perceived in multiracial and multicultural terms, especially as prominent individuals in these regions are increasingly drawn from a visibly wide set of origins; in other regions, the mainstream will remain heavily white, at least in the near future. A multiracial character for the mainstream could further expand access, including additional space for African Americans. However, mainstream expansion today is also consistent with high levels of average inequality among groups and with the exclusion of many nonwhites. The growing assimilation of some nonwhites is no reason to settle into complacency about the need to promote greater equality and inclusion.

The relatively modest magnitude of mainstream assimilation today compared to the sweeping assimilation of the descendants of European immigrants in the decades following the end of World War II highlights the dependence of assimilation processes on large-scale features of the societal context, economic and demographic. I discuss these within the framework "non-zero-sum assimilation," a theory I develop concerning the mechanisms driving assimilation: social mobility, which produces parity with many individuals in the mainstream; the growth of amicable personal relationships with such individuals; and mainstream cultural change that elevates the moral worth of minority individuals. It is the first mechanism that is most constrained today. In the post–World War II period, when the United States was briefly the preeminent global economic power, higher education and the occupational sectors it fed were expanded enormously. This expansion engendered non-zero-sum mobility on a mass scale for the second and third generations descended from the immigrants with previously stigmatized origins, such as those from Ireland, southern Italy, Poland, and Russia. (A claim made throughout the book is that assimilation is more extensive under conditions of large-scale non-zero-sum mobility, when upward mobility by minority-group members does not require downward mobility by some in the majority.) In the early twenty-first century, when economic inequality is much greater than it was in the middle of the twentieth century, the basis for significant non-zero-sum mobility that favors minorities is demographic rather than economic: with the aging and retirement of a large number of older, well-placed white workers, there are not enough younger whites to replace them. This process will play out most intensely during the coming two decades as the last of the large, heavily white baby-boom cohorts age out of work and civic leadership and many individuals with minority family backgrounds, including mixed ones, replace them. But contemporary assimilation is more selective: its magnitude—the extent to which it involves all parts of minority groups—will not match that of the earlier period.

In the last part of the book, then, I examine social policies that could enhance mainstream expansion today and also extend the option to more African Americans and others affected by severe racism. Prominent among these policies are those addressing high and growing economic inequality in the United States. The underlying rationale is that inequality throws sand in the gears of social mobility. Policies to reduce inequality will broadly improve opportunities, including for African Americans, but they will not by themselves blunt the severe and systemic racism that is evident in the distinctive trajectory of mixed individuals with black ancestry. Reparations have become a prominent part of the public discussion for redressing black-white inequality, and they need to be considered.

In addition, no discussion of the situation of black Americans can avoid the unique burdens imposed on them and their communities by mass incarceration. Finally, the defective legal statuses of many in the immigrant population—primarily but not exclusively unauthorized status—need to be rectified because we know that they handicap the next generation, even those born in the United States.

This book is the culmination of a decades-long effort to reinvigorate assimilation ideas, which have been criticized extensively for a bias in favor of the experiences of white immigrants from Europe and their descendants, and to demonstrate their continuing importance to the American story.[8] I began in the 1970s and '80s, at a time when many commentators were arguing for the durability of the ethnicities that had crystallized out of the European immigration of the late nineteenth and early twentieth centuries. My examination of the Italian American experience and of the sociological significance of ethnic identities among whites (which appeared simultaneously with Mary Waters's influential and similarly argued *Ethnic Options*) showed assimilation to be occurring on a massive scale even as ethnic symbolism retained some vitality. My collaboration with Victor Nee that resulted in *Remaking the American Mainstream*, published in 2003, reworked assimilation thinking to make it relevant for an America that is rapidly becoming more ethno-racially diverse because of immigration. My 2009 book, *Blurring the Color Line*, pointed to mechanisms, especially the non-zero-sum mobility created by demographic shift, that would promote an important degree of assimilation for nonwhites.[9] The role of this book, then, is to produce the evidence that such assimilation is indeed taking place.

This demonstration of the continuing importance of assimilation patterns is intended to counter the imagined majority-minority future arising from the widely disseminated demographic data. This demographically inspired concept, which suggests a society riven along ethno-racial lines, stimulates perceptions of threat for many whites and contributes in this way to the very polarization it envisions. The argument of this book is not that whites will retain a numerical majority status, although I do not rule out such a possibility, but rather that mainstream expansion, which would meld many whites, nonwhites, and Hispanics, holds out the prospect of a new kind of societal majority.

The book is intended to unfold in a series of logically arranged steps, like the unpacking of nested Russian dolls, to arrive at new insights about ethno-racial change in America. It begins with a puzzle: why, after the election of our first African American president, did the electorate swing to the opposite extreme and elect Donald Trump? Chapter 2, which lays out what we have learned about the 2016 election, underscores the critical importance of demographic "imaginings" among Americans and hence of the narratives and data about ethno-racial shifts in the population. The Trump victory utterly confounded the pre-election predictions based on polling and gave rise to a raft of political-science research in search of an explanation. In examining that research, the chapter highlights the "racial resentments" and acute sense of vulnerability of working-class whites as the critical factors. This analysis is supported by recent social-psychological research, which shows whites generally adopting more conservative political stances when confronted with scenarios of future demographic shift. However, the social-psychological research also shows that the white anxieties behind conservative reactions can be assuaged, opening the way to a consideration of alternative narratives about the American present and future.

The third chapter addresses the question: how do Americans arrive at ideas about ethno-racial change in their society? The notion that whites will become a numerical minority has been around at least since President Bill Clinton, in a 1997 speech, claimed that this would happen in a half-century. But the pronouncements more recently of what I call our "demographic data system" have been critical to Americans' acceptance of this idea. It is certainly true that, in an era of large-scale immigration, various observers could have arrived at this notion and publicized it. Without the data and interpretations coming from the Census Bureau and other parts of this system, however, the idea would have lacked the imprimatur that gives it legitimacy.

The chapter reviews Census Bureau data and pronouncements about population change and the ways in which they have been taken up by the mass media. A Census Bureau press release introducing the notion of a "majority-minority nation" about a decade ago was especially consequential. The chapter then explores the reactions to the census data from political and cultural commentators, from Pat Buchanan to Ezra Klein. The reactions on the right and the left are, not surprisingly, different: the right issues dire warnings about national decline, while the left exudes a confident sense of inevitability, combined with some degree of celebration of "the end of white America." The chapter also considers white Americans' everyday experiences with diversity, especially in their neighborhoods. I summarize the evidence about the sharply rising diversity in white neighborhoods over the last several decades and what we know about whites' responses to it.

The fourth chapter examines how our demographic data system has produced the majority-minority prediction for the next several decades and also why, despite the critical innovation of multiple-race reporting in the 2000 Census, it has failed to call an equivalent attention to the surge of ethno-racial mixing in families. The chapter introduces the reader to the Census Bureau's measurement of race and ethnicity and includes a brief tour of its history. The current questions and the construction of data from them are discussed, as are the bureaucratic, political, and legal constraints on census data, exemplified by the role of the Office of Management and Budget in developing standards for ethnic and racial data reporting. The chapter then brings into play the increasing extent of ethno-racial mixing in families, beginning with the steady rise in marriages across the major ethno-racial divisions. This mixing leads naturally to increases in the number of children with mixed backgrounds (whether formed through marriage or not); the great majority of them have one white and one minority parent. I present data from census data sets and birth certificates to demonstrate the rapid growth of mixed parentage among infants and the relative frequency of different ethno-racial combinations among them. The chapter concludes by examining how census data procedures have dealt with this momentous new development. For reasons I develop, those procedures have proven inadequate to give Americans an accurate understanding of ethno-racial mixing in families and its implications for the future. I show, for example, that the group with mixed minority-white parentage is the pivot on which the outcomes of Census Bureau population projections depend; if we change our assumptions about its classification, the projected future looks quite different.

If this mixed group is demographically important, we need to understand where its members fit into American society. The fifth chapter presents a coherent if complex picture of the socioeconomic position, social affiliations, identities, and experiences of those from mixed minority-white families. It does so in part by using some original data analyses, along with a comprehensive synthesis of the research literature on mixed Americans, including both qualitative and quantitative studies.

This picture is differentiated by the ethno-racial origin of the minority parent, and large differences can be seen in the starting points for mixed individuals during infancy. The strongest contrast lies between those with Asian and white backgrounds and those with black and white ones. The former are raised mostly by married-couple families that have high incomes because both parents are highly educated; the children grow up in suburban neighborhoods with many homeowning white residents. As adults, they mix easily with whites and frequently marry them; their fluid identities often shift between mixed and white. Qualitative research indicates that Asian-white young adults do not feel a strong distinction from whites. Black-white children are raised by families, often headed by single parents, that face more economic challenges. They are not as concentrated in urban neighborhoods as black-only children are, but they have experiences similar to theirs with the police. Although they tend, as adults, to identify with the black side of their background, they not infrequently marry whites.

Other large groups with mixed majority-minority backgrounds seem positioned in between whites and minority groups. This is true of the largest such group, those from families with one white (non-Hispanic) and one Hispanic parent. But in some fundamental ways, such as educational attainment, identity patterns, social affiliations, and marriage tendencies, the members of other mixed groups appear closer to the white side of their background than to the minority side.

Chapter 6 provides the conceptual, or theoretical, and historical background for an interpretation of the significance of mixing that is advanced in the seventh chapter. I review the two bodies of relevant social-science theories, race and assimilation theories. I do not hide that I rely more on assimilation ideas than on those from race theory. But in order to avoid the false simplicities of an abstract portrait of change, the book delves into history—specifically the history of the post–World War II mass assimilation of the so-called white ethnics—to look for clues about the current nature of assimilation and to reveal the real-life messiness of assimilation processes, which generally do not produce integration into the mainstream in a seamless way. This part of the chapter develops a theory to explain the midcentury mass assimilation, based on social-psychological principles; the idea of non-zero-sum mobility, which mitigates ethno-racial competition for valued statuses, plays a central role in this theory. As noted earlier, the historical examination also revises fundamentally the currently reigning depiction of that assimilation in the whiteness account, for example, by highlighting the ways in which the mainstream became more diverse and had its identity altered as a consequence of mass assimilation.

Based on the ideas developed in chapter 6 and the takeaways from assimilation history, the first part of chapter 7 develops an understanding of how large-scale assimilation can be occurring in an economically stressed time by applying to the present the non-zero-sum assimilation theory, which has three main elements (status uplift, social proximity to whites, and moral elevation). The chapter, for example, presents evidence that the patterns to be expected from non-zero-sum mobility created by demographic shift are occurring: they are evident in the penetration of more individuals from minority backgrounds or mixed minority-white ones into the upper reaches of the labor force and in the growing diversity of higher education, even at its most elite levels. This mobility particularly benefits the groups that have grown extensively through immigration since the 1960s. The second part of the chapter argues that these patterns should be understood as an expansion of the mainstream and are associated with greater openness to nonwhites and Hispanics than in the past. At this point, I consider how the character of the mainstream may be altered by this openness, contrasting the idea of assimilation as whitening with the ongoing mainstream diversification.

The eighth chapter considers how assimilation processes could be facilitated by social policy, and it concentrates on three major barriers to assimilation: the high and growing overall level of economic inequality, which is inhibiting social mobility; systematic racism, which causes groups like African Americans to be "underserved" by assimilation processes; and defective legal status, which affects a large part of the immigrant population and hinders the second generation as well.

In the ninth and concluding chapter, I summarize the various conceptual strands and empirical findings and then return to the opening theme of narratives for understanding demographic change and their political ramifications. Like other Western countries, the United States needs continued large-scale immigration to retain its vitality, but the current narrative about the changes wrought by immigration has polarizing political consequences, especially for the white majority, which will remain the dominant political group nationally well past midcentury. The United States—again like other Western immigration societies—is in need of a new narrative, one that is less threatening to the majority and that, at the same time, allows immigrants and their children to become a part of the mainstream "us" without complete abandonment of their distinctiveness. It is my hope in writing this book that ideas about mainstream assimilation can provide the material for fashioning such a narrative.

2

The Enigma of November 2016

> When Mexico sends its people, they're not sending their best.
> They're not sending you. They're not sending you.
> —DONALD TRUMP, ANNOUNCING HIS CANDIDACY
>   FOR PRESIDENT, JUNE 16, 2015

A day that began for much of the country with bright promise ended in shock and disbelief.

Many Americans turned on television sets during the afternoon and early evening of November 8, 2016, expecting to see the election of the first female president of the United States. For weeks, the opinion polls had pointed in that direction, even if the margin of Hillary Clinton's advantage was sometimes small, especially after FBI director James Comey revealed publicly eleven days before the election that the agency had reopened the investigation into her handling of her email while she was secretary of state. Yet she consistently maintained a significant lead. Poll aggregators, such as "The Upshot" at the *New York Times*, had been estimating her chances of victory as very high; the morning of the election, The Upshot gave her an 85 percent chance of victory. Donald Trump appeared to have no better than a one-in-six chance of becoming the next occupant of the White House.

About 11:00 p.m. EST, when Florida was called for Trump and bellwether states that Clinton had been expected to win comfortably, like Pennsylvania, remained extremely close, it became clear that what had seemed a virtual certainty that morning might not happen after all. At 2:30 a.m., when Trump took Wisconsin in an upset, the election was decided. There was not going to be a woman president, at least not yet. Donald Trump, a most improbable candidate for the White House, had triumphed—if not in the popular vote, at least on the scorecard that mattered, the Electoral College.

The stunning reversal of political fortunes led immediately to a search for causes. Some of the Clinton campaign's strategic decisions came in for severe criticism. In what retrospectively seemed like an excess of confidence, the campaign had largely ignored until the last minute, when it was too late, Rust Belt states like Michigan and Wisconsin that, as part of the so-called Blue Wall, had seemed safely in the Democratic column. Instead, it invested resources in states like Arizona, where Clinton had little chance of winning. Since Trump's Electoral College victory was achieved by about 100,000 votes spread among three states, Michigan, Pennsylvania, and Wisconsin, the campaign's inattention to some Blue Wall states looked quite foolhardy on Wednesday morning.

Fingers were quickly pointed also at the turnout. An article on November 10 in the *Washington Post* by Paul Waldman claimed that a plunge in the percentage of Americans going to their polling places was a key factor.[1] According to Waldman's clearly preliminary analysis, the percentage of votes by the "voting-eligible population" fell to 56 percent in 2016, substantially lower than in the preceding three elections. However, with a little more distance from election day, the evidence looked much less convincing. Based on an analysis of official voter files not available immediately after the election, Nate Cohn, in a March 28, 2017, article in the *New York Times*, argued that overall turnout was about what was expected beforehand and therefore did not tilt the electoral playing field toward a Trump victory.[2] True, the turnout of black Democrats was not as high as during the Obama elections, but that was to be expected—black turnout in 2016 was closer to historical patterns. Turnout among whites and

Hispanics was elevated, but because this effect was widely spread, especially among whites, the net gain for Trump was small. All in all, turnout was not decisive, according to Cohn.

But something Cohn highlighted became a central clue to the puzzle of the 2016 election: working-class whites, a group defined by the lack of a college education, gave Trump a much larger vote margin than did more educated whites. The split among whites along educational lines, it turned out, was wider than ever before. The election-day exit polls found that two-thirds of whites without a college degree voted for Trump; those with a degree were evenly divided between the two major candidates.[3] As Cohn pointed out, this split implied that some working-class whites who had voted for the nation's first black president in one or both of the prior elections had now voted, paradoxically, for Trump, whose campaign blatantly played upon white prejudices toward African Americans and other minorities. Cohn described this switch as one of "persuasion": Trump "flipped millions of white working-class Obama supporters to his side." But how?

Economic Dislocation or Racialized Identity?

The disaffiliation of working-class whites from the Democratic Party was something that had developed over time, before cresting in the 2016 election. The political scientist John Sides has examined what he calls the "diploma divide" among whites over a quarter-century.[4] Between 1992 and 2008, the party split among whites with no more than a high school diploma was stable and fairly even; for much of this period, working-class whites were more likely than more educated whites to identify with the Democratic Party. But after 2008, Democratic loyalty declined sharply among less educated whites, while rising among those with a college degree. The two lines crossed in 2010; since then, the older pattern has been reversed, and now college-educated whites are more likely to identify themselves as Democrats. According to Sides, "By 2015, white voters who had a high school degree or less were 24 percentage points more Republican than Democratic (57 percent to 33 percent)."[5] This disaffection

with the Democrats among working-class whites shifted the overall party split among whites in favor of Republicans. By 2015, the
majority of whites identified as Republican, and their margin over
Democratic-identifying whites was fifteen percentage points. At the
time of Obama's election in 2008, the party split among whites had
been even.

The search for an explanation of the diploma divide quickly
devolved into two competing viewpoints: economic dislocation
versus threats to white dominance of American society. The idea
that economic dislocation lay behind the shifting political affiliations of working-class whites was rooted in the changes in the labor
market landscape wrought by automation, deindustrialization, globalization, and intensifying income and wealth inequality. In the
past, less educated whites in some parts of the United States could
count on stable employment in well-paying unionized jobs in manu-
facturing industries such as automobile or steel production. By the
early twenty-first century, however, many of those jobs had disappeared: factories in the United States had closed, and production
had migrated elsewhere, or robots had taken over the assembly work
that humans had once done. Moreover, economists' studies show
that the share of the national income going to labor as opposed to
capital has been declining fairly steeply in the early years of the new
century, with a small uptick during Obama's final years in office. The
earnings differentials by educational credentials have been increasing, and real wages (that is, with inflation controlled) have been
stagnant or declining for workers without college degrees.[6]

In places where the labor market has been hollowed out by the
disappearance of major plants, many working-class residents are
forced to patch together an income stream from a variety of part-
time and sometimes temporary jobs. The sociologist Justin Gest
studied the working-class whites of Johnstown, Ohio, a city that
once prospered on the solid foundation of steel mills and factories.[7]
When the plants that brought this prosperity started to close in the
late 1970s, good jobs became scarce. The population, especially its
white portion, went into steep decline, plummeting from nearly
170,000 in 1960 to 67,000 half a century later. A city that had been

dominated by the descendants of the European immigrants who came to find work in the mills became evenly divided between whites and African Americans.

Johnstowners of both races now struggle to get by in whatever way they can. The city has a "huge underground economy," sustained by the many residents who scrape together an income from low-wage jobs, informal services to their neighbors, and the sale of scrap and odds and ends. The drug trade also is thriving. Working-class whites are under the spell of family memories of the "golden days" of the mid-twentieth century, and many of them still hope that something will turn up to bring that Johnstown back; fracking is the latest prayer for an economic miracle. One person who has observed focus groups with working-class whites says that "they just don't believe in promises, in the future of the community, leaders, they're very skeptical about everything . . . and they're highly antagonistic and have almost a fervor to get into an argument. They have a feeling that they've been battered. There have been so many promises made since the fall of the steel mills, and that's the root of it." A political party staff member characterizes these citizens as "socially conservative, slightly racist, with a huge chip on their shoulder, distrustful of most public and private institutions, extremely cynical, and extremely susceptible to demagoguery."[8]

Though the economic-dislocation explanation seems persuasive on its face, public opinion survey data have largely pointed elsewhere: toward the notion that threats to the dominant position of white men fueled much of the support for Trump, who ran a campaign that heavily targeted minorities, immigrants, and women. Trump regularly mocked women during the campaign, especially by describing them in bodily terms, implying that their physical attractiveness is the primary basis for their social value. In one of the most notorious of these incidents, after then–Fox News anchor Megyn Kelly questioned him during a televised debate about his history of offensive misogynistic statements, Trump responded in a subsequent interview by saying, "You could see there was blood coming out of her eyes. Blood coming out of her wherever."

Trump's cultivation of hostility toward minorities and immigrants was more systematic in scope and less focused on the mockery of individuals. Opening his campaign at Trump Tower in New York in June 2015, he attracted widespread media attention for his derogatory remarks about Mexican immigrants: "They're bringing drugs. They're bringing crime. They're rapists. And some, I assume, are good people." Debasement of immigrants, especially Mexicans, Central Americans, and Muslims, was a consistent feature of Trump's campaign speeches and tweets. And one of his most attention-grabbing campaign promises was to build a "big, beautiful" wall at the southern border and to make Mexico pay for it.

Trump did not spare American-born minorities from his verbal cruelty, twisted facts, and outright falsehoods. He frequently has portrayed African and Latine Americans as responsible for "the overwhelming amount of violent crime in our cities," claiming during the campaign that "there are places in America that are among the most dangerous in the world. You go to places like Oakland. Or Ferguson" (the Missouri city made prominent by the 2014 killing of the unarmed black teenager Michael Brown by a white police officer). And when black professional football players began kneeling during the national anthem as a way of calling attention to police violence against African Americans, Trump attacked the gesture, saying of protest leader quarterback Colin Kaepernick, "Maybe he should find a country that works better for him. Let him try, it won't happen."[9]

POLITICAL SCIENTISTS FOCUS ON
WHITE VULNERABILITY

According to many commentators, Trump's rhetoric toward women, immigrants, and minorities was music to the ears of many less educated white men, who felt threatened and even besieged by the changes taking place in American society, evidenced by the growing visibility in the public sphere of these once-subordinate groups. In an influential analysis, widely covered in the press, the political scientist Diana Mutz weighed the relative impacts of economic distress (the "left behind" thesis) and status threat in support for Trump. She found little evidence that any worsening in the financial position of voters had an effect on their decisions in the 2016 election. The evidence instead indicated the powerful electoral role of concerns about status. According to Mutz, these concerns are broader than just white male anxieties about the improving positions of women and minorities and the rising numbers of the latter due largely to immigration. She also pointed to the influences of globalization and the perceived weakening of America's position in the international order. Her analysis found a linkage of presidential vote to candidate positions on trade, immigration, and competition with China. Another important influence was the "social dominance scale," devised by psychologists to measure preference for "hierarchy over equality" and known to indicate also "animus towards outgroups." Mutz's overall conclusion is that Americans' "candidate preferences in 2016 reflected increasing anxiety among high-status groups rather than complaints about past treatment among low-status groups. Both growing domestic racial diversity and globalization contributed to a sense that white Americans are under siege by these engines of change."[10]

Other political scientists see the status concerns that drove the election outcome as operating primarily on the domestic landscape. John Sides's analysis is exemplary.[11] He focuses on the white voters who shifted their choice from Obama in 2012 to Trump in 2016, since these shifts, especially in the working class, were critical to Trump's victories in upper Midwestern states like Michigan that gave him a majority in the Electoral College. He finds that, of the factors predicting a GOP vote by whites, the ones that became more powerful between 2012 and 2016 were attitudes toward minorities—toward blacks, Muslims, and immigrants. Moreover, the electoral salience of these attitudes is likely to have shifted some white Obama voters toward Trump since, according to polling data, substantial numbers of this group had negative attitudes toward one or more minorities even before 2016. In general, partisan divisions in opinion, according to a book-length analysis by Sides and his colleagues Michael

Tesler and Lynn Vavreck, have been crystallizing around these attitudes, as Republicans hold increasingly unfavorable attitudes toward
immigrants and minorities compared to Democrats. One stunning
illustration of the political potency of white attitudes about race
is the correspondence between their 2016 vote and whites' views
on racial inequality—whether they see it as mainly attributable to
discrimination or to blacks' lack of effort. The likelihood of voting
for Trump among the former was close to zero; among the latter, it
was almost 100 percent.[12] This correlation was stronger in 2016 than
in the prior two elections.

This is not to say that the election outcome was driven exclusively by ethno-racial concerns. A study by Brian Schaffner and
his colleagues affirmed the political power of the racial attitudes of
whites but also brought sexism into play.[13] These political scientists
were interested in explaining the educational chasm in white voting patterns. The electoral gap between college-educated and non-
college-educated whites was about three times larger in 2016 than
it had been in prior decades. Attitudes about gender and race, along
with economic distress, were critical to the sudden widening of this
gap given that the Trump campaign broke what had been norms
in recent presidential contests with its overt appeals to sexism and
racism, thereby priming attitudes that are more likely to be held by
working-class whites. Calling upon scales of "hostile sexism" and
"denial of racism," the researchers found that these indicators were
much more powerful in explaining 2016 vote choice than economic
distress. Like Sides, however, when Schaffner and his colleagues
looked at those who switched from Obama in 2012 to Trump in
2016, it was the racism scale that mattered most.

Findings such as these, when translated for a wider public, have
often been framed as "racial resentment." For instance, a 2017 *Vox*
article by German Lopez carried the headline, "The Past Year of
Research Has Made It Very Clear: Trump Won Because of Racial
Resentment." In 2018, Diana Mutz was part of a panel assembled
by radio station KQED to discuss the topic "Racial Resentment and
White Cultural Anxiety Fuel Support of President Trump, Studies Find." Even Trump-friendly Fox News got into the act with a

May 28, 2019, report, "Trump Stokes Racial Resentment to Hinder Biden's Rise."[14]

Yet racial "resentment" seems too narrow a characterization of the boiling mix of white anxieties, grievance, and shaky sense of dominance that was stoked and harvested by the Trump campaign.[15] Its limitations emerge from the definition of racial resentment that German Lopez quotes: "a moral feeling that blacks violate such traditional American values as individualism and self-reliance."[16] Not only does the definition limit resentment to whites' feelings about blacks, omitting immigrants and other minorities such as Muslims who were targeted by Trump, but it scants another powerful element of the complex of feelings, perceptions, and beliefs that led many whites to Trump: their growing sense of vulnerability as their dominance over the American social and political landscape seemed no longer to be taken for granted.[17] The political scientists Nicholas Valentino, Fabian Neuner, and Matthew Vandenbroek expressed this vulnerability: "Whites now view themselves as an embattled and even disadvantaged racial group, and this has led to both strong in-group identity and a greater tolerance for expressions of hostility to racial out-groups."[18]

Reflecting on the research findings about 2016 voting patterns, Sides, Tesler, and Vavreck entitled their 2018 book *Identity Crisis: The 2016 Campaign and the Battle for the Meaning of America.* By invoking the term "identity," these political scientists intended to underscore the decisive role of group identities, as opposed to individual fortunes and their vicissitudes, in the 2016 electoral outcome. And the identities that mattered were those involving ethnicity, race, and religion. When voters see the world in terms of group identities, their own individual position, and whether they are doing well or not, can be subordinated to the perceived position and prospects of their group:

The existence, content, and power of group identities—including their relevance to politics—depends on context. One part of the context is the possibility of gains and losses for the group. Gains and losses can be tangible, such as money or territory, or they can be symbolic, such as psychological status. Moreover, gains and losses do not even need to be realized. Mere threats, such as the possibility of losses, can be enough. When gains, losses, or threats become salient, group identities develop and strengthen. Groups become more unified and more likely to develop goals and grievances, which are the components of a politicized group consciousness.[19]

In 2016, white identity was crucial. Whites, who in the late twentieth century could think of themselves simply as "Americans," without any qualifier, were becoming increasingly aware of themselves as one racial group in an increasingly diverse America.[20] Immigration, the rapidly changing demography of the country, and the election of Barack Obama as president all made them conscious that they were members of a distinct group and also that they could no longer assume that they were the incarnation of the nation. In this sense, one could say that the election was fought over who are the authentic Americans.

The sense of grievance felt by many whites has been increasing in the early twenty-first century. In a survey conducted just after the 2016 election, a majority of whites, and even more so Trump voters, agreed with the statement that "average Americans have gotten less than they deserve," but many fewer thought that this was true of black Americans. Sides, Tesler, and Vareck characterize these beliefs as "racialized perceptions of economic deservingness," which are again tied closely to group identity.[21] That is, the grievances felt by many whites have less to do with their own economic situation than with their perception of the treatment of whites as a group relative to other groups. Many whites believe that whites are suffering because other groups are favored, especially by government and by "elites."

In fact, many whites now view their racial group as victimized by discrimination. How widespread the belief is remains a bit murky. One 2019 survey suggests that a large minority of whites believe this.[22] However, a survey conducted in 2017 by National Public Radio, the Robert Wood Johnson Foundation, and Harvard's School of Public Health found that a majority of whites believe that their group suffers from discrimination.[23] Many fewer, however, think that they personally have experienced anti-white discrimination.

This sense of white vulnerability cannot be detached from ideas about how America is changing. Right around the time of the first Obama election, news media started reporting the headline from Census Bureau projections that whites would become a minority of the population by the middle of the century (discussed in depth in the next chapter). This idea was dubbed the "majority-minority" society or nation, the term indicating that current minority groups— American Indians, Asians, blacks, and Hispanics—would together constitute a majority of the population for the first time in American history.

SOCIAL PSYCHOLOGISTS ILLUMINATE WHITE REACTIONS TO DEMOGRAPHIC CHANGE

White vulnerability has been pinpointed in an important strand of social-psychological research that uses prospective population shifts as a way to prompt whites' anxieties about the weakening of their position vis-à-vis minorities. The core hypothesis is that reminding whites about their future as a demographic minority— an outcome projected to occur in the nation as a whole during the 2040s—stimulates these anxieties, leading many whites to express hostility toward out-groups and adopt more conservative political positions. The social-psychological mechanism involved is not inherently specific to whites: rather, any group suffering a threat to its status is presumed to adopt a defensive posture as a way of protecting its position as much as possible. Among white Americans today, politically conservative positions are defensive in the sense that they are protective of established hierarchies and work against groups that are attempting to climb social ladders.

Research by Maureen Craig and Jennifer Richeson exemplifies this strand.[24] In one series of experiments, the researchers assigned randomly chosen individuals to a treatment group that read a passage about whites' future minority status (or present minority status in California), while those in the control group read an unrelated passage. Afterwards, the subjects completed a questionnaire that included questions about their opinions on policy issues. The findings from various experiments of this type demonstrate that whites for whom the projected demographic shifts are made salient express more conservative attitudes on policy positions, regardless of their political party affiliation and even when the policy issues are unrelated to racial concerns. In some of these studies, the experimenters also tested the perception of a threat to whites' status. They found that exposure to material about demographic shift heightened whites' concern about their group's status and also that this heightened concern mediated their increased conservatism. That is, when the perception of threat was controlled for, either statistically or through experimental design, the political impact of the prompting about demographic change disappeared.

Closely related is research by Rachel Wetts and Robb Willer.[25] They examined the nexus among the perception of threat to white status, "racial resentment" defined empirically in terms of a scale of anti-black prejudice (whose items contrast the view that blacks are held back by historical oppression and contemporary discrimination with the stereotype that they do not work hard enough), and attitudes toward social welfare. They posit a sequence of causal linkages among the three factors that leads from perceived threats to heightened resentment, to negative views of social welfare. The study, which combined survey analysis with experiments, confirms it. In the experimental portion, the researchers again presented population projections to a treatment group to make salient for whites the demographic threat to their status. This stimulus increased their prejudice, made their views of social welfare more negative, and heightened their willingness to reduce funding for it. Wetts and Willer's analysis indicates that increased "racial resentment," which can be thought of as the perception that undeserving "others" are getting ahead, mediates the relationship between status threat and welfare attitudes.

There is also evidence to support the idea that threats to status provoke protective reactions in groups other than whites. The social psychologist Maria Abascal conducted an experiment in which both whites and blacks were presented with a scenario of rapid Hispanic demographic increase. Consistent with other experiments with white subjects, whites in the experimental condition (those exposed to material about Hispanic population growth) were more likely to identify with the white racial group than were whites in the control group, who were more likely to identify as American. However, blacks in the experimental condition were less likely to identify with the black racial group and more likely to identity as American. How to explain this discrepancy? According to Abascal, black reactions are conditioned by their place in the US hierarchy. They seek to ally themselves with the more powerful racial group "on the basis of an American identity that Hispanic presumably do not share," thereby "using this boundary to reinforce the exclusion of Hispanics."[26]

The social-psychological studies of white reactions to scenarios of demographic change have identified ways to assuage the anxieties that push whites in more conservative directions. For instance, Craig and Richeson found that adding a paragraph to assert that whites would remain atop the future racial hierarchy negated the conservative impact of the projected demographic shift.[27] Wetts and Willer probed whites' support for welfare programs based on experimentally manipulated descriptions of the beneficiaries of the programs. When presented with assertions that whites are the main beneficiaries, white subjects were more supportive of social welfare. The researchers inferred that the "anti-welfare sentiment among whites" demonstrated by the experiments arose "because they [whites] perceive such programs to mostly benefit minorities."[28]

How demographic change is narrated matters for how whites react, in short. This has been strikingly shown in related research by Morris Levy and Dowell Myers, who frame their approach in terms of "news accounts of growing diversity." They divided subjects into three groups, each presented with a different version of a concocted news story about Census Bureau projections. The one that most resembles the widespread reporting on demographic change is described by Levy and Myers as *exclusive*: the projections foresee whites transitioning to a demographic minority during the 2040s. A second story, labeled *diversity*, simply discusses rising racial diversity without alluding to a future minority status for whites. The third story, an *inclusive* one, is novel: reconfiguring the projections to include among whites those individuals who are partly white and identify themselves as such, it foresees whites persisting as a demographic majority. (This story is in fact based on alternative projections produced by the Census Bureau but rarely discussed in the news media.) Levy and Myers hypothesized that "framing the rise in diversity as a modern manifestation of America's history of ethnic blending and blurring that would preserve a white majority, albeit one transformed through racial mixing, blending, and multiracial identification, might assuage and counteract some of the threatened feelings that result from receiving news about large-scale increases in diversity."[29]

Levy and Myers then asked their white subjects how they felt about the story they read. The feelings of those who read the exclusive story were predominantly anger and anxiety. The diversity story did not elicit such negative feelings. The inclusive story produced the most positive feelings: the readers of this story felt mainly hope and enthusiasm. Interestingly, this was even more true of Republican-leaning whites than of whites in general. These findings point to a conclusion that how demographic change is understood not only matters but may matter a lot.

Conclusion

Demographic imaginings are inflaming American politics and contributed, perhaps decisively, to the startling outcome of the 2016 presidential election. Many whites fear that their once-secure status as part of the dominant societal group is now being undermined as immigration brings in more and more nonwhites. A consequence, they imagine, is a nonwhite majority in the not too distant future. Such a majority could even turn whites into victims, and more than a few whites believe that there is already discrimination directed against them. These fears led some of them to vote for a populist nationalist like Donald Trump, whose campaign slogan, "Make America great again," promised to roll the country back to a time when whites felt comfortably in the saddle.

This sort of populist nationalism, fed by upwelling majority-group anxieties about cultural and demographic changes resulting from large-scale immigration, is not just an American phenomenon but has emerged as a major political force throughout the West. (Canada appears so far to be the exception.) In tandem with the 2016 election of Trump as president came: in the United Kingdom, the 2016 vote in favor of Brexit and the success of the newly formed Brexit party in the 2019 European Parliament elections; in France, Marine Le Pen's second-place showing in the 2017 presidential election and her party's emergence as the main opposition in the 2019 European Parliament elections; and in Germany, the Alternative für Deutschland, a right-wing party formed in 2013, becoming the third-largest party in the Bundestag in the 2017 federal elections. In all these cases (and others), immigration was a principal target of the political rhetoric of the populist parties and movements. In Europe, however, in some contrast to the United States, this rhetoric plays very heavily on fears of cultural change, often cast grandly in terms of a submergence of Western civilization under waves of Muslim immigrants and their descendants. The Princeton Islamic scholar Bernard Lewis put this rhetoric baldly when he declared that by the end of this century Europe will be "part of the Arab West, the Maghreb."[30]

Perhaps the growing consensus among political scientists in the United States that "racial resentment" tipped the election to Trump shortchanges the role of economic factors, the feeling of some Americans of being "left behind." This role can be hard to see in the typical survey data because it is tied to specific places whose local economies have been hollowed out by deindustrialization and globalization, leaving the residents who remain—many others, especially young people, having departed from the area—with an experience of deflated opportunities (regardless of their personal financial situation). As some have observed, Trump voters were frequently the more affluent residents of poor places.[31] The survey evidence that supports racial resentment generally lacks adequate place-specific data to detect the role of this alternative political geography.

This role emerges with a sharper focus from a data flyover of the US landscape. Eduardo Porter, an economic correspondent for the *New York Times*, entitled a column shortly after the election "Where Were Trump's Votes? Where the Jobs Weren't."[32] Porter based the claim on a series of observations. To start with, the economic recovery since 2008 had not brought whites of prime working age (twenty-five- to fifty-four years old) back to the labor market position they had occupied before the recession: in the aggregate, they still showed a large jobs deficit, while other major ethnic and racial groups of prime working age had gained more jobs than they originally lost. This disparity was very much tied to the groups' geographic distributions. In broad strokes, post-recession economic activity was concentrated in metropolitan regions, while rural areas and small towns have been much less economically dynamic. Whites are disproportionately located in the latter.[33]

One can home in on the "hot spots" in the geography of economic hollowing-out through the clusters of "deaths of despair": the growing numbers of middle-aged whites who are dying from drug abuse, alcoholism, and suicide. The identification of this phenomenon barely predates the 2016 election. In 2015, the economists Anne Case and Angus Deaton first called attention to the increasing mortality among American middle-aged whites, which strikingly contradicts the otherwise universal trend of declining mortality in rich countries. Among middle-aged American whites, the increased mortality is concentrated among the less educated; for those with a college degree, mortality rates are falling. Subsequently, Case and Deaton proposed an explanation for why so many middle-aged, less educated whites are dying from drug overdoses, cirrhosis of the liver, and suicide: their story is not about income decline as much as it is about the cumulative disadvantages arising from "progressively worsening labor market opportunities at the time of entry for whites with low levels of education."[34] These disadvantages extend to marriage and other socially supportive relationships and to health. Thus, this explanation encompasses observations about the deterioration of white working-class family life that have been made elsewhere.[35]

The Case and Deaton account, moreover, implicitly invokes the role of place, because labor market opportunities are inherently tied to a locality unless a prospective worker is willing and able to relocate.

There is in fact a direct connection among places, deaths of despair, and Trump electoral support, as demonstrated by the sociologists Shannon Monnat and Warren Brown. Because Trump was victorious in the Electoral College but did not win the popular vote, "small advantages in key places enabled Trump to accumulate the set of electors needed to claim victory." Many of these places were found in the industrial (or formerly industrial) Midwest, where Trump's vote totals were superior to those of the 2012 Republican candidate, Mitt Romney, and Clinton's were inferior to those of Obama. As Monnat and Brown note, the electoral tide in favor of Trump was found not so much in the poorest places but in places that "are generally worse off today than they were a generation or two ago." Consequently, Trump's support surged in "counties with more economic distress, worse health, higher drug, alcohol and suicide mortality rates, lower educational attainment, and higher marital separation/ divorce rates."[36] For instance, Luzerne County in Pennsylvania delivered more than half of Trump's margin of victory in the state. The county fits this profile and notably experienced a threefold rise in drug overdose deaths during the preceding decade and a half and a doubling in the number of suicides. Similar county profiles can be found in the other Midwestern states that Trump won by a small margin and that were critical to his Electoral College majority.

There is no inherent conflict between the two dominant strands of explanation for the Trump victory. Racial resentment and the sense of being left behind are compatible: working-class whites in places that are experiencing economic and demographic decline, combined with increases in deaths of despair and health problems from drug and alcohol abuse, can imagine the worsening of their surroundings as due to the gains of "undeserving others"—minorities and immigrants. This is the significance of describing whites' perceptions of economic dislocation and inequality as "racialized," as John Sides, Michael Tesler, and Lynn Vavreck do.[37] Indeed, the political rhetoric coming from the right encourages a zero-sum vision in which minority gains come at the cost of white losses. For example, Rush Limbaugh proclaimed shortly after Obama's election to the White House, "The days of them [minorities] not having any power are over, and they are angry. And they want to use their power as a means of retribution."[38]

This compatibility of the explanations is brilliantly captured by an extended metaphor in Arlie Hochschild's book about the experiences and worldviews of working-class whites on the political right in Louisiana.[39] Hochschild sought to understand the "deep story" of her subjects, the narrative that "tells us how things feel" and how "the party on the other side [politically from her] sees the world." She found this narrative in the metaphor of "waiting in line." That is, the experiences of these working-class whites correspond with that of waiting one's turn in a long line of people hoping to reach the "American Dream . . . the idea that you're better off than your forebears just as they superseded their parents before you." Her subjects once felt that their position in the queue was determined by their being white and Christian, placing them ahead of "people of color." But they are not moving ahead—indeed, they are losing out—because now others are "cutting in line" and getting unfairly ahead of those who are following the rules. Who are the line-cutters? They are mainly Americans of color, immigrants and refugees, and women. By and large, they are benefiting from government policies and programs not open to whites, such as affirmative action. The line-cutters are epitomized by the Obamas, who unexpectedly have risen to the pinnacle of American society. How could this have happened without the interference of government propelling them forward?

The working-class whites in the corner of Louisiana where Hochschild did her research, like many others who voted for Trump, probably do not have much, if any, personal knowledge of the "others" whom they perceive to have received unfair advantages because of public policies. But they don't need it to feel that this deep story is true. Their experience is one of decline, if not in their personal circumstances then certainly in the lives of others in their communities. If they and those they know are being left behind, others must be getting ahead. The world as condensed and interpreted by the media they are exposed to provides the ideas that help them to understand the forces, largely outside of their personal ken, that are holding them back. This is a feat of the imagination, of the narratives that have been developed from media stories and personal discussions that help individuals understand the world around them and interpret the personal events occurring in the "small world" within their direct experience in terms of patterns and trends in the larger, outside world.

The idea of a majority-minority America that most Americans now believe will be our future in a few decades is one of those critical narratives. It envisions whites as destined inevitably to become a numerical minority of the country. A corollary is that the power and status that individual whites feel are associated with their membership in the dominant American population will slip away. These aspects of whiteness, it appears, are especially meaningful for working-class whites, whose employment and socioeconomic situation depend to a great degree on large impersonal forces, such as decisions by companies and government, to which they have no access and over which they have no influence. Even working-class whites who feel personally secure may still feel uneasy for their children and grandchildren, who will face unknown and unpredictable circumstances.

The social-psychological research alerts us to how narrative framing matters and to the sorts of alternative framings that might provoke less political polarization, both among whites and in the country as a whole. The growing diversity of the United States is certainly making whites more conscious of their membership in an ethno-racial group that is just one part of the American population. But their growing consciousness of whiteness may not have to become racially politicized in the way that was true in 2016.[40] A less inflammatory alternative narrative may be possible.

3

The Power of the Demographic Imagination

Demography is destiny.

—SCAMMON AND WATTENBERG (1970)

A half-century from now, when your own grandchildren are in college, there will be no majority race in America.

—PRESIDENT BILL CLINTON, SPEAKING AT THE 1997 UNIVERSITY OF CALIFORNIA-SAN DIEGO COMMENCEMENT

Any American paying attention to the news in the new century could be forgiven for thinking that whites, the dominant racial group in the United States ever since the nation's founding, were teetering on a demographic precipice and about to topple into a numerical minority, with potentially huge implications for their position of dominance. Power in a society is, of course, not strictly equatable with numbers but rests also on relative economic status and positioning within the political system. In these respects, the dominance of whites is much more secure than is implied by demographic strength alone. Nevertheless, in a democratic society, population sizes are undeniably related to electoral weight and ultimately to power.

The demographic news for several decades has been a steady drumbeat of exploding ethno-racial diversity, of expanding minority populations, combined with the aging and numerical decline of whites in the aggregate.[1] Immigration has been a powerful driver of change. Large-scale immigration to the United States had been shut down by restrictive legislation in the 1920s and then by worldwide economic depression and war in the following two decades. Immigration began to resume after the end of World War II and received a mighty boost from passage in 1965 of the Immigration and Nationality Act (or Hart-Celler Act) under the influence of the civil rights movement. That legislation finally dismantled the regime of regulating immigration by national origins and implicitly by ethnicity and race.[2] The national-origins quotas that restricted immigration from southern and eastern European countries were gone, and so too were the draconian racist limitations on immigration from Asia. The United States had opened up to immigration from anywhere on the globe, subject to a uniform country quota set initially at twenty thousand per year.

The volume of immigration to the United States has steadily climbed since then, with the totals for recent decades exceeding the numbers at the high point of the previous era of mass migration. The bars in figure 3.1 show the official counts of immigrant arrivals by decade, numbers that in recent decades have to be augmented by the much-harder-to-count numbers for immigrants without official authorization, who arrive either through clandestine border crossing or visa overstay. The overall number of unauthorized residents in the United States has declined somewhat since the recession of 2008, but the unauthorized still represent about one-quarter of all the foreign-born.[3] The population percentage represented by the foreign-born, shown by the line in figure 3.1, also reveals the powerful demographic role of immigration. Even though the American population that immigrants are joining is much larger than it was a century ago, the percentage of the foreign-born in the population has nearly attained its historical high points in the late nineteenth and early twentieth centuries.[4]

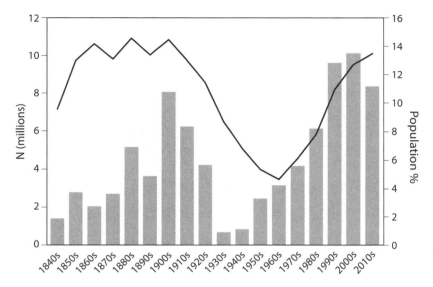

FIGURE 3.1 Legal Immigration (Bars) and Foreign-Born Population (Line) by Decade, 1850–2017

Note: Each point on the line indicates the foreign-born percentage at the end of the decade.
Sources: Office of Immigration Statistics, *Yearbook of Immigration Statistics* (various years); National Academies of Sciences 2015.

Equally important has been the shift in the geographic, and hence ethnic and racial, origins of the immigrants. Until the middle of the twentieth century, the great majority of immigrants were from Europe and Canada. As of 1960, more than 80 percent of the foreign-born in the United States had come from these regions. By the 1980s, only 13 percent of legal immigrants each year were from Canada or Europe, and four-fifths came from Asia, Latin America, and the Caribbean, with Africa joining the mix in the 1990s. Moreover, the predominant continent of origin has shifted over time: although in the early decades of the post-1965 immigration, the greatest numbers came from Latin America—above all, from Mexico—by 2011 that immigration had subsided and was eclipsed by immigration from Asia.

The long-run significance of immigration for population change lies even more in the ensuing generations than in the immigrants themselves. Given the relative recency of the immigration surge

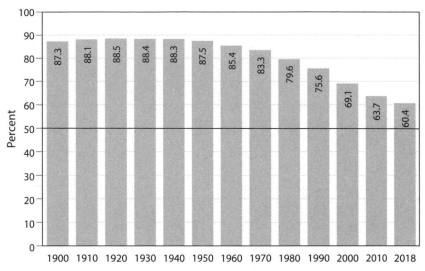

FIGURE 3.2 Population Percentage of Whites (Non-Hispanic), 1900–2018
Note: From 2000 onwards, only single-race whites are counted. The figure for 1930 is an inter-
polation; that for 2018 is the Census Bureau's estimate.
Sources: Gibson and Jung 2005; Gratton and Gutmann 2006.

following the 1965 immigration act, the generation that matters the
most at this moment is the second, composed by definition of individuals born in the United States to one or two immigrant parents.
In the middle of the 2010s, the second generation constituted about
12 percent of the population; in other words, the immigrants plus
their children made up one-quarter of the entire population.[5] There
are still some older whites in the second generation, but at this point
its youthful membership is largely Asian and Hispanic in its ethno-
racial origins. Recent black immigrants from Africa and the Caribbean have not yet produced an equivalently large second generation,
and whites overwhelmingly belong to the third and later generations, meaning that the immigrants in their family backgrounds were
grandparents, great-grandparents, or earlier ancestors.[6]

Trailing a bit behind the headlines about immigration has come
news about slippage in the size of the white group relative to nonwhites, both in the nation as a whole and in many of its cities,
states, and regions. Perhaps most saliently, the national percentage
of whites—defined by demographers as non-Hispanic and white

alone by race, a group overwhelmingly made up of Americans whose forebears immigrated from somewhere in Europe—has been falling from census to census since the mid-twentieth century, and at an accelerating rate (figure 3.2).* In 1970, the white percentage was still 83 percent, at a time when the United States was a nation divided mostly between two major racial groups, white and black. American Indians and Asians were each less than 1 percent of the population in that year; Hispanics were only 4 percent. By then, the influence of the new era of immigration had barely registered in the national demographic profile. By 2000, the white percentage had fallen fifteen points, to 69 percent. And it has continued to drop since then; in the latest available census measurement as I write this book, for 2018, whites, according to the conventional definition, were barely above the 60 percent threshold. During this period of decline in their share of the population, whites were actually still growing in numbers, if more slowly than nonwhites. But now some demographers find that this growth may be coming to an end. In 2016, for the first time in US history, white deaths exceeded white births in most US states, suggesting that the white population is no longer experiencing what demographers refer to as "natural increase."[7]

Demography Envisions the Future

Given the apparent decline of the white share of the American population, it comes as no surprise that the nation's demographic data system envisions whites as an eventual numerical minority. I refer to a "demographic data system" rather than simply to the Census Bureau because the bureau is not the sole actor, even if it is the nation's official custodian of demographic data and the public face of the system. Functioning under bureaucratic, legal, and political constraints, the Census Bureau does not have full freedom of action when it collects and reports data. By law, it is required to follow the

---

*Here, as elsewhere in the book, I use the terms for groups in common discourse and forgo the cumbersome if precise qualifier "non-Hispanic" for racial groups. I make exceptions where there is ambiguity.

guidelines of the federal Office of Management and Budget (OMB) for ethnicity and race data, and those guidelines, as the next chapter relates in detail, have played a critical role in shaping the data as publicly presented. Also part of the system are the demographers who help Americans, through reports, articles, and books intended for a broad audience, to understand the patterns in demographic data and their implications.

This system and the Census Bureau as its public face play a critical role in the wide acceptance of the majority-minority perspective on the nation's future. Of course, many whites, especially those in communities experiencing economic and population stagnation if not decline and those adhering to white nationalist ideologies, are capable of independently coming to the view that their group is in decline. Without the imprimatur of the demographic data system, however, the anxious imagining that the white group may soon be eclipsed numerically by minorities would amount to little more than opinion. The demographic data and interpretations issued by the system rescue these ideas from the realm of opinion and transmute them into common knowledge.

The Census Bureau regularly prepares population projections that divide the population into its major ethno-racial components: American Indians, Asians, blacks, Hispanics, and whites. This division is required for credible projections because the demographic drivers—fertility, mortality, and migration—vary substantially among these groups. Starting with the projections prepared in 2000, a momentous transition began to appear of whites from a numerical majority to a minority. The 2000 projection foresaw this transition as occurring in 2059.[8]

Mass media were slow to pick up on what was initially an unheralded feature of the projections. Perhaps the nomination in the summer of 2008 of the first nonwhite candidate to head a major-party ticket for president sharpened sensitivities to the rapidity of demographic change. At any rate, in the *New York Times*, the first announcement of the possible future minority status of whites appeared that summer in an article by the demography reporter Sam Roberts, under the headline "In a Generation, Minorities

May be the US Majority."[9] Citing the Census Bureau's projections issued that year, the article stated that "the census calculates that by 2042, Americans who identify themselves as Hispanic, black, Asian, American Indian, Native Hawaiian and Pacific Islander will together outnumber non-Hispanic whites." The claim, incidentally, is not accurate, because of ambiguities that plague the projections, but we will get to that later. Roberts cited increasing immigration levels and higher birthrates for the shortening of the time to the transition (from 2059) and quoted an expert at the Population Reference Bureau: "No other country has experienced such rapid racial and ethnic change." ("In peacetime" probably should have been a qualifier.)

The word was out. Subsequent population projections would receive much more public attention. The Census Bureau redid the projections in 2009, and then the next big release, based on 2010 census data, took place in 2012. The press release highlighted the growth of ethno-racial diversity over the half-century time span of the projections and invoked the concept of a "majority-minority nation," which was projected to occur, it asserted, by 2043.[10] In its report, the *New York Times* did not employ this phrase, but did say in its headline that "census officials" foresaw "a plurality nation."[11] According to the Census Bureau's acting director, Thomas Mesenbourg, "The next half century marks key points in continuing trends—the US will become a plurality nation, where the non-Hispanic white population remains the single largest group, but no group is in the majority."

Based on reporting by the Associated Press, numerous newspapers and other media throughout the country picked up on this important development in the demographic future. The *Pittsburgh Tribune Review* reported the news with the headline "Whites No Longer a Majority in the US by 2043, Census Bureau Projects." The *Pantagraph* of Bloomington, Illinois, was even more terse: "Census: Whites in Minority by 2043." The *Bismarck Tribune* ran the Associated Press article, with the same headline. The *Charleston Daily Mail* in West Virginia varied the headline slightly.[12]

For the next set of population projections, the Census Bureau published a report in 2014 as part of the regular *Current Population*

Reports series to accompany its bare-bones press release. The report, written by two Census Bureau demographers, made clear in its first paragraph that by midcentury whites would be a numerical minority of the population: "More than half of all Americans are projected to belong to a minority group (any group other than non-Hispanic white alone)." The report went on to declare that, "by 2060, the share of this group [non-Hispanic whites] is projected to be *just* 44 percent. . . . According to these projections, the majority-minority crossover will occur in 2044" (emphasis mine).[13]

For the most recent projections, issued publicly in 2018, the Census Bureau press release tried to avoid the majority-minority issue. The headline emphasized the aging of the nation. In discussing race and ethnicity, the statement muddied the waters by calling attention to the growth over time of the "White-alone population, regardless of Hispanic origin," though it also acknowledged the shrinkage of the "non-Hispanic White-alone population."[14] In any event, the genie was out of the bottle. Others lost little time in identifying the crossover year to a majority-minority nation (when whites would become a minority). William Frey, the Brookings Institution's well-known demographer, posted a report a day after the Census Bureau's release with the headline "The US Will Become 'Minority White' in 2045, Census Projects."[15] In truth, this deduction wasn't too difficult, since detailed tables produced by the bureau to present the projections showed that the percentage of non-Hispanic whites would dip below 50 percent in that year.

Projections are of course about the future, but during the Obama administration the Census Bureau began to issue estimates about the existing population that amounted to signposts on the way to the majority-minority country. These focused on the child population, since the demographic dynamic engendering a majority of minorities was emerging from a sharp age disjunction between the heavily white older population, dwindling because of mortality, and the increasingly diverse population of children.

The first releases concerned infants (children who have not reached their first birthday). Starting with the births in 2011, the Census Bureau declared that the majority of infants were members of minorities. Subsequent corrections to the data showed that whites retained a narrow majority among the infants born in that year. However, a majority-minority situation among infants was established for the babies born in 2013, and it has been repeated every year since then. In 2016, according to census estimates, minority births exceeded white births by about sixteen thousand—granted, a very small margin when the total number of infants is almost four million.[16]

If the margin was small, the news was big. Here was indisputable evidence of the ineluctable emergence of the future majority-minority society. National Public Radio's article "Babies of Color Now the Majority, Census Says," invoked the Census Bureau projections: "Nonwhites are expected to become the majority of the nation's children by 2020. . . . This is now the reality among the very youngest Americans: babies." Responding to the earlier, erroneous Census Bureau report, a *Washington Post* article had made the same claim in 2012: "The census has forecast that non-Hispanic whites will be outnumbered in the United States by 2042, and social scientists consider that current status among infants a harbinger of the change." *USA Today*, with a broader reach, asserted that "minorities are now a majority of births; Census shows how fast the nation is changing."[17]

In short order, the Census Bureau reported that minorities dominated among America's young children. This announcement came in 2015 for those under the age of five. *US News & World Report* promptly blared, "It's Official: The US Is Becoming a Minority-Majority Nation," opening its article with, "They may not know it, but for kids under the age of 5, the day the United States became a minority-majority nation has already arrived."[18] Just a few years thereafter, the demographer William Frey pointed out that the latest census population estimates now showed minorities to be the majority of children under the age of ten. Labeling the children born since 2007 as "generation Z-Plus," he stated that "we are on the cusp of seeing the first minority white generation."[19]

In brief, since 2000 the Census Bureau has publicized the majority-minority outcome in its projections, as well as in population estimates for children that are consistent with the majority-minority forecast. The bureau's efforts have been greatly amplified by the media attention its data releases receive. This has established in the public mind the notion of an inevitable transition in the not too distant future to a nation where whites will be a demographic minority, with essentially unknowable but presumably huge consequences for the relative positions of whites and nonwhites.

Extrapolating from the Data

Of course, many commentators, on both the political right and left, have taken these ideas much further. On the far right, the common assertion is that immigration is a mechanism for forcing unwanted demographic change on American whites. The *Daily Stormer*, for example, takes as an "obvious and admitted fact that all White nations are being purposefully multiculturalized to the end of making them racial melting pots."[20] Fox commentator Laura Ingraham opines that "massive demographic changes have been foisted upon the American people," with the consequence that "in some parts of the country, it does seem like the America that we know and love doesn't exist anymore."[21]

An atmosphere of crisis bordering on hysteria pervades the discussion of immigration and demographic change among some conservatives. The right-wing commentator Pat Buchanan has evoked the bogeyman of "Third-World America." In 2018, he identified as "the great issue of our time" the demographic changes wrought by immigration, and he wondered whether America could stop the "invasion" of other countries before "they change the character—political, social, racial, ethnic—character of the country entirely." However, Buchanan is more worried about "Western suicide" than about what others seem to see as cultural and demographic homicide. The *New York Times* columnist Charles Blow has not unfairly characterized these views as "white extinction anxiety."[22]

This anxiety has bubbled up in a nightmare vision that goes far beyond the demographic projection of a white minority. Known as "replacement theory," or "the Great Replacement," this fevered vision is not limited to the United States but is also believed by anti-immigration extremists in western Europe.[23] The core claim of replacement theory, popularized in recent years by the French thinker Renaud Camus, is that a demographic process is under way to replace native white populations of wealthy Western countries with immigrants and their descendants who come from the Global South. An especially sinister twist is the additional idea that this process is being directed from above by Western elites pursuing their own interests, or even by Jews. These ideas echoed, for instance, in the chant by white nationalists demonstrating in Charlottesville, Virginia, shortly after Trump occupied the Oval Office—"Jews will not replace us."[24] More ominously, they have motivated multiple acts of mass violence; the shooter who in 2019, targeting Mexicans, killed twenty-two people at an El Paso Walmart posted a manifesto just before the violence referring to population replacement.

To the left of center, by contrast, there is generally a preternaturally calm confidence in the inevitability of a majority-minority society in the near future. Blow's column on white extinction anxiety continues by asserting that "white people have been the majority of people considered United States citizens since this country was founded, but that period is rapidly drawing to a close." Citing reports about the harbingers of profound demographic shift from the Brookings Institution, among others, Blow concludes, "This is happening. America will soon be a majority-minority country." The panic about this transition, he notes, is limited to those "who conflated America with whiteness."[25]

The journalist Ezra Klein, the editor of the webzine *Vox*, presents the projections from the demographic evidence in a similarly matter-of-fact way, while underscoring its political significance. Calling demographic shift and whites' reaction to it "the most important idea for understanding American politics in 2018," Klein ticks off the indicators of imminent shift as identified by the Census Bureau and demographers: the majority of infants now are nonwhite; the white population is aging, and its most common age is nearly sixty; and accordingly, in most states, deaths among whites outnumber births. Only whites are projected to decline in numbers in the future;

other groups will grow. The unavoidable conclusion is that in a few decades, "for the first time in the nation's history, non-Hispanic whites will no longer make up a majority of the population."[26]

Oddly, given the facticity of this presentation, Klein notes, if briefly, that "race is what we make of it, and what we make of it shifts and mutates." But he does not pursue this thought, which could undercut the apparent implications of demographic shift. Klein focuses instead on current perceptions, observing that everyday experiences in diverse environments tend to magnify the relative sizes of minority groups and depress the number of whites. And such perceptions among whites stoke their anxieties about loss of status, as the social-psychological research cited in the last chapter has demonstrated, and nourish a more conservative politics.[27]

On what could be called the multicultural left, there are also grace notes of celebration at the idea of an imminent majority made up of minorities. The reason for celebration is precisely what drives fear into the hearts of many whites—the end of white dominance in all its manifestations. In 2009, Hua Hsu, writing in the *Atlantic*, delivered a paradigmatic statement: "The End of White America?" Hsu was interested not so much in demographic change, which he took for granted, as in the cultural expressions of an opening up of the mainstream that would accompany that change. He declared early on that, "where the culture is concerned, it [white America] is already finished. Instead of the long-standing model of assimilation toward a common center, the culture is being remade in the image of white America's multiethnic, multicolored heirs."[28] More recently, in *The New Yorker*, Hsu sees whiteness as having become increasingly problematic for those who have invested in it: "Whiteness is no longer an unequivocal badge of privilege"; for some, in fact, it "is invoked only in a dance of disavowal."[29]

In "The End of White America?" Hsu identifies numerous instances of this cultural remaking, such as the hip-hop artist and entrepreneur Sean Combs. In the 1990s, following on his career successes, Combs crashed into the circles of wealthy whites, eventually inviting them to his ironically themed "white parties," where everyone was required to wear white. According to Hsu, "Combs is both a product and a hero of the new cultural mainstream, which prizes diversity above all else, and whose ultimate goal is some vague notion of racial transcendence, rather than subversion or assimilation."[30] Hip-hop itself is the supreme manifestation of cultural refashioning because of its worldwide popularity among youth of all races and because it is manifestly a creation of the African American imagination.

In this new multicultural world, whiteness appears to have been sidelined and white culture seems to be characterized by its vacuousness. For that reason, according to Hsu, "many white Americans are eager to divest themselves of their whiteness entirely." His article was written before the notoriety surrounding Rachel Dolezal, who was forced to resign in 2015 as president of an NAACP chapter in the state of Washington when her parents revealed that she was a white passing as black. Dolezal has become an emblem of a strategy of attempting to leave whiteness behind for a more authentic experience as a member of a minority group.[31] Other whites have adopted an ironic stance toward whiteness, exemplified by the popular blog at the time, *Stuff White People Like*.

If, however, many educated whites are attempting to flee from whiteness, working-class whites are often fleeing "*into* whiteness," a development whose significance for the polity was hard to recognize at the time. Hsu in 2009 identified key features of a cultural configuration that morphed into "Make America Great Again" in 2016. Certainly, one salient feature is nostalgia for a less diverse America, a time experienced by many whites as racially untroubled, "where the '50s never ended." For some working-class whites, this culture coalesces around country music and NASCAR racing. But there is an aggrieved aspect, a feeling of "cultural and social dislocation," a "sense that the system that used to guarantee the white working class some stability"—"dignity" might be the better word—"has gone off-kilter."[32]

Hsu ends on a hopeful note: "The coming white minority does not mean that the racial hierarchy of American culture will suddenly become inverted. . . . There will be dislocations and resentments along the way, but the demographic shifts of the next 40 years are likely to reduce the power of racial hierarchies over everyone's lives, producing a culture that's more likely than any before to treat its inhabitants as individuals, rather than members of a caste or identity group."[33]

Experiencing Diversity in the Everyday

If the reality of a majority-minority nation is somewhere off in the future, that reality has already come to some states and many cities. As of 2018, five states have majority-minority populations: Hawaii, which has never had a white majority; California, by far the largest of the five, where non-Hispanic whites became a numerical minority during the 1990s and have now fallen to less than 40 percent of the population; New Mexico, where Latines are almost half of the population; Nevada, which became majority-minority in 2016; and Texas, another large state, which had transitioned to a majority of minorities by 2005.

Immigration is propelling the spread of diversity across the national landscape. The early waves of the post-1965 immigration concentrated their force on a small number of so-called gateway regions, like Los Angeles, Miami, and New York. But with time, and as concentrations of immigrants continued to grow in these regions, where they competed with each other for jobs and housing, immigrants have been appearing in large numbers in places where there had been no sizable immigrant inflow for a while, sometimes for a century or more, such as small-town Iowa and North Carolina. The new destinations also include Sunbelt metropolitan areas such as Atlanta and Las Vegas, where the Hispanic population in particular has grown rapidly. The spread of immigrants is fed by migration from more established immigrant regions, as well as by new arrivals from abroad.[34]

This burgeoning diversity obviously must affect the everyday experience of most Americans, both white and minority. The United States is still a very segregated society, but segregation has been declining over time. Combined with the rising level of ethno-racial diversity, this has led in particular to steadily changing residential contexts for many whites. Although it is often noted that whites are the most segregated ethno-racial group in the sense that they live typically in neighborhoods with the highest concentrations of fellow group members, their segregation has been declining and they have become steadily more exposed to nonwhites in their neighborhoods. Immigration specifically has had a large impact in diversifying the communities where whites live. The average white in a metropolitan region—80 percent of whites reside in such regions—now lives in a neighborhood that is 75 percent white (down from 88 percent in 1980).[35] In other words, one of four neighbors of a white metropolitan resident belongs to a minority group. This statistical fact implies that many whites and minorities experience an everyday visual diversity on the street or in public places that is likely to affect their perception of changes taking place in the larger society.

In much of the United States, whites have difficulty escaping diversity. One of the new phenomena linked to immigration is the emergence of what could be called "super-diverse" or "global" neighborhoods, where whites and multiple minorities, especially those of immigrant origin, congregate. This phenomenon is not limited to the United States, as these neighborhoods appear in many European cities, such as Amsterdam, London, and Paris, as well as in Canadian cities such as Toronto. But there are many examples in the United States; some of the best known are located in New York City's borough of Queens, in neighborhoods such as Jackson Heights and Astoria.

The phenomenon has now spread far beyond the country's gateway regions, where immigrants have tended to settle initially. A recent study of virtually all metropolitan areas found that, by 2010, most white residents (nearly 80 percent) lived in neighborhoods with a significant presence of at least one minority (Asians, Hispanics, or blacks), and nearly half were in neighborhoods with at least two minority groups.[36] In a surprising development, given the long history of rigid segregation between whites and blacks, whites most commonly experience living with multiple minorities where significant numbers of blacks live alongside Asians or Hispanics or both. Moreover, for white families wanting to avoid minorities, the bastions of whiteness are eroding: as of 2010, only 22 percent of whites in US metropolitan areas lived in white-only areas (which might still have had some minorities, but not enough to be registered as a "significant" presence by the study's criteria). For whites in the most economically dynamic regions of the country, such as the regions centered on Los Angeles or New York, an all-white neighborhood is increasingly rare. White families can find mixed neighborhoods with relatively high percentages of whites, but it is nearly impossible to avoid diversity altogether.[37]

The increasing diversity of the residential environments where the great majority of whites live is bound to affect their perception of demographic shift. According to a growing body of research, the experience of local growth in minority populations influences the perception of their size in a community.[38] Well known, moreover, is that Americans, both white and minority, tend to exaggerate minority population sizes and to underestimate the size of the white majority, to the point that many appear to believe that whites are already a numerical minority in the nation. The General Social Survey, a highly regarded national poll, revealed in 2000 that roughly half of Americans perceived whites as a numerical minority, or at least as a smaller group than blacks and Hispanics combined; perceptions of either sort were more common among minority-group members than among whites. Respondents had more realistic estimations of minorities in their local communities, but those living in communities with a larger minority presence perceived minorities as larger in relation to whites in the nation as a whole.[39]

The perception of the relative sizes of minority and white populations is linked in turn to whites' attitudes toward immigrants and racial minorities. This is consistent with the social-psychological research described in the previous chapter, which used population projections of whites' future as a demographic minority to show the effects of status threat on whites' political stances and attitudes toward minorities. The role of status threat equates with the notion that whites' prejudice toward minorities is often defensive—part of a posture by many whites to maintain their sense of superior group position in relation to nonwhites.[40]

An imaginative study by Ryan Enos, a Harvard political scientist, illustrates vividly the impact of diversity in the everyday on whites' political attitudes.[41] He sent pairs of Spanish-speaking, Latine-appearing confederates over the course of several days to suburban train stations around Boston. Surveying the white commuters on the train platforms before and after exposure to these "strangers," Enos found a shift in their attitudes, toward more exclusionary positions concerning Mexican immigration and the children of undocumented immigrants. The experiment powerfully demonstrates the impact of even subtle ethno-racial changes in the everyday environment on white attitudes toward minorities.

Yet the linkage of the increasing diversity of residential contexts and the attitudes held by the majority is not as straightforward as it seems, because an increase in the number of minorities in close proximity unleashes another social-psychological mechanism that undercuts hostility: namely, interpersonal contact. The hypothesis that contact between majority and minority can undermine prejudice is a hallowed part of social psychology, going back to one of the discipline's foundational works, Gordon W. Allport's 1954 book *The Nature of Prejudice*.[42] The contact hypothesis, perhaps precisely because it is so appealing, has been subjected to innumerable tests over the decades, and it has been validated, subject to some important conditions. The most important of these conditions is that, to be effective in countering prejudice, interpersonal contact should involve individuals of equal social status in a context of cooperation rather than conflict. A meta-analysis of more than five hundred studies of the contact hypothesis finds three mechanisms that reduce prejudice—increased knowledge of the other group, heightened empathy, and a reduction of anxiety about intergroup interactions.[43]

The contact hypothesis may help to account for some of the paradox in the geographical distributions of white attitudes. Contrary to the simplest reading of the idea that large minority populations and increases in their relative sizes fuel white hostility, many of the most diverse places in the United States, such as Los Angeles and New York, places with huge numbers of immigrants, are also the most politically liberal; in these places, white as well as minority voters support Democrats, and often very liberal ones, by large margins. Conversely, the places where whites support Republicans by large margins include many where diversity is relatively low and immigrants are still few, such as the Iowa district that is about 95 percent white and has repeatedly elected Representative Steve King, an outspokenly anti-immigrant congressman. But complicating the picture, even these places now also include areas that have recently experienced diversifying change through the arrival of sizable groups of immigrants, especially working-class Hispanics.[44]

In the places with established diversity, as opposed to diversity of very recent vintage, there almost certainly tends to be much greater interpersonal contact across the majority-minority divide. Whites live in neighborhoods that have many more nonwhite residents with whom they have formed amicable neighbor relationships—the kind of situation described by Tomás Jiménez in his study of the impacts of immigrant diversity on whites, *The Other Side of Assimilation*. Or whites encounter nonwhites in workplaces, where their shared status as coworkers creates the potential for respectful interactions. Places with established diversity also tend to have numerous public spaces that promote civil cross-group interactions, as well as some degree of cosmopolitanism—a point argued by the sociologist Elijah Anderson in his book *The Cosmopolitan Canopy*.[45]

Strong evidence of contacts bridging the divide comes from the high intermarriage rates in such places, since such marriages can be conceived as the visible tip of a much greater, less perceptible mass of relationships. Intermarriages on a sizable scale imply the presence of numerous interactions, acquaintanceships, and friendships that do not lead to romance. And intermarriage, which occurs most frequently between whites and minorities, is currently at high levels in the more diverse parts of the United States. A Pew Research Center analysis of the recently married of 2015 reveals a large range of intermarriage rates across metropolitan regions, from 42 percent in Honolulu to 3 percent in Asheville, North Carolina, and Jackson, Mississippi. In the regions with large immigrant populations, especially those where residential segregation is lower overall, intermarriage rates tend to be between 20 and 30 percent; for example, they are 22 percent in the Los Angeles area and 31 percent in Las Vegas. However, in the Chicago and New York regions, where both diversity and segregation are high, the rates are just below 20 percent. Intermarriage rates are lower still in regions where diversity is low, either largely white or largely white and black, such as Asheville and Jackson. This pattern is not limited to the South but is also found in, for example, the Pittsburgh region, where the intermarriage rate is 10 percent.[46]

Conclusion

Demographic anxiety is hardly new in American history. In the early twentieth century, another period when native-born white Americans were uneasy over high levels of immigration, which was then coming from southern and eastern Europe, eugenicists like Madison Grant, author of *The Passing of the Great Race* (1916), rang the tocsin about the undesirability of ethno-racial changes potentially spurred by the immigrant flow. For Grant, Jews and other southern and eastern European ethnics posed a great danger for the racially Nordic character of the United States through "mongrelization."[47] Grant's was an explicitly racist theory, based on notions of inherent superiority and inferiority. Lothrop Stoddard, one of Grant's disciples, extended the racist vision in his 1920 book *The Rising Tide of Color*, which envisioned the white races as numerically submerged by the rapid worldwide growth of nonwhites.[48] This "white extinction anxiety," to borrow Charles Blow's telling phrase, made its way into *The Great Gatsby*, where F. Scott Fitzgerald has Tom Buchanan proclaim, "Civilization's going to pieces. . . . I've gotten to be a pessimist about things. Have you read *The Rise of the Colored Empires* by this man Goddard? . . . Well, it's a fine book, and everybody ought to read it. The idea is if we don't look out the white race will be— will be utterly submerged. It's all scientific stuff; it's been proved."[49]

Scientific or not, it is still unusual to see public discussion rely as heavily on demographic detail as it does today. In a 2018 issue of the staid *National Geographic* devoted to "Race," Michele Norris, in an article entitled "As America Changes, Some Whites Feel

Left Behind," writes about Hazelton, Pennsylvania, which between 2000 and 2016 went from a heavily white to a majority-Hispanic community. This focus allows her to explore how whites respond to demographic change, and in the course of the article she presents a series of graphs derived from census data and projections, with such headings as "Tipping points: By 2020 50.2% of American children will be from today's minority groups. By 2044, 50.3% of Americans of all ages will be from those groups."[50] Norris's presentation of specific demographic data to the tenth of a percentage point assumes a scientific inevitability and predictability about ethno-racial shift and is not alone in doing so.

Americans appear sharply divided in their views of demographic and cultural change. The cleavage is profiled by various years of the American Values Survey, produced by the Public Religion Research Institute. Aside from unsurprising disparities on issues of obvious relevance to partisan politics, the survey shows differences related to the idealization of the past and pessimism about the future. Essentially, these differences mark off a subgroup of the white population that can be roughly delineated by class position (working-class) and party affiliation (Republican). In 2018, for example, the survey inquired whether "the impact of the US becoming majority nonwhite by 2045 will be mostly negative." Although a substantial majority of Americans think that the impact will be positive, differences in views are closely aligned with race, education, and party affiliation. A clear majority of Republicans (61 percent) believe that the impact will be negative, while only a small minority of Democrats (19 percent) agree with them. Moreover, the great majority of nonwhites (about 80 percent of blacks and Hispanics) welcome a majority-nonwhite society. Whites are more apprehensive, especially those without a college degree, about half of whom view the changes as negative. A similar, if not so extreme, division was evident when respondents reacted to the nostalgic query, "Since the 1950s, do you think American culture and way of life has mostly changed for the better or has it changed for the worse?"[51]

Views on immigration are entwined with these perspectives on the past and future. Especially revealing of difference is a question on preserving American culture in the face of immigration: "The American way of life needs to be protected from foreign influence." Party affiliation again points to a wide division: the great majority of Republicans (76 percent) agree with the statement, while only half as many Democrats (39 percent) do so. Ethnicity and race, combined with education, also influence attitudes in this respect. Most minorities, especially Hispanics, disagree with the statement, but most white Americans without college degrees agree, especially the men among them.

These perspectives as revealed by survey data are consistent with the notion that many whites, especially those without university degrees, feel a status threat from the ethno-racial changes they perceive as taking place in American society. These changes are epitomized by the widely accepted notion that whites will be a demographic minority in the not too distant future. Exacerbating the sense of threat is the fact that many Americans "telescope" these changes: they see them as nearer at hand than the population projections indicate, or even as having already occurred. This mistake is not limited to the less educated. Even so astute a commentator as the widely renowned historian Gary Wills, writing at the end of the twentieth century, could get the timing wrong:

> The explosion of ethnic diversity guarantees that affirmative action of some sort will be needed so that everyone feels a stake in a country that is literally changing complexion everyday: whites will be a minority by early in the next century.[52]

Telescoping may help to make more understandable the belief of many whites that they are the victims of discrimination.

In understanding how we have reached this point, we should remember the role of narratives—the stories we tell ourselves to help us think about events in the present that we experience or hear about and what they portend for the future. The narrative that dominates public discourse and is very widely believed by Americans of all races is that of the majority-minority society: the changes of today are harbingers of the inevitable demographic reality that whites will soon be a numerical minority of the population. What will ensue when and if that happens is unknown, but many Americans—and not just whites—believe that whites' societal dominance will erode, if not end, and that whites will lose their position as the prototypical Americans. They will become a sociological, not just a numerical, minority, vulnerable to the power of others.

4

The Demographic Data System and the Surge of Young Americans from Mixed Family Backgrounds

The question is unavoidable: why should anyone *not* believe the data and projections of the Census Bureau? These point to a rapidly unfolding shift in the ethno-racial complexion—a "browning," or "beiging," it is sometimes said—of the United States.[1] This change appears in population projections, but these are, after all, just calculations about a hypothetical future, though based on current data and current patterns in basic demographic processes like fertility.[2] The calculations could easily prove wrong because these patterns are not fixed but shift over time. For example, white fertility may reverse course and go up; or immigration to the United States could decline, as some Americans appear to want to happen.

But the changing complexion of the population is also apparent in data about the present, especially in differences between older and younger Americans. Older Americans are disproportionately white, and younger Americans nonwhite. In particular, children under age ten—"generation Z-plus," as they have been dubbed by the demographer William Frey—are now majority-minority, the first cohort of Americans for whom this is true.[3] Since this will likely be true of future birth groups, and since the white population apparently has already begun to decline, isn't the future majority-minority nation an inevitability?

Adding to the weight of an answer to this question in the affirmative is the well-earned reputation of the Census Bureau for scrupulous rigor and objectivity. Importantly, however, one must never forget that all data are constructed to varying degrees: measurement procedures, such as the classification of observations into categories or the assignment of values to them, intervene between social reality and the consumer of the data. This point is all the more important because the Census Bureau is a government agency whose data are subject to a variety of bureaucratic, legal, and even political influences. The data are never purely the product of scientific concerns, that is, the quest to gain knowledge.[4] Most of the time, these influences may not do much to affect our ability to perceive social reality "through" the data, but there can be moments when unanticipated developments cause social reality to diverge sharply from the data. The early twenty-first century is such a moment.

The development producing this divergence is the rapidly increasing mixing in families across major ethno-racial boundaries and the resulting surge of young Americans who come from mixed family backgrounds. Of course, ethno-racial mixing is nothing new in the United States and was observed as early as the colonial era. In the post–World War II period, the rise of marriage on a large scale across ethnic and religious lines among whites played a leading role in the story of mass assimilation, which forged a white mainstream that included the descendants of late nineteenth- and early twentieth-century immigrants from Ireland and southern and eastern Europe.[5] Throughout American history, moreover, whites' dominant status has been expressed in sexual encounters across racial lines that have produced children, particularly between white men and minority women. When these children were mixed white and black, they were consigned to the African American population by virtue of the "one-drop rule." When the children were mixed white and American Indian, they had a greater chance of being absorbed into the white population.[6]

The current situation is novel in the degree of social recognition accorded mixed ethno-racial parentage as an independent status rather than one that must be amalgamated to one group or another (as in the one-drop rule). The Census Bureau's important decision to allow multiple-race reporting starting in 2000 acknowledges this new reality and also has contributed to it by creating statistical "facts" concerning racial mixture that seep into public consciousness.[7] Nevertheless, the rising level of mixing—specifically, the growing number of young people from mixed family backgrounds—poses a potent challenge to our conventional statistical schemes for ethnicity and race and to our perceptions of the present and near future of American society. As I show in this chapter, demographic data in their current state fail to adequately grapple with mixing and, as a result, seriously distort contemporary and near-future ethnoracial realities.

This chapter is a pivot in the book's argument, as this preliminary discussion hints. On the one hand, it continues the investigation into the dominant narrative about the American future, the majority-minority society, and reveals its basis in flawed data that distort social reality. On the other hand, by highlighting a momentous demographic development—the surging numbers of young people from mixed minority-white family backgrounds—it puts the argument on a different trajectory for the rest of the book. Subsequent chapters examine the significance of this development for the future, first empirically and then interpretively. Only after this examination will the full meaning of the current majority-minority narrative as a "demographic illusion" be apparent.

How the Census Measures Ethnicity and Race

Race has been central to the US census since its origins at the nation's founding. Because of the need to apportion congressional representation among the states, the Constitution mandates a decennial census in article 1, section 2, stipulating that the census count all "free Persons" and all "other Persons" after excluding "Indians not taxed" (presumably because they were not under the jurisdiction of any US government body). All "other persons" were, of course, slaves, who famously counted as three-fifths of a free person for purposes of apportionment. The first census, conducted in 1790, in fact collected data in five categories: free white males age sixteen and older; younger free white males; free white females; all other free persons; and slaves. Race was embedded in the counting then not just because of slavery, but also because of the distinction drawn between whites and other free men and women, who were thus distinguished by color. Whiteness was identified with full citizenship in the new nation, and in fact the nation's first naturalization law (1790), which stipulated the rules by which immigrants could become citizens, restricted this right to anyone who was a "free white person."

Every census since the first one has also collected data by race. But the categories in which it is tallied have expanded over time as Americans' perception of their diversity as a people has grown more complex. A separate category for American Indians was added in 1860, and the first category for Asians ("Chinese") was introduced in 1870.[8] Some broad racial categories grew more detailed over time, affecting the counting of Americans of African descent in particular. During the late nineteenth century, the census counted African Americans according to the degree of their black and white ancestries, going so far as to distinguish in 1890 among "mulatto," "quadroon," and "octaroon," with the latter two indicating "one-fourth" and "one-eighth" African descent, respectively.

These intricate descent categories, incidentally, were assigned by census enumerators, not chosen by the individuals themselves, although enumerators must have often inquired in the household about the degree of black descent of its members when that seemed to be in question. The practice of having enumerators fill out the census forms for households continued past the middle of the twentieth century. Only in 1960 did the Census Bureau adopt the practice of sending the forms to households to complete on their own. This shift, no doubt mandated by practical exigencies in a growing country, had powerful ramifications for ethno-racial counts. When enumerators placed individuals into categories, the emphasis was on ethno-racial membership as perceived by others. When households and their members completed the forms, subjective identifications received much greater weight.

The impact of immigration streams from outside of Europe did not register on the ethno-racial categories of the census until the late nineteenth century. The list of Asian groups began its expansion with the addition of Japanese in 1890 and the introduction of three new categories in 1920: Filipino, Korean, and "Hindu." The latter two disappeared in 1950 but made a return in 1980, when "Hindu" was replaced by the religiously neutral "Asian Indian." By then, Vietnamese had been added as a category, along with Hawaiian and other Pacific Island origins.

Latin Americans appear even later in America's ethno-racial accounting.[9] Mexicans made a cameo appearance as a distinct category of race in 1930; previously, they had been counted among whites. Their classification as a separate race elicited strenuous objections from the Mexican government and Mexican American groups, which successfully insisted that they be returned to the white category. In 1970, the census form sent to a sample of households included a first attempt at a systematic measurement of Americans with Mexican and other Latin American ancestral origins. The question was distinct from race, and in asking about a person's "origin or descent," it provided the categories Mexican, Puerto Rican, Cuban, Central or South American, "Other Spanish," and "No, none of these," from which to choose.[10] The Census Bureau discovered that this specific question caused some confusion because, for example, some non-Hispanic residents of the Midwest and South checked "Central or South American."

So, in 1980, a modified question about Hispanic origins appeared on the census form received by every household. The "Central or South American" response category had been dropped, and the question was now: "Is this person of Spanish/Hispanic origin or descent?" With this addition to the so-called short form, the questions answered by every household, ethno-racial origins now claimed two questions on the full-count census form, one for race and one for what the Census Bureau regarded as "ethnicity." Since then, though the question wordings and categories have been regularly modified and their order has been switched (initially, the race question appeared first and now the Hispanic-origin question does), a two-question format for collecting the data has been a consistent feature of the census, the American Community Survey (a roughly 1 percent annual sample of the nation that began in 2005), the Current Population Survey, and numerous other surveys.

One other innovation is of great consequence for the story I am telling. In 2000, the Census Bureau yielded to pressure from below, from ordinary Americans who did not want to be forced to choose between parts of their family backgrounds, either for themselves or for their children.[11] For the first time, the census form allowed respondents to mark more than one race to indicate complex racial identities and backgrounds. Initially, the option to check the boxes for multiple races did not seem of great moment. Many Hispanics claim multiple races, but often on the basis of the mixing of indigenous peoples, Africans, and Europeans that happened in Latin American societies rather than after migration to the United States. Apart from Hispanics, just 1.9 percent of Americans claimed to be of mixed race in the 2000 Census. By 2010, that figure had risen to a still modest 2.3 percent. However, the mixed-race part of the population is expected to be one of the fastest growing, and for good reason.

The two questions in the 2010 Census for collecting data about ethnicity and race are shown in figure 4.1. The 2020 questions will be similar, although the plans, as I write, call for fill-in areas, which will allow whites and blacks in particular to provide greater specificity about their ethnic origins, such as Italian or Jamaican.[12]

The mutations of the census questions about ethnicity and race point to a difference from the other demographic characteristics on the census form, like sex and age. Especially because of mixing in families in the past and present, answering questions about ethno-racial origins calls for more interpretation of the social circumstances of an individual's life and family origins, and it invokes identity in the sense of a presentation of self that can be shaped by individual

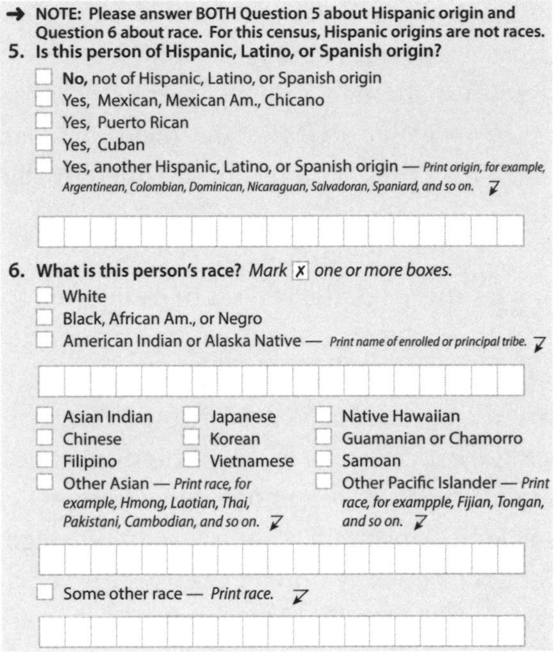
→ NOTE: Please answer BOTH Question 5 about Hispanic origin and Question 6 about race. For this census, Hispanic origins are not races.

5. Is this person of Hispanic, Latino, or Spanish origin?

- ☐ **No,** not of Hispanic, Latino, or Spanish origin
- ☐ Yes, Mexican, Mexican Am., Chicano
- ☐ Yes, Puerto Rican
- ☐ Yes, Cuban
- ☐ Yes, another Hispanic, Latino, or Spanish origin — *Print origin, for example, Argentinean, Colombian, Dominican, Nicaraguan, Salvadoran, Spaniard, and so on.*

6. What is this person's race? *Mark* ☒ *one or more boxes.*

- ☐ White
- ☐ Black, African Am., or Negro
- ☐ American Indian or Alaska Native — *Print name of enrolled or principal tribe.*
- ☐ Asian Indian
- ☐ Japanese
- ☐ Native Hawaiian
- ☐ Chinese
- ☐ Korean
- ☐ Guamanian or Chamorro
- ☐ Filipino
- ☐ Vietnamese
- ☐ Samoan
- ☐ Other Asian — *Print race, for example, Hmong, Laotian, Thai, Pakistani, Cambodian, and so on.*
- ☐ Other Pacific Islander — *Print race, for exampple, Fijian, Tongan, and so on.*
- ☐ Some other race — *Print race.*

FIGURE 4.1 Questions about Race and Hispanic Origin Used on the 2010 Census
Source: U.S. Census Bureau (Humes et al. 2011).

choice as well as by "reflected appraisals" in the eyes of others. That race and ethnicity are not fixed and obvious in the same way that, say, age is has been demonstrated by the inconsistencies that appear in reports for the same individuals over time. (Sex also increasingly involves elements of choice, but not yet to the same degree as race and ethnicity.) Census Bureau researchers matched records for the same individuals in the 2000 and 2010 Censuses and, together with the demographer Carolyn Liebler, compared ethno-racial responses. For about 6 percent of the population, the responses were different.[13]

PUBLIC REPORTING

Collecting data is one thing; processing the data into presentable form can be something else. The two questions, with the detail they allow—especially the option of identifying with more than one race—can give rise to numerous complex combinations, such as persons of Mexican ethnicity and Chinese race. On its website, the Census Bureau provides counts for some of these detailed and complex categories and makes data available for large samples of individuals (the so-called PUMS data, or Public Use Microdata Samples) from which other counts not provided by the bureau can be calculated.

However, the public pronouncements about census data take advantage of a far more condensed set of categories and generally focus on mutually exclusive ones. Six of the categories stand out: single-race whites; single-race blacks, Asians, and American Indians; persons of mixed race; and Hispanics. (There is also a small category for Hawaiians and other Pacific Islanders, and another small "other race" category for those who cannot be placed anywhere else.[14] To avoid overburdening the discussion, these two categories are not considered.) As is frequently noted in Census Bureau publications, Hispanics "may be of any race." Hence, individuals who indicate any Hispanic ancestry are classified in this group, whatever their race. The Census Bureau's public statements that minorities outnumber whites among US babies and that projections show whites becoming a minority of the population in the mid-2040s are undergirded by these categories. In other words, the "whites" who are or will be a minority are non-Hispanics who check only "white" on the race question. Others are also white in some sense—for instance, they may be white and Asian by background, or have one white and one Hispanic parent—but are counted as not white for the purpose of describing the population in public statements.

Table 4.1, which is taken from the Census Bureau's report on the 2017 projections, illustrates this data scheme and its usual interpretation. The subheading to the table is actually the headline: "The non-Hispanic White population is projected to shrink." But in fact the headline concerns only those whites who select white as their sole race; those who are white and another race are not deemed relevant to the claim. There are two lines for the single-race white population, but the subheading directs attention to the second of them, to non-Hispanic single-race whites. In other words, the first line, which shows the white population increasing over time, includes Hispanics,

TABLE 4.1. Population by Race and Ethnicity: Projections 2030 to 2060

The non-Hispanic White population is projected to shrink by 19 million people by 2060.

	Population (in thousands)						Change from 2016 to 2060	
	2016		2030		2060			
Characteristics	Number	Percent	Number	Percent	Number	Percent	Number	Percent
Total population	**323,128**	**100.0**	**354,840**	**100.0**	**403,697**	**100.0**	**80,569**	**24.9**
One race								
White	248,503	76.9	263,302	74.2	274,576	68.0	26,073	10.5
Non-Hispanic White	197,970	61.3	197,888	55.8	178,884	44.3	−19,086	−9.6
Black or African American	43,001	13.3	48,934	13.8	60,471	15.0	17,470	40.6
American Indian and Alaska Native	4,055	1.3	4,657	1.3	5,567	1.4	1,512	37.3
Asian	18,319	5.7	24,382	6.9	36,778	9.1	18,459	100.8
Native Hawaiian and Other Pacific Islander	771	0.2	912	0.3	1,124	0.3	353	45.8
Two or More Races	8,480	2.6	12,652	3.6	25,181	6.2	16,701	196.9
Hispanic	57,470	17.8	74,751	21.1	111,022	27.5	53,552	93.2

Source: U.S. Census Bureau (Vespa et al. 2018).

as do all of the other lines for racial groups. Accordingly, the note at the bottom of the table found in the report warns that "percentages will not add to 100 because Hispanics may be of any race."

Why not interpret the line for whites including Hispanics? It tells a very different story, indicating that whites will still be a strong majority of the population, about two-thirds, in 2060. This story gets no traction for two reasons. For one, there is a strong proclivity in census data presentations, as well as in the public understanding of them, to see the ethnic and racial data as reports of identities and group affiliations and to presume that one identity must be dominant for individuals whose ancestral origins supply multiple possibilities. To put the matter differently, group belongings tend to be seen as mutually exclusive: affiliation with one precludes affiliation with another. There is also a conceptual tidiness involved: mutually exclusive, exhaustive categories classify every individual in one and only one of them.

The second reason has to do with empirical knowledge about the difficulties that many Hispanics have in answering the question about race. Since their primary identity is often within the umbrella of Latine identities, they can be unsure how to answer the race question. For example, immigrants can be confused by US racial categories, which do not match those at home, and often write a nationality label in the "other" race space. Hispanics may also choose "white" for a variety of reasons, including as an attempt to signal their Americanness.[15] (For example, many later-generation Mexican Americans in south Texas identify as "white" because of family memories of Mexicans' past legal status as white, which originated in the citizenship guarantee of the 1848 Treaty of Guadalupe Hidalgo at the end of the Mexican-American War.) In other words, in the current two-question format for recording ethno-racial background, it is a mistake to assume that Hispanics' choice of "white" for their race generally conveys the same information about identities and group affiliations as it does for Americans whose ancestors immigrated from Europe.

This ambiguity in race reports by Hispanics has a deeper implication. The current questions make it impossible for individuals filling out census forms to indicate meaningfully—in a way that the Census Bureau can recognize—that they or their children have mixed

Hispanic and non-Hispanic ancestry. There is a fundamental lack of parallelism in the reporting of race and Hispanic origin. Matters would be different if Latines were not forced to choose a race but could do so only when they thought it relevant, when, for example, they come from mixed Anglo-Hispanic families.

THE OFFICE OF MANAGEMENT AND BUDGET AND THE CENSUS

As noted in the last chapter, the federal Office of Management and Budget is also part of the nation's demographic data system. The OMB's role is especially critical to this book's story because it defines standards for the collection of ethnicity and race data. This may seem peculiar because, as its name implies, the OMB is not an agency that is primarily concerned with the generation of scientific knowledge. One mission of the OMB, however, is to ensure that important kinds of data are consistent across federal agencies and departments, and ethnic and racial data are crucial for civil rights enforcement.[16]

The standards that regulate census ethnic and racial data today were promulgated by the OMB in 1997, in Directive 15. The standards, to be fair to the OMB, were not developed in a remote and bureaucratic way, but on the basis of extensive discussion with stakeholders, including the Census Bureau. And they took into account concerns that were already affecting the bureau's thinking about the impending 2000 Census, such as the introduction of a multiple-choice option for the race question. The directive stated that

> respondents shall be offered the option of selecting one or more racial designations. Recommended forms for the instruction accompanying the multiple response question are "Mark one or more" and "Select one or more."

That memorandum identified the major categories to be used for the reporting of such data.[17] These are the categories in table 4.1. The memorandum also defines these labels in terms of the ancestries or origins underlying them: for example, whites are equated with "origins in any of the original peoples of Europe, the Middle East, or

North Africa." The directive does not require that the original data be collected solely in terms of these categories; more detailed ones may be used, but these must be capable of being aggregated into the required categories for reporting.

The OMB standards mandate a two-question format, one question for race and the other for Hispanic ethnicity. Both questions are to be answered by self-reports. However, there is an unresolved ambiguity about this reporting. Often, the census form for a household is completed by a single household member, and the degree to which that person's reports on other household members would coincide with what they would claim themselves is unknown. Since they all live together, and most often constitute a family, the correspondence is presumably very high, but it is probably not perfect.

The multiple-race option raised concerns among civil rights groups and in Department of Justice discussions with stakeholders prior to the 2000 Census. The census counts of minority groups are essential for civil rights jurisprudence, such as litigation over employer discrimination and enforcement of the Voting Rights Act. With a mixed-race option, civil rights advocates feared that minority counts could be reduced, with the consequence of weakening arguments, say, that employers were discriminating because they had failed to hire an appropriate number of minority workers given the minority presence in geographically proximate labor markets. Any removal of mixed-race individuals from minority counts seemed especially unjust in light of the past relegation of mixed-race blacks to the black group via the so-called one-drop rule.

The OMB issued "guidance" on this issue in March 2000, just prior to the census.[18] The guidance was tailored specifically to civil rights monitoring and enforcement and laid out principles for classifying individuals of mixed race for those purposes. In particular, the OMB said that individuals of mixed minority and white origins should be allocated to the minority category. Just as with the one-drop rule, in other words, the minority side was to take precedence over the white side in the federal statistical system, at least for civil rights purposes. (The irony involved was not lost on some critics.) Though this intent might seem to limit the principle, it is easy to see why its impact would be larger within the broad scheme of census data reporting. How could the census publish two contradictory versions of the data for the same place? This guidance tipped the scales against a more expansive definition of whites in particular. If two versions of ethno-racial counts existed for the same geography, one with higher counts of whites than the other, and hence lower counts of minorities, the consequences would be great confusion (which one is right?) and the undermining of civil rights litigation (why should the court accept these data, the defendant could argue, when the Census Bureau has published another version more favorable to me?).

With this OMB recommendation, a track switch had been thrown, perhaps unintentionally, but thrown nevertheless. Data, at least in the form shown to the broad public and reported by the media, were to be shunted in a distinct direction. The decision to give preference to the minority side in reporting data has had huge consequences, as we will shortly see.

The role of the OMB in preparation for the 2000 Census may appear to suggest a largely collaborative relationship with the census, rather than a constraining one. A different picture appears in the run-up to the 2020 Census. Aware of shortcomings in the two-question format—especially because many Hispanics, forced to answer a race question that they do not find meaningful, place themselves in the "other" race category—the Census Bureau tested in 2015 a new composite question. In the one-question format, a "Hispanic, Latino, or Spanish" category would be added to the list of races, and respondents would still have the option of marking one or more categories. An additional element in the test was a new race category for "Middle Eastern or North African" (or MENA). This part of the test responded to demands from individuals and interest groups that the groups from this part of the world, whose members frequently experience prejudice and discrimination in American society, not least because many are Muslim, must be distinguished from whites, so that their disparate status could be analyzed.

The test was a success in the eyes of the Census Bureau.[19] Latine use of the bothersome "other" race category (which, because it is not an OMB category of reporting, has forced the Census Bureau to reallocate its occupants to the OMB race categories for other governmental agencies) was greatly reduced. Moreover, most Hispanics no longer checked any racial category, corroborating the widespread belief that "Hispanic, Latino, or Spanish" is the main identity for much of this population. A side benefit was that Latines who checked racial boxes—mostly "white"—did so meaningfully, according to interviews conducted by the Census Bureau. These Latines were generally reporting mixed family origins; those who reported "white" in the new one-question format were usually indicating a family background that included European-descent forebears. In the two-question format, mixed backgrounds could not be reported because of the assumption that a Hispanic "may be of any race"; as noted, a Hispanic identity therefore took precedence over everything else.

The new MENA race category also worked as anticipated. Consequently, the Census Bureau staff recommended using the new composite question in the 2020 Census.[20] However, the OMB appears not to have cooperated. Use of the new question would require a change in the OMB standards for race and ethnicity, but no new standards were issued. In January 2018, the Census Bureau announced that it would retain the two-question format for the 2020 Census and no new categories would be added. The National Public Radio journalist Hansi Lo Wang reported that, according to census experts, the decision "suggests the Trump administration will not support Obama-era proposals to change how the US government collects information about race and ethnicity."[21]

If so, politics has constrained the census on a very consequential issue.

A Momentous Challenge to Demographic Reporting: The Surge of Young Americans from Mixed Family Backgrounds

INTERMARRIAGE

Mixing in families is rising sharply. To a degree not true in the past, this mixing is socially acceptable and legitimated through marriage, giving it an impact on family relations and on the next generation

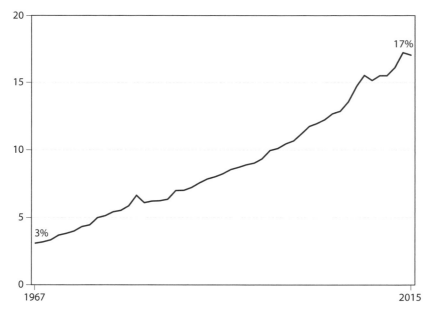

FIGURE 4.2 The Rise of Intermarriage since *Loving v. Virginia* (1967)
Note: The line shows the annual rate of marriage across the major lines of race and Hispanic origin among newlyweds.
Source: Livingston and Brown 2017, data courtesy of Anna Brown.

that is novel and potentially consequential for ethno-racial boundaries. In the not very distant past, marriage across racial lines was legally prohibited in many states.[22] It was only in 1967, in the wonderfully named decision *Loving v. Virginia*, that the Supreme Court effectively threw out the remaining antimiscegenation laws.

Since then, the rate of intermarriage has climbed steadily. This is not to say that marriage is the only route to family mixing; mixed families are also forming and procreating without a legal bond. But the best trend data are for marriage, and there is no reason to suspect that the mixing to be seen in marriage is not also occurring in the families of unmarried partners. In fact, the degree of mixing outside of marriage may be even greater, since some mixed couples who anticipate family resistance may hesitate to marry.

Figure 4.2 shows the trend line of the percentage of ethno-racial intermarriages that took place each year between 1967 and 2015, as calculated by the Pew Research Center.[23] When *Loving v. Virginia*

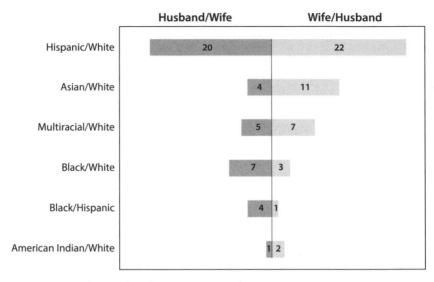

FIGURE 4.3 Prevalent Newlywed Intermarriage Combinations
Note: The bars represent the percentages of opposite-sex newlywed intermarriages for each combination. Read the label combinations in the following way: for Hispanic/white, the left-hand bar shows the percentage of married couples in which the husband is Hispanic and the wife is white, while the right-hand bar shows the percentage in which the wife is Hispanic and the husband is white.
Source: Livingston and Brown 2017.

was decided, that rate was quite low—just 3 percent of newlyweds married someone from a different ethno-racial background. But the percentage has increased almost in a straight line since 1967 and in 2015 stood at 17 percent, with no hint of stopping. Recently, one of every six newlyweds was intermarrying. This is what demographers call an "incidence" rate. The impact on the "stock" of existing marriages is necessarily slower, since most of those marriages occurred in years when the intermarriage rate was lower than it is now. Nevertheless, today 10 percent of all married persons have a partner of a different race or ethnicity from their own.

The predominant form of intermarriage unites minority and white partners. Marriages between Hispanics and non-Hispanic whites make up more than 40 percent of all recent intermarriages (see figure 4.3). Marriages between whites and Asians are the next most common combination, at 15 percent. Altogether, intermarriages with one non-Hispanic white partner constitute more than 80 percent of the whole. This predominance indicates that whites are desired partners for many young minority-group members, because in intermarriages whites are overrepresented relative to their numbers in the pool from which newlyweds mostly come. There is, in other words, an ethno-racial "status" dimension in marriage choice: some minority-group members find majority-group partners attractive because they represent the dominant group in US society.

Another indication of this dimension is found in the education levels, a status-related characteristic, of the minority-group members who intermarry. Overall, intermarriage for them is related to education. The linkage is especially strong for Hispanics. For instance, while only one-sixth of Latines with a high school diploma or less intermarry, the rate is almost 50 percent for those with a baccalaureate. For black men, who are more likely than black women to intermarry, the incidence of intermarriage also climbs steeply with education level, though not quite as much as for Hispanics. Asians deviate somewhat from the pattern, but it is nevertheless true that Asians with some college exposure have higher frequencies of intermarriage than those with at most a high school diploma. In contrast to these patterns, whites exhibit little change in intermarriage tendency across education levels.[24]

The intermarriage rate has reached a point where a large and growing minority of Americans now have someone from another ethno-racial group in their family network. Intermarriage has a ramifying impact on kinship networks and hence on the contact across ethno-racial lines at family events like weddings and funerals. In a Pew survey around 2010—when 8.4 percent of all marriages were intermarriages—35 percent of Americans said that they had a close relative married to someone from another racial group. Since the overall rate of intermarriage has continued to climb, the figure is presumably near 40 percent now. The intergroup contact within families may help to account for the rapid growth in the acceptability of intermarriage. In a related national Pew survey, almost two-thirds declared that they "would be fine" with a family member marrying "someone outside their own racial or ethnic group." A quarter-century earlier, intermarriage was much less acceptable.[25]

This penetration of ethno-racial diversity into family networks is limited, however, by geography. As observed in the last chapter, intermarriage must be so limited because it obviously depends on diversity within the pool of possible mates. For that reason, there is enormous variation across metropolitan regions in the overall percentage of intermarriages among new marriages. According to the calculations of the Pew Research Center, in Honolulu, Hawaii, where the intermarriage rate was highest in 2011–2015, the "pool of potential partners," comprising the unmarried and the just married, was "made up of 42% Asians, 20% non-Hispanic whites, and 9% Hispanics." The next-highest intermarriage rate was found in the Las Vegas area, whose pool of possible partners was 46 percent white, 27 percent Hispanic, 14 percent black, and 9 percent Asian.[26] However, ethno-racial diversity per se is not enough to guarantee a high level of intermarriage. It is lower than diversity alone would predict in regions that are highly segregated. And in those metropolitan areas that have been untouched by post-1965 immigration and whose populations are divided largely between whites and blacks, the intermarriage rate remains low.

MIXED CHILDREN

The rise of mixed families obviously implies that more and more children are growing up with parents and other relatives like grandparents, aunts, uncles, and cousins who come from different ethno-racial backgrounds. In the second half of the twentieth century, family mixing by whites from different ethnic backgrounds and the surge of younger whites with mixed, and increasingly complex, family origins played a major role in eroding ethnic distinctions (such as between British Americans and Italian Americans) that had once seemed salient and important.[27] An obvious question, then, is what to make of the similar surge of young people from mixed racial backgrounds or from mixed Latine and non-Latine families.

To get a grasp of the magnitude of mixing, the best data come from birth certificates, which usually show the backgrounds of both mothers and fathers. The fathers' data in particular are more commonly available on birth certificates than in census data because, in the latter, the fathers are identifiable only when they live in the same household as their children. On birth certificates, their data are present as long as their paternity is acknowledged. Even the birth certificate data, however, are not complete. For births in 2017, fathers' data were missing on 14 percent of the certificates.[28] These cases should not be laid aside just because a key datum is missing. A common assumption in social-science analyses is that the cases with missing data are in the aggregate like those where the data are present; the discussion is then based on the cases with complete data. That does not seem like a good way of proceeding here because the sociological significance of a child's mixed family background lies to a substantial degree in the family connections it provides to different groups. In other words, a mixed family background is significant not just because of what is embedded in DNA: it also necessarily establishes close kinship ties to two or more ethno-racial groups by virtue of birth. If the father is not acknowledged, these ties cannot happen. Hence, in determining the overall frequency of mixing among births, the cases with missing paternal data should be included and counted as unmixed.

With that said, 14.1 percent of births in 2017—one of every seven—were to parents from different ethno-racial backgrounds. White parents were a very substantial part of this mixing. Three-quarters of the mixed births were to a white-minority parent combination; or in other terms, this combination then accounted for 10.6 percent of all births in the United States. That is a large proportion: about three-quarters of the black-only births, for example.

Figure 4.4 shows the main ethno-racial combinations involved in contemporary mixing. Mirroring the patterns of intermarriage, the most common combination by far is one non-Hispanic white and one Hispanic parent. This combination accounts for nearly 40 percent of all mixed births, and it is almost evenly divided between Hispanic fathers and Hispanic mothers. The next most common combinations

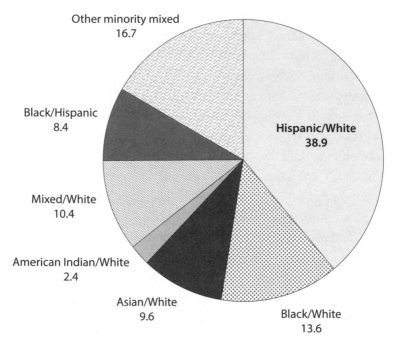

FIGURE 4.4 Ethno-Racial Mixes among 2017 Births
Note: The figure shows the composition of the 14.1 percent of 2017 births of children whose parents came from different major ethno-racial groups.
Source: National Center for Health Statistics, 2017 birth certificate data.

are white and black parents (14 percent, usually with a black father), white and racially mixed parents (10 percent), and white and Asian parents (also 10 percent, usually with an Asian mother). Other combinations involving a white parent, such as white and American Indian parents, occur roughly in accordance with the size of the minority population, but since the minorities are small parts of the national population, the parental combinations are also few in number.

Of the combinations involving only minority parents, one stands out: black and Hispanic parents (usually with black fathers). That combination accounts for 8 percent of all mixed births. The numbers for other combinations (not shown) are much smaller: 4 percent for black and racially mixed parents; 4 percent for Hispanic and racially mixed parents; and 3 percent for Asian and Hispanic parents.

In calling attention especially to children with one white parent and one minority one, I am focusing on what could be described as "first-generation" mixing for whites.[29] In particular, as far as we can tell from the birth certificate, the white parent's background is unmixed. (More accurately, it is likely to be a mix of European ancestries but with no known nonwhite ancestry.) First-generation mixing comes close to guaranteeing that the child will have contact with white relatives as well as minority ones. This is, then, the most rigorous measurement of mixing we can obtain in demographic data.

White ancestry also is involved in some other births as a result of mixing, but in prior generations; that is, a child may have one or more white grandparents or great-grandparents. Such mixing could be described as second- (or later-) generation mixing. Where mixing occurred generations in the past, we cannot be confident, given the racial segregation of American society up through much of the twentieth century, about the attachments to a specific strand of a family background. In the past, the family may have had to associate exclusively with one part of its potential kinship network. Examples abound. Senator Elizabeth Warren, for example, has controversially cited her American Indian ancestry, but this mixing in past generations of her family has become detached from any kinship connections in the present to American Indian individuals. It shows up only in her DNA.

For the future, however, we cannot disregard second-generation mixing. It is already not insubstantial: if we include babies who have any white ancestry in their parents' backgrounds in the count of mixed minority-white births, then the percentage of them rises to 12 percent, or one of every eight infants. Moreover, the role of second-generation mixing will grow, since today's young Americans from mixed family backgrounds will play a greater and greater role in future parenting. Distinguishing between the mixing of the past and that of the present and near future requires an assumption that there is something novel about mixing in the twenty-first century. That assumption will be put to the test in the next chapter.

Just as intermarriage has been rising over time, so has the percentage of births mixing minority and white family backgrounds. The trend line from 1980 is shown in figure 4.5, along with that for mixed births in general. (In this chart, I am forced to rely on census data

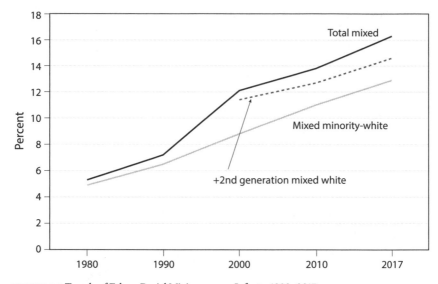

FIGURE 4.5 Trends of Ethno-Racial Mixing among Infants, 1980–2017
Note: Infants are defined as children under the age of one.
Sources: PUMS samples from the 1980–2010 decennial censuses and 2017 American Community Survey data, courtesy of IPUMS (Ruggles et al. 2019).

because of changes in ethno-racial reporting standards in birth certificate data.)[30] Both have risen fairly steadily across a three-decade
period, but only in the early 2000s did the percentage of minority-
white births approach one-tenth of the total. In recent years, the
two lines have begun to diverge somewhat: that is, as the fraction
of overall mixed births has steadily climbed, more of them have not
involved a white parent (someone who is exclusively non-Hispanic
and white). This is occurring partly as a result of mixing in prior
generations between minorities and whites, since more parents are
now mixed themselves. But it is also due to the changing demography of young adult Americans, more of whom belong to minority
groups. There is no sign of a leveling-off of mixing; unless something
unanticipated slows it down or brings it to a halt, there is every
reason to expect that mixed backgrounds will continue to increase
among children born in the United States. The greater frequency of
these births since 2000 makes the phenomenon of a mixed family
background—and, pointedly for ethno-racial divisions, of a mixed

white and minority family background—a distinctive if so far mostly unheralded feature of the early twenty-first century.

A DEEPER DIVE INTO HISPANIC MIXING

Hispanics are critical to the mixing across major ethno-racial boundaries in families. Not only are they the other parents for half of the mixed minority-white infants, according to figure 4.4, but they are involved in about 60 percent of all minority-only mixes. They often are the vital nodes holding together the lattice of linkages involving mixed Americans that increasingly crisscross America's ethno-racial divides.

The frequency of their mixing with non-Hispanics has a major consequence for young Americans with Hispanic ancestry: they frequently have some other ancestry as well. Of all the infants with a Hispanic parent in 2017, one of every four (28.0 percent) had a non-Hispanic parent, and one of every five (20.0 percent) had a non-Hispanic white, or Anglo, parent.

This pattern is not new. In the past, Hispanics were even more central to family mixing. In 1980, for example, when the overall level of mixing was quite low—just 5 percent of infants had ethno-racially mixed parentage (see figure 4.5)—nearly one-third of infants with a Hispanic parent had a non-Hispanic parent as well.[31] Moreover, at that moment, nine out of ten (89.3 percent) of these parents were white. The apparently lower level of mixing today is due to two factors: the higher percentage of Hispanic parents who are immigrants, and the larger size of the young adult Hispanic population. Both increase the likelihood that Hispanics will partner with other Hispanics. Still, by any measure, the level of mixing remains robust.

Not all Latine groups contribute equally, or in the same way, to mixing. One reason lies in the racial diversity of Latines. The racial composition of these groups, generally a consequence of mixing prior to coming to the United States, affects their ability to mix with different parts of the native-born, non-Latine population. Many members of some Hispanic groups with frequent African ancestry, such as Dominicans and Puerto Ricans, are likely to be constrained in their ability to mix with whites, but their way may be smoothed to romantic bonds with African Americans. Others are racially distinct because they are largely indigenous in appearance, as is true of Central Americans and, to a lesser extent, Mexicans. At the opposite pole are the groups whose members commonly are of predominantly European descent; this is the case for some South American groups, such as Argentines and Chileans, and of course it is also true of Spaniards. Members of these groups presumably find it easy to mix with whites.

Another factor is history. Groups with a colonial experience in the United States—Mexicans and Puerto Ricans in particular—have suffered from some degree of enduring disadvantage, which impedes their participation in the mainstream society. The Mexican case is especially complicated: many Mexican Americans today come from families that directly experienced a colonial relationship to American society, having resided for multiple generations in places such as San Antonio, where relations between Hispanics and Anglos were colored well into the twentieth century by the hierarchical patterns established by nineteenth-century conquest. Other Mexican Americans come from families with a recent immigration experience, and they may behave like the descendants of other new immigrants. But here too there is a disparity, based on undocumented status. Having undocumented parents, as Frank Bean and his colleagues have demonstrated, is a source of disadvantage even for those who are US citizens by birth.[32]

Mexicans do exhibit a lower level of mixing, as this unique set of disadvantages implies, but the difference from other Hispanics is not great. Nearly one-quarter (23.1 percent) of infants with a Mexican parent have a non-Hispanic parent, and one of every six (17.2 percent) has an Anglo parent. The fact that many Mexican parents are also immigrants, who tend to partner with other Mexicans, skews the figures downward, but not greatly it seems. Restricting the calculations to the infants of US-born mothers reveals that one-third (34.4 percent) of those with Mexican ancestry have some sort of non-Hispanic ancestry as well, and that one-quarter (26.0 percent) have an Anglo parent.[33] For other infants of Hispanic descent and with US-born mothers, the degree of mixing is notably higher: close to half of these infants (44.8 percent) have a non-Latine parent, and almost one-third (30.7 percent) have an Anglo parent.

Puerto Ricans confound the expectation that, like Mexicans, their mixing would be relatively low. Of all births to Puerto Rican parents, more than 40 percent (43.7 percent) involve a non-Hispanic partner. In one-quarter of births (25.6 percent), the partner is non-Hispanic and white; for another one-eighth (12.6 percent), the partner is African American. Cubans, the fourth-largest Latin American group, are the only other group whose origin is distinguished in the birth certificate data. Their levels of mixing are very similar to those of Hispanics overall.

The frequent mixing of Hispanics and non-Hispanics in families has subtle but major implications for Census Bureau population projections. Between 2016 and 2060, the number of Hispanics is projected to almost double, at which point they will constitute more than one-quarter of the total population, putting them far ahead of other minority groups in terms of size (see table 4.1). However, with their high level and lengthy history of mixing with whites and others, a substantial portion of Hispanics in the future will possess close family ties to Anglos and other non-Hispanics. The Hispanics of the middle of this century will not be insulated from the influences of other groups in American society.

MIXED CHILDREN AND CENSUS DATA

The mixing of white with minority parents has a profound and little-known impact on the public reporting of demographic data. Understanding it requires a bit of wading into the weeds of census ethno-racial classifications. Consider, for example, the widely publicized statement by the Census Bureau, discussed in the preceding chapter, that the majority of babies born in the United States are now members of minority groups. This statement relies on a classification in which most mixed babies with a white parent are categorized as minority—not white, in other words. In identifying children as

TABLE 4.2. The Ethno-Racial Identifications of Infants by White-Minority Parent Combinations, 2017

	White fathers			White mothers		
	% white	% mixed	% minority	% white	% mixed	% minority
Other parent is . . .						
Black	6.1	77.1	13.1	6.9	71.7	13.4
American Indian	22.6	19.1	57.2	25.7	40.6	33.7
Asian & Pacific Islander	13.9	76.9	7.1	18.2	71.6	17.9
Other race	57.0	23.9	19.1	25.7	48.5	25.8
Mixed race	23.4	75.5	0.0	24.7	74.6	0.0
Hispanic	23.8	0.7	75.1	12.5	0.5	86.8
TOTAL	20.9	31.9	46.2	14.3	33.4	50.4
TOTAL w/o Hispanic	17.4	69.7	11.0	16.3	70.5	9.2

Notes: "Non-Hispanic" is assumed for all race categories; percentages may not add to 100% because a small "other" category has been omitted.
Source: American Community Survey, courtesy of IPUMS (Ruggles et al. 2019).

mixed, the Census Bureau does not look to the ethno-racial backgrounds of parents, since one or even both may be missing from the household (the latter in the case of foster children or children being raised by grandparents). Instead, it looks to how the ethno-racial background of the child is reported by adults on the census form.

The surprising fact is that not all mixed children, even when they are infants, are reported as such to the census.[34] (Birth certificates are not helpful here because they do not indicate how parents view their newborns.) Table 4.2 shows the distribution of infant identities as reported by one white and one minority parent in 2017. Overall, about one-third of the infants were reported as mixed, though this figure is lowered by the distribution of identities when the minority parent was Hispanic. By conventional census coding, the identities of Anglo-Hispanic children are mostly Hispanic—that is, they are assigned the identity of the minority parent—and they are therefore reported as minority in table 4.2. They are coded this way essentially by default because the two-question format currently used by the

Census Bureau requires that any indication of Hispanic ancestry lead to classification as Hispanic regardless of what is reported on the race question and regardless of the intentions of the parents. If we remove the white-Hispanic parent pairs, where census conventions create confusion about parental intentions, then the percentage of infants identified as mixed jumps to 70 percent.

Since the children reported as mixed are classified as nonwhite by the census, the table makes apparent how few mixed children appear on the white side of the ledger: just 17 percent. If we apply this figure to what we know from the birth certificate data to have been the share of mixed white-minority births in 2017—10.6 percent—the implication is that almost 9 percent of *all* 2017 births involved white parents but would be nevertheless classified as "minority" by the Census Bureau. Based on this classification decision, the Census Bureau would conclude that whites were a minority among 2017 infants. But the number of "minority" births to white parents is clearly large enough to alter the conclusion with a different classification rule, one that recognizes that partly white infants are not necessarily "babies of color."

A priori, these babies are in between: they are both white and minority, with family roots on both sides of a still salient societal divide. In this respect, the idea that US babies are now mostly minority is an illusion fostered by arbitrary classification decisions— arbitrary at least with respect to the daily lives of these young children. The reader will remember that this classification decision has its origins in an OMB-issued "guidance" to be used for civil rights purposes.

The decision has had far-reaching consequences for census data and lies behind the population projections that yield a majority-minority society by the mid-2040s. Understanding this statement again requires wading into the weeds. In a projection, an individual's ethno-racial classification is fixed: it does not vary over time. The classification as white or not white occurs at first encounter, which can be: (1) when the individual appears in the base, or initial, population data; or (2) when he or she is projected to be "born" (in the future obviously). In either case, the projection relies on an initial ethno-racial description. In the case of an existing individual, this comes from actual data (responses to the two-question format); in the case of a projected birth, the Census Bureau projection program invokes the current patterns by which parents describe their children in ethno-racial terms to make a classification.[35] Either way, the great majority of individuals from mixed majority-minority family backgrounds will be classified as not white. And incidentally, according to the 2017 projections, most of these individuals will be born in the future, some of them of course to present-day Americans with mixed white and minority ancestry. Because most of these prospective parents are already classified on the not-white side of a binary division, their children are likely to be classified this way as well. The classification decision will propagate.

Consequently, individuals of mixed majority-minority parentage are the pivot in the projections. That is, whether or not a majority-minority society is forecast by 2060 depends on the classification of the mixed group. This unsettled outcome emerges when the projections are recast with alternative category placements of the mixed majority-minority group.

Figure 4.6 displays the projected white part of the population, using more and less inclusive conceptions of who counts as white.[36] The lowest line represents the Census Bureau projection: the percentage that is non-Hispanic and solely white by race dips under 50 percent in the mid-2040s. The middle line adds in the projected non-Hispanics who are white and another race. In this case, the transition to a majority-minority society does not occur until the mid-2050s, and by 2060 the white portion of the population is still at 49 percent. The upper line includes a plausible estimate of the group that is part Hispanic and part Anglo, namely, the number of non-Hispanics of mixed minority and white race. (One justification for the plausibility of this estimate is the approximate parity of the two groups among infants in figure 4.4.[37]) Although the upper line steadily declines—the white part of the population decreases throughout the projection—it does not cross the 50 percent threshold by 2060. The majority-minority society does not occur by that point.

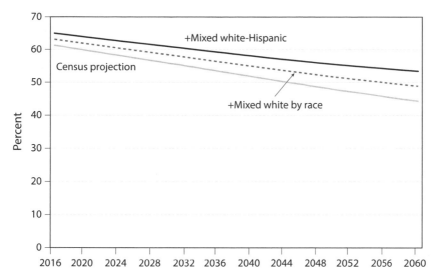

FIGURE 4.6 Projections of Whites as a Percentage of the Population, According to More and Less Inclusive Conceptions of Whiteness

Note: The increment added to the white population by Anglo-Hispanics is a rough estimate (see text for justification).

Source: Population projections from US Census Bureau 2017.

The downward slope of the upper line may leave the impression that the majority-minority society is just a matter of a little more time, but that conclusion is more uncertain than it seems. Consider the infant population, a strong indicator of the future. Figure 4.7 shows its projection under alternative assumptions. The lowest line represents, again, the census-defined white group, which appears to plummet as a percentage of all infants, starting out below 50 percent in 2016 and dropping to 34 percent by 2060. However, the upper line, which again includes the projected number of non-Hispanics who report both white and nonwhite races and the estimated number of Hispanics with Anglo ancestry, presents a very different picture. Although it descends, it does so slowly, dropping by just five percentage points over the life of the projection. And in 2060, white and partly white infants still make up a majority.

What the example of infants demonstrates is the powerful growth of the mixed-white population in the projections. By the 2050s, one of every three babies with white ancestry will also have Hispanic or racially nonwhite ancestry when second-generation mixes are

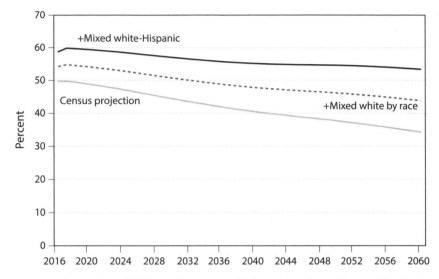

FIGURE 4.7 Projections of Whites as a Percentage of Infants, According to More and Less Inclusive Conceptions of Whiteness
Note: Infants are defined as children under the age of one. The increment added to whites by Anglo-Hispanic infants is a rough estimate (see text for justification).
Source: Population projections from US Census Bureau 2017.

counted. These mixed infants will be almost one-fifth of all infants, of any ethno-racial background. Consequently, assumptions about the ethno-racial assignment of mixed minority-white individuals have a large impact on the projections. The assumption in public demographic data that they are not to be counted with whites determines the outcome of the majority-minority society by the mid-2040s.

Conclusion

I am *not* advocating that the mixed group be counted exclusively with whites. Their position in a majority-minority binary scheme is profoundly ambiguous: they start life with close family links to whites and to minority kin. In this respect, they are an in-between group that through kin relationships spans a societal chasm.

In any event, it should be apparent that our understanding of what the United States might look like in coming decades hinges on what we are willing to assume about the mixed minority-white group. This raises the obvious question of what we know about them. The United States is still a very racially segregated society, and even if Americans from mixed majority-minority backgrounds span its divides through their family connections, as adults they may still lean in one direction or another in choosing where to live and whom to have as friends and, even more pertinently, as a life partner, as well as how they identify themselves. The next chapter delves into these critical questions.

What we have seen so far calls into question the appropriateness of a binary ethno-racial scheme applied to the US population. The public presentation of census data and projections has emphasized the division between the white majority and minority groups, implying that these two blocs are exhaustive and mutually exclusive—everyone fits in one and only one category. Admittedly, a scheme like this can suffer from some degree of error and still provide a very useful approximation. However, the findings in this chapter show that the degree of error is no longer small, and it is growing. At present, more than 10 percent of infants born in the United States have one white and one minority parent. That fraction has been increasing steadily and is virtually certain to increase further in the near future. As the current youngsters from mixed families age and new births continue to feed into the mixed population, the share of all Americans from such backgrounds will increase. With their numbers, they are guaranteed to have a major impact on our society, and the ambiguity of their social location between the majority and minority social formations will firmly refute any binary scheme for predicting the American future.

By relying so heavily on publicly presented census data, Americans have accepted a distorted picture of changing on-the-ground social realities. The census data in their public form emphasize a binary division, but a finer sifting of them uncovers much more mixing across this divide than is generally recognized. The headlines blare about minorities predominating among births, then among children under a certain age, and soon among all children. The social realities could be quite different: in stark contrast to the headlines, a substantial fraction of these "minority" children will have a white parent.

5

What We Know about Americans from Mixed Minority-White Families

> Growing up, I understood myself to be black, and yet I was also exposed to whiteness through my mother and most (though certainly not all) members of her family in nonantagonistic, positively nurturing ways.
> —THOMAS CHATTERTON WILLIAMS (2019)

The young Americans with majority and minority family backgrounds are the critical unknown for the American future in ethnoracial terms. They are the pivot of the population projections of the future ethno-racial composition of the country—epitomized by the highly publicized forecast that whites will be a numerical minority of the population by the mid-2040s, in a quarter-century. A priori, the social locations of these mixed individuals would seem ambiguous or athwart conventional ethno-racial categories, but the Census Bureau classifies the great majority of them among nonwhites for its major public data presentations. This decision determines the forecast of a majority-minority society in the near future and even tarnishes conclusions about today's youth population, such as the statement that the majority of babies belong to minority groups. These are the demographic data that are broadcast widely by the media.

Mixed family backgrounds have a new significance in the twenty-first century. The number of young people with such origins is surging as a result of the rise of mixing in families, signaled by the steady climb of the intermarriage rate. The advent of multiple race reporting in Census 2000 has brought novel attention to them. And this public attention has contributed to an independence for mixed status that it has long lacked in the mainstream society. It should be obvious that we need to know much more about the lives of mixed Americans in order to place them within the ethno-racial configuration of the United States or to understand how they may be changing it. Most broadly stated, the question is: Where are mixed Americans located within the American social terrain? A full answer to this question requires answers to a series of subsidiary questions: What are their experiences and, in particular, to what extent do they confront discriminatory or even exclusionary social boundaries in their daily lives and at critical junctures in their educational and work careers? With whom do they affiliate, or in other words, who populates their network of close connections and who constitutes their families? How do they identify themselves? This last question should not be read simply as, which boxes do they check on a census form, but must include consideration of how stable, salient, and personally significant is their ethno-racial identity.

We are not at a point where questions about Americans with mixed minority and white backgrounds, the focus of this chapter, can be answered in full detail and with authority. But we do now possess a body of research that, in broad strokes, presents a consistent picture. Our situation is akin to that of a jigsaw puzzle solver who finds that some pieces are missing but who can still assemble enough of them to see the general nature of the picture. The research does not offer up a Solomon-like decision on how to split mixed individuals between the white and minority divisions, as public discourse about the population, now and in the future, so often attempts to do. On the whole, mixed individuals remain in between, but the degree to which they resemble whites in social characteristics and in their social integration with them is striking in a number of ways.

There is a huge and important exception: individuals of black and white parentage tend to have experiences like those of African Americans, and consequently they lean strongly toward the minority side in their identities. This distinctiveness indicates that American racism remains severe toward individuals with any sign of African ancestry, even when they have close white relatives. It is conceivable that it affects others as well, such as Anglo-Latines with a strongly indigenous phenotype, but we lack enough evidence to draw such a conclusion yet.

The Evidence

Assembling the evidence on mixed Americans requires cobbling together the findings from a variety of studies that employ diverse methods with mostly offsetting weaknesses and strengths. There are three main sources of evidence: the first consists of large-scale population surveys from the Census Bureau, including decennial census data; the American Community Survey (ACS), an annual demographic survey of an approximately 1 percent sample of the population; and the Current Population Survey (CPS), a smaller monthly survey conducted for the purpose of estimating employment data.[1] Also important here are so-called vital statistics data, in particular birth certificate data, as used in the preceding chapter. In addition to drawing on studies that have used these data, I present my own analyses in what follows. Nongovernmental surveys are the second source of evidence, such as the especially useful surveys conducted by the Pew Research Center. Pew has published in-depth reports on its two most relevant surveys, one of multiracial Americans and one of Hispanics.[2] Third, some studies that are indispensable for the insights they give into the subjective aspects of mixed backgrounds are based on small, nonrandom, in-depth interview studies, mostly with individuals of Asian and white ancestry and of black and white parentage.[3]

An issue that still plagues this research is the selectivity involved in the reporting of mixed family origins. Questions about race and ethnicity (or Hispanic origin) can invoke subjective and contingent understandings of who one is—identities, in other words. So, when asked these questions, only some with mixed backgrounds will claim to be mixed; others will place themselves in single categories. In the preceding chapter, we saw this in the parental reporting about mixed infants (table 4.2); later, we will see that this is true also of adults from mixed family backgrounds.

Moreover, the ethno-racial identities of mixed individuals are more fluid than are those of individuals of unmixed ancestry. This implies that, if we ask the same individuals about their family backgrounds at two different times, there will be more inconsistency for the individuals who are mixed than for those who are unmixed. Some mixed individuals rotate in and out of mixed categories. We know from a clever study that matched individuals in the 2000 and 2010 Censuses that many individuals who sometimes report as mixed at other times appear as unmixed, and that this inconsistency is not unusual.[4] We do not know enough to say whether some characteristics, such as perhaps high education levels, predispose people to report mixed ancestry with greater consistency. A complicating factor in census data involves who completed the form: sometimes the individual in question filled out the form, and at other times it may have been someone else in the household, typically, a family member. But if certain characteristics correlate with the likely reporting of mixed backgrounds—and this seems plausible a priori—then a sample of individuals who report mixed origins at any point in time overrepresents those with these characteristics and underrepresents those without them.

Especially useful therefore are studies that identify mixed backgrounds by tracing family ancestry rather than by asking individuals to identify themselves ethno-racially, since the latter approach can confound family background with identity.[5] The two Pew Research Center surveys fit this bill since they ask separately about the ethno-racial origins of each parent and even more distant ancestors; accordingly, they will play a prominent role in the discussion here.

A two-city study of Mexican Americans also meets this criterion by design, since the adult children of the original families in the sample collected in the mid-1960s were interviewed decades later in the 1990s.[6] Regardless of how the children then identified, we know whether their family origins were mixed or not.

Many other studies suffer from the ambiguities of selectivity in ways that we are not able, at this point in our knowledge, to take into account and compensate for. This is true of census-collected data since the standard two questions, on race and Hispanic origins, can encourage identity responses, as the fluidity in the responses of mixed individuals suggests. If this is true for the census, there is absolutely no reason to assume that it is not true also of other surveys and studies. The problem also affects the in-depth interview studies, which solicit respondents by advertising for individuals with particular kinds of mixed backgrounds: individuals for whom being mixed is not salient at that moment may simply not volunteer. In other words, the mixed population as glimpsed in any data collected at a specific point in time through standard questions about race and ethnicity, like those on the census, is a selective representation of a larger, partly hidden population of people who grew up in mixed families.

Given this issue, it is critical to reach conclusions about the social significance of backgrounds by cross-validating findings across studies with different methodologies. In what follows, I will point up what I see as the main consistencies and inconsistencies in the evidence.

Starting Out in Life

If there is anything consistent in the social-science knowledge about adult social positioning, it is that where we start in life is a very good predictor of where we wind up. Over and over again, studies of intergenerational inequality have arrived at such findings as: that parental education predicts children's education, or that parental occupational status predicts children's status. Recently, as economists and sociologists have gained access to social security and income tax files, they have found that parental income predicts children's adult income to a surprisingly high degree, given that Americans tend to think of their society as open and encouraging mobility, an idea that is proving to be increasingly problematic.[7] Hence, an examination of the family characteristics of infants with mixed parentage is informative; moreover, we largely avoid the problem of selectivity because, for most infants, we know their parents' ethno-racial backgrounds and thus can identify mixed infants with little ambiguity.

PARENTAL EDUCATION

In discussing intermarriage in the previous chapter, I noted that intermarriage generally involves minority parents with above-average levels of education. This is also true of the minority parents of mixed minority-white infants. This broader statement, which includes unmarried parents, implies that, on average, an infant growing up with one minority parent and one white one will be more advantaged than an infant with two parents of the same minority origin. However, the pattern of educational selectivity in mixed families is not uniform: it is much more pronounced for minority mothers than for minority fathers. The educational mix, moreover, varies considerably by ethno-racial origin of the minority parent. For instance, the parents of Asian-white babies have much more education than the parents of black-white babies.

The birth certificate data contain information about the educational attainment of the parents, as do the American Community Survey data. However, the former are preferable because they cover parent pairs who are not living together. So the discussion that follows is based on these data (but the conclusions would not be much affected if the ACS data were used instead).

The most educated parents of mixed infants are those of Asian-white babies. These children mostly—by a more than two-to-one majority—have Asian mothers and white fathers (corresponding with a well-known gendered pattern of intermarriage). From the 2017 birth certificate data I find that, as an Asian mother's education increases, her likelihood of having a child with a white father grows:

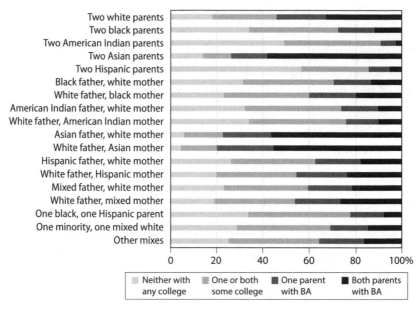

FIGURE 5.1 Parental Education of Infants from Different Mixed and Unmixed Family Backgrounds
Source: National Center for Health Statistics, 2017 birth certificate data.

of those with a high school diploma or less, 7 percent had a child with a white father; of those with a baccalaureate or more, 15 percent did. This pattern is weaker for Asian fathers. Nevertheless, given the generally high educational attainment of Asians, the implication is that most Asian-white children will grow up in highly educated families. In fact, for about 80 percent of these babies, one or both parents have at least the baccalaureate degree; for the majority, both parents possess this credential. The situation of Asian-white infants is very similar to that of infants with two Asian parents, although the latter are a bit more likely to have parents who did not attend college. All these data appear in figure 5.1.

Asian-white infants start life with a superior position compared to infants with two white parents. Although a majority of white-only babies have at least one parent with a baccalaureate, only for about one-third is this true of both parents. The situation at birth of black-only infants looks quite a bit less favorable compared to both of these groups. For slightly more than one-quarter, at least one parent completed college; only for 12 percent is this true of both. Even more disadvantaged are other unmixed infants, those with two American Indian parents or two Hispanic ones. Among the former, fewer than 10 percent have a parent who completed a college degree; for the latter, fewer than 15 percent do. To be sure, the education level of the parents of Hispanic-only infants is influenced by the presence of many immigrant parents in this group.

The parents of mixed black and white infants or mixed American Indian and white infants display in the aggregate superior education levels to the corresponding minority parents of unmixed infants, but not by large margins. For the larger category of black-white infants (where the father is black), the advantage is marginal; where the mother is black and the father white, the advantage is more pronounced. The advantage is also apparent for American Indian–white infants compared to those with two Indian parents. However, for none of these mixed infants does the education of their parents come close to the levels typically enjoyed by infants with two white parents. In these cases, the situation of mixed infants is in between but closer to that of minority-only infants.

For two other large groups of mixed minority-white infants, however, parents' education levels are much higher than they are for infants with two parents from that minority origin. These groups— where one parent is Hispanic and the other Anglo (i.e., non-Hispanic white), and where one parent is racially mixed and the other white— are truly in between. For both mixed groups overall, somewhat more than 40 percent have at least one parent with a baccalaureate. One-fifth of Hispanic-white infants have two highly educated parents and one-quarter of mixed race–white infants do. In both cases, the parental educational distribution is a bit more favorable when the father is white than when the mother is.

However, mixing per se does not of itself provide much of an educational lift in infants' homes. When we look at infants who are not the progeny of first-generation minority-white mixing (first-generation mixing involves, as a reminder, one exclusively non-Hispanic white parent), the parents' educational characteristics generally are not favorable (see the bottom three entries in figure 5.1).

For infants with one black and one Hispanic parent, parental education is on average similar to that for infants with two black parents. Second-generation mixes, where one parent is a mixture of white and one other race, reveal a slightly improved educational distribution in the home. The final group ("other mixes") involves mostly minority origins, but a white strand may also be present in the ancestry of a parent in combination with multiple nonwhite strands. There is again a small improvement in the educational distribution of the parents, making it similar to the overall distribution for black-white infants. But it is less favorable than most of the distributions for first-generation minority-white mixes.

These patterns alert us to an issue to keep an eye on: namely, the distinction between first- and later-generation white-minority mixes. Later-generation mixes (where the white ancestor is a grandparent or great-grandparent) do not appear to provide the same advantages as first-generation white mixes. Does this happen because the advantages of minority-white mixing tend to deteriorate across generations, or is the pattern in current data a product of past, more unfavorable treatment of mixed individuals, which may have changed in the early twenty-first century because of the new status of mixing? One clue lies with the large group of infants with a white parent and a racially mixed one: their relatively favorable situation suggests higher social status and greater integration with whites for mixed majority-minority young adults today.

PARENTAL MARITAL STATUS

Parental marital status is another critical aspect of the starting point for infants. Parents who are married represent the most stable and solid beginning; infants with parents who do not live together are usually the most disadvantaged. Children raised in a home with two parents are the most likely to grow up in economically comfortable circumstances, and they also have the best chance of receiving nurturing parental attention. Cohabiting, unmarried parents can provide these advantages, but the families headed by them are less stable in general than ones headed by married couples. That parents

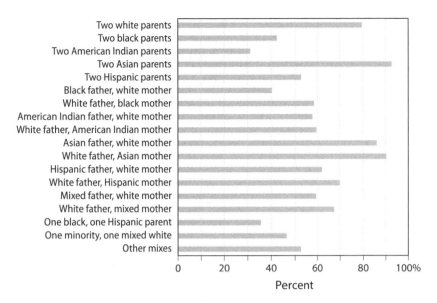

FIGURE 5.2 Rates of Parental Marriage for Infants from Different Mixed and Unmixed Family Backgrounds
Source: National Center for Health Statistics, 2016 birth certificate data.

are married when a child is born is obviously no guarantee that a favorable family context will persist, nor are all single-parent situations disadvantaged, since other relatives, like grandparents, can provide economic and emotional security and adult attention. But in terms of averages and probabilities, having married parents is preferable to having cohabiting ones, and the latter family is preferable to a home with a solo parent.[8]

At the moment of birth, there are large differences in the marital status of parents across categories of mixed and unmixed infants according to ethno-racial origins. (The data on marital status in figure 5.2 come from birth certificates, which do not tell us whether unmarried parents are living together or not.[9]) These differences reflect to a significant degree the economic prospects of parents, since marriage has become less and less an option for working-class and poor adults. Based on the educational differences among parents we just discussed, one could guess then that marriage would be most likely for the parents of Asian-only and Asian-white infants, and this is true: around 90 percent of both groups are born to married parents. The next most favored are infants with two white parents, 80 percent of whom have married parents. At the other end of this range are infants born to various pairings of minority parents— American Indian, black, or Hispanic. The likelihood that their parents are married is typically in the 30 to 50 percent range.

The largest category of mixed infants, with one white and one Hispanic parent, is in between. About half of the infants who are only Hispanic have married parents, while this is true for about two-thirds of the children who are white and Hispanic. Also in the middle are infants with white and racially mixed parents, more than 60 percent of whom have parents who are married. This is virtually the same rate for the infants born to white and American Indian parents (59 percent), whose rate of parental marriage is much higher than for infants with two American Indian parents, since fewer than one-third of these infants are born to a married couple.

The least favorably positioned group of mixed minority-white infants has black and white parentage. Only 45 percent of these infants have married parents, a figure that is scarcely different from that for black-only infants. This low marriage rate is mainly attributable to the situations of white mothers with black fathers; by far the larger group of parents of black-white infants, only 40 percent of these couples are married. The smaller group of white fathers and black mothers of black-white infants is much more likely to have wed. The overall low rate of marriage for the parents of black-white infants suggests that these children will start life with greater economic disadvantages than other mixed infants. That suspicion, we will see, is borne out by the data on family income.

The mixed infants who do not have one white parent are also not well off in terms of parental marriage. This is especially the case for the children of one black and one Hispanic parent, only 36 percent of whom have parents who are married. The other mixed infants who are not the progeny of first-generation minority-white mixing are more likely to live in a home headed by married parents. Even so, in the most favorable case ("other mixes"), the marriage rate of these parents is below that of all of the first-generation minority-white mixes except for the black father–white mother combination.

PARENTAL INCOME

The incomes of the families into which infants are born are also obviously consequential for their start in life. It is not possible with the available data, however, to examine income while also sorting out the family situations of mixed and unmixed infants, because for incomes we have to rely on the Census Bureau's American Community Survey, which is household-based. When both parents are not in the household, it is not possible to completely and unambiguously identify mixed infants (who, in census data, are equated with children under the age of one). The income comparisons that are the most credible involve households with two parents in residence (regardless of their marital status). The drawback of these comparisons is that two-parent families tend to have higher incomes than those of solo parents.* Since we already know that the risk of living in a single-parent family is much higher for some categories of infants, these comparisons may paint an overly rosy picture. We can improve things somewhat by paying attention to discrepancies in how solo parents describe their own and their infants' ethno-racial backgrounds. Doing so allows us to identify some mixed infants in single-parent households.

Though the variability of median parental income across the combinations of two parents' ethno-racial backgrounds is high, the basic story line for the mixed families echoes the preceding patterns with an important twist: the incomes of most combinations tend to be in between those of the corresponding minority families and those of whites, but sometimes their median incomes are even above that of white families, especially when the father is white. Indeed, the income differences in some combinations between a pairing with a white father and a pairing with a minority father are quite substantial. Since they are not matched by equivalent differences in parental educations (see figure 5.1), these income differences appear to reflect the still considerable advantages of white men in the labor market.

*Since unmarried parents may or may not be defined by the census as part of the same family, this analysis is based on the sum of the two parents' individual incomes (called "parental income") rather than on census-defined "family" income.

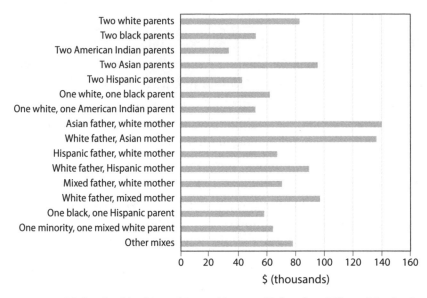

FIGURE 5.3 Median Combined Annual Parental Income of Infants from Different Mixed and Unmixed Family Backgrounds
Note: Data restricted to infants with both parents in household.
Source: 2017 American Community Survey data, courtesy of IPUMS (Ruggles et al. 2019).

The combined parental incomes of Hispanic-white infants exemplify these points (see figure 5.3). There is a huge difference—almost two-to-one—between the median income of $83,000 for a family with two white parents and $43,000 for one with two Hispanic parents. The families of infants with a white father and a Latina mother exceed whites in median income, with $90,000, while the families of infants with a Latino father and a white mother have a median income, $67,000, that falls in the middle. The families of infants with a white and a mixed-race parent have a similar income pattern. When the white parent is the father, the median parental income is nearly $100,000, well above that for white-only infants, and when the mixed-race parent is the father, the parental income is about $70,000. It is not clear what the minority comparison for this figure should be, but it is clearly above the median incomes for the minority families of unmixed infants (other than Asians).

The most affluent mixed families are those with Asian and white parents. Regardless of the race of the father, these families have very high median incomes, well above $100,000. Their incomes are not only higher than the income of the average white-only family but also substantially higher than that of the average Asian-only family, which in turn is more affluent than the average white family.

In the critical case of black-white infants, it also makes no difference whether the black parent is the father or the mother. (The estimate in the figure combines both because of the small sample size of the subgroup with white fathers and black mothers.) Their median parental incomes are in the vicinity of $65,000, a figure clearly above the median for black-only infants but well below that for white-only ones. However, the two-parent data overstate the economic circumstances of families with black-white infants because at least 40 percent are single-parent families, which can be identified when white mothers state that their children are black or mixed black and white (and, less frequently, black mothers assert equivalent mixing for their infants). The economic positions of these families are much more parlous. When the single parent is a white mother (the usual case), the median parental income is $24,000, which is equal to the 2017 federal poverty line for a four-person family. No other group of mixed minority-white infants is so frequently found in single-parent families.

The patterns for American Indian–white infants are similar but skew lower in income. The two-parent families, with median incomes in the $45,000 to $50,000 range, are much less affluent than white-only families but not as impoverished as American Indian–only ones. The single-parent rate for these mixed infants is also high at 25 percent, but not as high as for black-white infants. However, the median income of single parents with American Indian infants is very low, just $10,800, well below the poverty line.

In the bottom three categories of figure 5.3, mixed infants who do not have a white parent, parental incomes generally are not strong. Yet they do suggest a general advantage of mixture in the sense that they are consistently higher than the incomes of families of unmixed infants of minority background. The combined incomes of the parents of black and Hispanic infants (the median is $58,000) are the weakest of the three, but higher than the corresponding incomes of black-only or Hispanic-only families of infants. The median of the combined incomes of the parents of minority–mixed white infants is somewhat higher, at $64,000, about the same as the overall figure in the chart for black-white infants. The median for the heterogeneous category of the other mixes is the highest, at $78,000, putting this category above the Hispanic father–white mother group or the mixed father–white mother one.

In reflecting on these complexities, it is important to keep in mind a point made concerning black-white infants—namely, the risk that the income figures for two-parent households greatly overstate the affluence of a mixed category by omitting single-parent situations. Because of the limitations of census ethno-racial data, it is not possible in general for these complex mixes to identify systematically single-parent households with infants having the appropriate mixtures of parentage. But we saw in the last section that the last three groups of mixed infants have parents with relatively low rates of marriage, which are below all rates for a white parent paired with a minority one except for black fathers paired with white mothers. Of course, household-based data like those in figure 5.3 do include some unmarried couples, but when the rate of marriage is low, the chance that some will be single-parent families is obviously greater.

A final consideration is geography, since average income, along with the cost of living, varies considerably by metropolitan region, which may account for some of the variation among the family groups in figure 5.3. For instance, the relatively high incomes of the parents of some categories of mixed infants could arise from concentration in high-cost, high-income metropolitan regions. A straightforward way of examining this possibility is through a regression analysis of parental income on metropolitan region as a fixed effect. This analysis reinforces the primary finding that the situations of mixed minority-white infants tend to be in between those in white-only and minority-only families, but for the exceptional situations of Asian-white couples. However, the income advantage of infants with two Asian parents compared to those with two white parents disappears when metropolitan region is taken into account, indicating that this income advantage is mainly a consequence of the concentration of Asian parents in high-income regions. The income advantage of infants with mixed Asian and white parentage remains.

RESIDENTIAL CONTEXT

The United States is still a highly segregated society where different economic and ethno-racial groups are residentially concentrated in different spaces and neighborhoods.[10] Segregation, which especially separates more affluent whites from more disadvantaged groups, is a primary mechanism for the intergenerational transmission of privilege and disadvantage because children belonging to different groups are exposed to very different conditions as a result of living in different places. Schooling epitomizes these consequences of segregation. Since schools through the twelfth grade are locally based, children from different ethno-racial groups are educated separately: in fact, rates of school segregation are arguably greater than rates of residential segregation, and unlike the latter, school segregation has not declined in recent decades. Given the unusually important role of local taxes in funding schools, the schools attended by children from affluent white families are generally better funded than those attended by working-class and poor minority children, with implications for the physical condition of school buildings, the educational resources within them, and the qualifications and experience of teachers.[11]

Residential segregation historically has been greatest between blacks and whites. Segregation levels between these two groups are still quite high, though they have been steadily if slowly declining for the last half-century. Segregation is somewhat lower between whites and Hispanics, and for US-born, middle-class Hispanics it is lower still. Segregation is modest between Asians and whites.[12] The question here is: where do the mixed minority-white families with infants fit in the segregated residential space of US society?

The spatial divisions of the country can be fit into a serviceable, if rough, scheme that takes account of how urban a space is and whether a residence is owned or rented. The combination of these

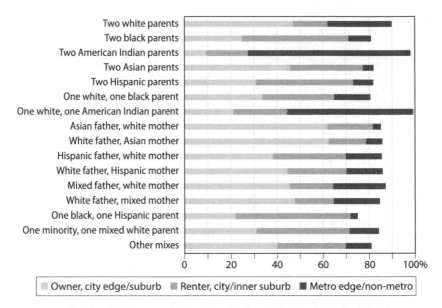

FIGURE 5.4 Residential Contexts of Infants from Different Mixed and Unmixed Family Backgrounds
Note: Residential contexts are defined on the basis of IPUMS classifications of residential space; see note 13 for more details. To simplify the graph, some categories are omitted. Data are limited to infants with both parents in household.
Source: 2017 American Community Survey data, courtesy of IPUMS (Ruggles et al. 2019).

two factors maps out socially very different residential spaces in the United States.[13] Minorities are more likely than whites to live in urban and inner-suburban areas (hereafter abbreviated as "urban") that are dominated by rental housing; whites are more likely to live in suburban or city-edge areas (abbreviated as "suburban") dominated by owner-occupied homes. Whites are also present in disproportionate numbers in rural areas and small towns outside or on the edge of metropolitan regions.

As figure 5.4 shows, nearly half of two-parent families with black infants live in rental spaces in cities or inner suburbs, and only one-quarter live in owner-occupied homes in suburban areas. (As in the discussion of income, we are forced to restrict the data presentation to two-parent families of infants because we can only confidently identify mixed infants in the relevant census data when both parents are present in the household.) The concentration of families with white infants is almost precisely the reverse of that for black infants' families: nearly half are in homeowner suburban areas, while only 15 percent are urban renters. Another one-quarter are located in rural areas and small towns, mostly in homes they own. The spatial distribution of two-parent families of Latine infants is similar to that for families of black infants, but their representation in homeowner suburban spaces, at nearly one-third, is greater.

Some categories of mixed minority-white infants are at least as concentrated in homeowner suburban areas as white infants and their families are. This is true, for example, of infants with a white and a mixed-race parent. Like whites, they are also represented in rural areas and small towns, where one-fifth to one-quarter are found. Infants with a white parent and an Asian parent are even more concentrated in homeowner suburban spaces than white infants are; however, unlike whites, they are infrequently found outside or on the edge of metropolitan regions. Like Asian infants, they and their families live, with few exceptions, in metropolitan regions.

Hispanic-white infants are more likely to reside in homeowner suburban areas than in rental urban areas, but their residential distribution does not favor the former as much as that of white infants does. Nevertheless, they reside much less often in urban rental spaces than do black and Hispanic infants. In other words, they are closer to white families in terms of residence than they are to the main minority ones. Also in between, but closer to their minority side, are black-white infants (represented in figure 5.4 again by a combined figure that does not distinguish which parent is black and which is white).

Families with an American Indian parent are not numerous, but they are in a class by themselves, undoubtedly because many live on or near reservations. Almost three-quarters of the families of infants with two American Indian parents live in rural areas or small towns. The figures are not as high when one parent is American Indian and the other white, but nevertheless, more than half are found in such areas. The rest are almost evenly divided between urban rental areas and suburban homeowner ones. This is not a spatial distribution conducive to advantage.

The families of other mixed infants (those who do not have a white parent) reveal disparate spatial distributions reminiscent of the findings about income. At one extreme, more than half of infants with one black and one Hispanic parent reside in urban rental areas, and fewer than one-quarter are in homeowner suburban areas. Their distribution across different types of residential space resembles that of unmixed black infants. The spatial distribution for infants with minority–mixed white heritage is a bit more favorable, but like that for unmixed Hispanic infants. However, the spatial distribution for those in the remaining, residual category improves more substantially. They resemble infants with one white and one Hispanic parent. Again, for these categories, we should keep in mind that their parents have relatively low marriage rates, so that the data on the presence of two parents in figure 5.4 risk giving an unusually positive picture.

Of course, having a distribution across residential space similar to that of white families does not guarantee residence in the same neighborhoods as whites. However, in the case of homeowners in the suburbs or city-edge areas, whites are dominant overall among families with infants, suggesting that many mixed or minority families in such areas reside in areas that also are occupied by whites, though not necessarily dominated by them.[14] A question that follows is about the nature of the relations between children from mixed families and their white peers.

Ethnographic and survey studies can get us closer to what mixed youth experience growing up in different kinds of residential spaces. Unfortunately, we have very few of these studies. An in-depth interview study by the sociologist Hephzibah Strmic-Pawl is particularly insightful about Asian-whites.[15] Sixty percent or more of her Asian-white interviewees lived in predominantly white neighborhoods as children, and a similar figure attended majority-white schools. Nearly two-thirds described their friends as "all or almost all" white. Repeatedly, when asked what their childhoods were like, these respondents answered like one young man, whose mother was white and whose father was Japanese: "I want to say it was just the same as any other kid would have been. Not a whole lot different." The general sense of these reflections is summarized by Strmic-Pawl in the comment by Dan, whose mother was Chinese and whose father was white: "I felt normal. . . . I never felt that I was different than any other kid." Curiously, many of these same respondents were teased about the Asian side of their background by white friends, but they accepted these micro-aggressions as part of what was "normal." Race, in other words, did not mark their childhood experiences in a way that made them feel like outsiders in mostly white social milieus.[16]

Strmic-Pawl's study also includes young adults with black and white parentage, but she does not delve into their childhood experiences as much, perhaps because her respondents consistently conveyed a sense that managing racism and race-inflected encounters was a major theme throughout their life experience. They oriented themselves in relation to majority and minority polarities very differently from the Asian-white interviewees. The basic sense of their orientation is described by Strmic-Pawl as "salient blackness," and presumably its development began during childhood.

The differences described by Strmic-Pawl are consistent with the friendship patterns to be found in Add Health, a rigorously conducted, nationally representative study that began when the subjects were adolescents. Grace Kao, Kara Joyner, and Kelly Balistreri analyzed the best-friend nominations of the respondents. For single-race adolescents, especially whites and blacks, the tendency to have a best friend of the same race was very high. By comparison, the friendship choices of racially mixed adolescents were less predictable. Black-white adolescents were disproportionately likely, due in part to the racial mix of the schools they attended, to choose black friends. However, their friendship choices were more diverse than we would expect from Strmic-Pawl's interviews: half of black-white adolescents in the study chose a black best friend, and 20 percent chose a white one, with the remaining friendship choices scattered across other groups. This distribution is much less racially homogeneous than the friendship choices of monoracial blacks. Asian-whites chose mainly white best friends (about 70 percent), and relatively few (11 percent) chose Asian best friends. Mixed Asian-white youths tended to befriend whites in part because of the racial mix of the schools they attended, which were majority white on average, but the tendency exceeds the percentage of whites among fellow students and thus appears to reflect preferences to interact with whites.[17]

There are no studies that examine the childhood experiences of mixed Hispanic-white individuals. However, the same Add Health data inform us about the friendships of light-skinned Hispanics, among whom most mixed Anglo-Hispanic adolescents are undoubtedly found. The analysis by Grace Kao and her colleagues found that the majority of these youth (57 percent) chose white best friends, and another 13 percent chose Hispanic friends who were described as "racially white."[18] Unlike the best-friend choices of Asian-white adolescents, however, their choice pattern mirrored the composition of the schools they attended. There is no suggestion of any additional factor in their preference. These data conform to the notion that Anglo-Hispanic youth tend to reside in neighborhoods with many whites, are unlikely to stand out there phenotypically, and seem as likely as Asian-whites to fit in.

Adults with Mixed Parentage

EDUCATIONAL ATTAINMENT

What does growing up in a mixed family mean for an adult's socioeconomic position? Does the relatively advantaged childhood situation of most mixed children compared to children in minority-only families translate into equivalent advantages when they are grown? Educational attainment is a useful marker of adult position, especially given the relative youth on the whole of the mixed minority-white group due to the recency in the surge of mixing. Their youth implies that their occupational position and income are not fully established, but that educational attainment is likely to be a good predictor of these eventual outcomes.

Census data are the best tool for investigating educational attainment because of numbers. That is, credible educational statistics have to be derived from sizable counts of individual cases in each mixed category; only census data, specifically, the American

Community Survey, meet this requirement. However, the downside of using census data comes from selectivity—namely, reports of ethno-racial origins (on the standard questions about race and Hispanic origin) are not fully reliable for mixed individuals because of the fluidity and contingency of their self-presentations. However, we can counteract the selectivity in the ACS data to some extent by drawing on the responses to a question about ancestry. Many mixed individuals who put themselves in a single ethno-racial category on the standard questions (for example, checking only "black" on the race question and "not Hispanic" on the ethnicity one) indicate a more complex ancestry on this additional question (specifying "Irish," for instance). By combining the data from these questions, we can obtain a more comprehensive picture of the situation of mixed minority-white Americans, with "expanded" categories. We can even identify many mixed Anglo-Hispanic adults in this way, by including in this category those who: identify as Hispanic on the Hispanic-origin question but cite European origins such as German on the ancestry question; or identify as non-Hispanic white but name a Latin American ancestry. There is a complication to this strategy: we cannot be sure how many in any expanded mixed category are first-generation mixed (one parent who is white and one who is a minority) and how many are reporting mixing that occurred in the grandparent generation or earlier. But we have no choice in this case and have to depend ultimately on the consistency of our findings about education with patterns we can see in other data.

Figure 5.5 shows the percentages pursuing education beyond high school for groups of US-born men and women between the ages of twenty-five and thirty-nine who have mixed or unmixed origins. In examining educational statistics, we have to take into account that educational levels have been rising over time; and so younger adults, who as a group include proportionately fewer unmixed individuals, have higher average levels than their elders. Additionally, in recent decades, the educational achievements of young women have exceeded those of their brothers. To avoid confounding differences among ethno-racial categories with age and gender differences, we need to compare categories that are equal in these other respects.

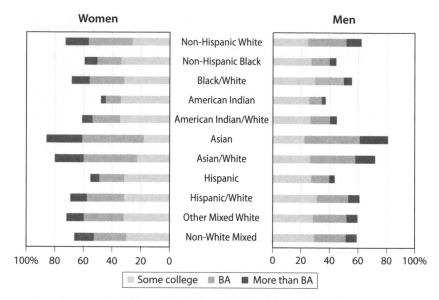

FIGURE 5.5 Postsecondary Educational Attainment of Mixed (Expanded) and Unmixed US-Born Men and Women Ages Twenty-Five to Thirty-Nine
Note: To counteract selective reporting of mixed backgrounds on the race and Hispanic-origin census questions, these expanded mixed categories take into account ancestry data as well. See text discussion.
Source: 2017 American Community Survey data, courtesy IPUMS (Ruggles et al. 2019).

The figure shows the still very large differences among categories of unmixed Americans that favor whites and Asians. Forty-seven percent of white women have earned at least a baccalaureate, as have two-thirds of Asian women, compared to one-quarter of their black peers. The education levels of American Indian and Hispanic women are even weaker. Among men, the percentages of those who have earned a baccalaureate or higher degree are lower on the whole, but the advantages of whites and Asians are arguably greater. The share of white men with a college degree (37 percent) is twice as large as it is for black men (17 percent). The disparity in this respect between Asian men and those in other unmixed nonwhite groups is greater still. The weakest position is occupied by American Indian men, only 11 percent of whom have a baccalaureate.

There is less inequality among the mixed categories, as their educational levels are generally in between the white and corresponding minority figures, sometimes closer to the white figures

and sometimes closer to the minority ones. This intermediate position is exemplified by individuals who come from black-white backgrounds. One-quarter (26 percent) of the men have a college degree,
a figure that is clearly higher than the 17 percent for black-only men
but substantially lower than the 37 percent for white-only men.
The education level of black-white women is similarly positioned,
as 37 percent have a baccalaureate or higher versus 47 percent for
white women and 26 percent for black women.

Some other groups of mixed origin reveal better educational levels, such as the Anglo-Hispanic category. Thirty percent of these
men have earned the baccalaureate or higher, a figure almost double
that for Hispanic men (16 percent). The heterogeneous group of men
in the "other mixed white" category has a rate of college completion
of 31 percent, which is edging a bit closer to the rate for white men.
This category has no precise counterpart among those in the preceding sections because of differences in the classification possibilities
in census data between children (who live with parents) and adults.
It contains individuals who indicate that their white racial origins are
part of a complex mixture (for example, American Indian–black–
white). These individuals might have an exclusively white parent or
a mixed white one; that is, they could be first- or later-generation
mixed white. Interestingly, the group of men with minority-only
mixed family origins has an almost identical rate, suggesting that
mixing per se may be conducive to educational levels above those
of the major minority groups. Among women, the Anglo-Hispanic
category and the categories for complex racial mixtures that include
white also seem closer to whites in educational terms, while the
category containing nonwhite racial mixtures is a bit behind and
positioned in between whites and minorities.

Asian-whites represent another important category of mixing,
especially because their parents are often highly educated. Their
educational achievement levels are also in between those of whites
and of their minority origins, but in the other direction. That is, for
both men and women, their rates of baccalaureate attainment are
well above those of white-only peers but below those of Asian-only
ones. At the other end of the educational spectrum is the group with

American Indian and white backgrounds. The exclusively American Indian group, as noted earlier, has the lowest rate of baccalaureate attainment of all the categories in figure 5.5. The mixed American Indian and white group has a better educational record, but not by much: just 18 percent of these men and 26 percent of the women have earned at least a baccalaureate. This record is well behind that of whites, even though as a result of expansion the majority of those in this mixed category are individuals who are solely white by race but claim some American Indian ancestry.

It is worth delving more into the educational records of individuals of Anglo-Hispanic family background because, as the last chapter showed, they account for almost half of all family mixing between whites and minorities. Moreover, since Latines are overall a notably disadvantaged, albeit diverse, population, the social positioning of mixed Anglo-Hispanic individuals is of critical significance for assessing the role of mixing in ethno-racial change. In other words, evidence confirming the patterns in figure 5.5 would be valuable.

Also particularly valuable would be large-scale surveys with data on both maternal and parental ancestries. Such data would be superior to census data, which do not allow us to infer that a mixed minority-white individual had a white parent as opposed to a white ancestor in a prior generation. One survey that fits this bill is the annual CIRP Freshman Survey, conducted by UCLA's Higher Education Research Institute (HERI). In several of the early years of this century (2001–2003), this survey of the nation's entering college class asked not only about the ethno-racial backgrounds of the students but also about those of their parents, making it possible to identify first-generation mixed students without ambiguity.

This sample is large, but obviously the data tell us only about college entry, not about ultimate educational attainment. (Only four-year colleges are considered here because the data I was able to analyze do not represent the two-year sector very well.) We can see in the data what sort of college students began at, because the survey also ranks the colleges that students attended according to their degree of selectivity; the ranking is rather generous, since about half of the freshmen in the survey were allocated to "high selectivity" schools. Nevertheless, college completion rates generally are higher at more selective colleges.

These data demonstrate that, among students with Latine ancestry, those with a white parent were more likely to begin college and much more likely to enter the selective tier of higher education.[19] (A similar pattern, but on a more modest scale, can be discerned for black students.) The advantage in beginning college becomes apparent when the ratio of Hispanic-only to Anglo-Hispanic students among freshmen at four-year colleges is compared to its equivalent in an appropriate birth cohort. The closest birth cohort is that in the 1980 Census, taken when there were 2.5 Hispanic-only infants for every Anglo-Hispanic baby. Among first-year college students some twenty-plus years later, there were 1.8 Hispanic-only freshmen for every Anglo-Hispanic one—the smaller ratio indicating a disadvantage for Hispanic-only youth in attending college.[20]

More strikingly, students from mixed Hispanic-white families were distributed across the tiers of the four-year system similarly to white students. In the early 2000s, more than half (54 percent) of students with two white parents attended highly selective schools, compared to one-quarter (27 percent) of students with two black parents and one-third (31 percent) of students with two Hispanic parents. For students with one white and one Hispanic parent, however, the fraction in the highly selective tier was, at 53 percent, no different from that for whites; it also made no difference whether the Hispanic parent was the father or the mother. Because of the mixed students' high rate of entering selective schools, the Hispanic population at these schools was almost evenly divided between them and Hispanic-only students. This was a ratio very different from the ratio to be found in the college-going age group.

Moreover, a white parent was a huge advantage for a student with Hispanic ancestry in gaining access to elite schools: these are the public and private universities classified by the survey as having very high selectivity. About 9 percent of the white-only freshmen attended elite schools in the early 2000s, compared to 5 percent of black-only students and 6 percent of Hispanic-only ones. However, 11 percent of the mixed white-Hispanic students attended elite schools. To be sure, though higher than the white rate and about double the rate for Hispanic-only students, the rate for mixed Hispanic students still fell below the rates for Asian-only and mixed Asian-white students, both at 18 percent. And mixed black-white students also exceeded by a bit the rate for the mixed Hispanic students. But only among Hispanic students was the cadre entering elite schools evenly divided between those of only minority parentage and those of mixed majority and minority parentage.

Other data give insight into the educational records of Americans of Mexican descent, a critical part of the total population with Hispanic ancestry, and not just because they are the majority of it. A number of researchers who have examined intergenerational progress have claimed that educational advances cease after the second generation, leaving the educational credentials of the third and subsequent generations well behind those of whites.[21]

In evaluating later-generation Mexican American disadvantage, we need to pay particular attention to what the economists Brian Duncan and Stephen Trejo have described as "ethnic attrition," that is, the loss to the Mexican category of individuals from mixed family backgrounds who no longer identify as Hispanic, or at least no longer do so consistently. A solid body of research reveals that ethnic attrition is considerable in magnitude and selective in its characteristics, removing numerous later-generation individuals with relatively high educational attainment from the Mexican group as identified, say, in census data.[22]

Research by Duncan and Trejo refutes the view that the educational attainment of Mexican Americans stalls after the second generation by showing that ethnic attrition by later-generations individuals with mixed Mexican-Anglo ancestry is partly responsible for this seeming stagnation. Recently, they and their colleagues have updated this research with an analysis of the National Longitudinal Survey of 1997, which examines over time a cohort of Americans born in the years 1980 to 1984.[23] Because the survey collected information on the birthplaces of grandparents, it allows the researchers to identify all third-generation Americans with Mexican-born grandparents, regardless of how they identify, and also to distinguish between those with solely Mexican ancestry and those who come from mixed family backgrounds.

This analysis indicates that, in the third generation, the educational attainment of unmixed Mexican Americans is quite a bit lower than that of individuals whose ancestry is a mix that includes Mexican. The researchers characterize education in terms of total years of schooling, as opposed to credentials earned. They find that unmixed Mexican Americans have an average of 13.0 years of education (equivalent to one year of college). But individuals with mixed Mexican ancestry average 13.8 years, nearly one year more. This mixed group still falls somewhat short of the white average of 14.5 years but is much closer than is the Hispanic average overall. Once again, the mixed group is in between.

EXPERIENCES WITH ETHNO-RACIAL BOUNDARIES

A fundamental experience of ethno-racial difference occurs when individuals encounter a social boundary—that is, when they receive signals, subtle or blunt, upon entering a social milieu or interacting with others that they do not belong or are not equal to the others present. They can have this experience in the course of interactions with other individuals or in an institutional context, as when youth who have received an inferior education in a segregated school system discover that they have been inadequately prepared to compete with peers at the university level. In principle, both minorities and whites can come up against social boundaries, but these experiences are much more consequential for minorities because the white majority controls the social spaces most connected with resources and privileges.[24] For minorities, the signals can make them feel that they do not belong in such spaces.

A signal of this kind is delivered obviously by discriminatory acts, such as individuals being denied jobs or promotions that they believe they deserve, or nonwhite youth being harassed by the police. A harsh signal is received also when a mixed family is given what seems like intentionally poor service in a restaurant. Less blatant signals are sent in the form of what are now known as "micro-aggressions":

slights and snubs that disrupt the smooth flow of everyday interaction to reveal otherwise masked derogatory views. Many Asian-
whites, for example, have been teased during childhood for their
Asian features, such as the epicanthic folds that make their eyes
look different from the white mainstream norm.[25] These signals of
nonbelonging and difference, especially when they accumulate and
become unexceptional, can create a sense in the individuals receiving them that they are permanent outsiders from certain scenes and
groups that matter: in other words, that they are minorities.

The path-breaking Pew survey on multiracial Americans (2015)
is particularly informative about a number of these experiences.
According to it, about 60 percent of Asian-whites and black-whites
say that they have been the target of slurs or jokes, as do about half
of American Indian–whites. Other experiences, however, differ-
entiate more strongly among mixed groups. Nearly 60 percent of
black-whites report receiving poor service in restaurants and elsewhere because of their racial background. By contrast, only half as
many Asian-whites and American Indian–whites say the same: 25
and 30 percent, respectively. These figures are no different from
that for the general public, also surveyed by Pew: slightly more
than 30 percent of adult Americans believe that they have received
poor service because of their racial background. And harassment
by the police sharply distinguishes black-whites from others:
41 percent of them say that they have been "unfairly stopped," compared to just 6 percent of Asian-whites and 15 percent of American
Indian–whites.[26]

Anglo-Hispanics are positioned in between black-whites and
the other mixed groups in how they report on such experiences:
more than half have been targeted by slurs at some point, and about
40 percent have had the experience of poor service.[27] One-quarter
report being stopped by the police without good reason. In addition,
individuals with a mixed Anglo-Latine background experience a high
incidence of employer discrimination: more than one-third complain of this, including 14 percent who say that it happened within
the past year; in Pew's baseline of the general public, one-quarter

said that they had experienced employer discrimination, and just 5 percent said that it had happened within the past year.[28]

The interviews with Asian-whites and black-whites by Strmic-Pawl give additional insight into some of these differences and how they are interpreted by those experiencing them. Her Asian-white respondents experienced mostly micro-aggressions, such as teasing about Asian facial features or cultural traits (food brought from home to school, for example), but chiefly during childhood rather than their adult years. In their view, they had little experience with institutional forms of racism. By contrast, for black-whites, racism, both institutional and individual, appears to be omnipresent, though it is offset by frequent experiences of black solidarity, even when this comes in the modest form of "identity recognition . . . communicated in micro-interactions," such as head nods and fist bumps.[29]

Experiencing a boundary, the sense that one is different from others because of the signals they are sending, depends on the ability of those others to perceive one's ethno-racial origins. This in turn depends on outward markers of origins, especially appearance and name. The recent social-science literature, which has focused on racelike aspects of distinction, gives us little basis for any conclusions about cultural bases of distinctiveness, such as name, clothing, or speech.[30] But we do have data about how mixed individuals perceive the distinctiveness of their appearance: both Pew surveys ask their respondents how they think they would be perceived by someone passing them on the street.

For multiracial individuals, the key factor is whether or not they have some black ancestry. Sixty-one percent of black-white individuals believe that they would be seen as black, while just a tiny fraction, only 7 percent, say that they would be taken for white. (Most of the rest believe that they are seen as "multiracial.") By contrast, among Asian-whites, just 23 percent think that they would be seen as Asian, while 42 percent say that they would be seen as white. Thirty-three percent of Anglo-Hispanics think that they would be seen as Latine, and 58 percent say that they would be seen as white. Individuals from American Indian and white family backgrounds are the most convinced that passersby would take them for whites: nearly 90 percent say so.

SOCIAL AFFILIATIONS

Although individuals from mixed families formed by white and minority parents start life connected by kin to two different groups with different experiences and positions within the US ethno-racial hierarchy, they do not necessarily remain equally connected to both sides as they grow up. Parents may separate, or they may never have lived together, weakening the relationship to grandparents and other relatives on the nonresident parent's side. In addition, a mixed child may encounter a less than warm reception among some relatives.

The Pew survey on multiracial Americans yields data about the social affiliations of mixed individuals, including their contacts with their relatives. It reveals that these contacts are typically not equal: individuals from mixed family backgrounds often have more contact with one side of the family than with the other. However, there is a crucial racial divide in this asymmetry, one that we meet again and again: it lies between individuals of black and white parentage and other individuals from mixed minority and white family backgrounds.[31]

Individuals of Asian and white descent on average have more contact with white relatives (61 percent) than with Asian ones, although contact with Asian relatives could be limited, as the Pew report notes, if the Asian parent is an immigrant whose relatives live abroad. For those who are mixed American Indian and white, the pattern of contact with relatives is even more tilted toward the white side, although the asymmetry may arise partly from the generational distance of the American Indian ancestor: many of the American Indian–white mixes in the Pew survey are found among whites who have an American Indian ancestor in the grandparent generation, or even earlier. For those who are black and white, the asymmetry is reversed: nearly 70 percent say that they have a lot of contact with black relatives, while only 21 percent say the same about white relatives. Forty-one percent reporting having no contact at all with relatives of the white parent. Hostility, open or veiled, on the part of these relatives is likely to be one reason for isolation from the white side of their families.[32] Adults who are partly black are much more likely than others to say that they have been treated badly by relatives because of race, though only one-fifth of black-white multiracials say this.

Many other contacts starting in childhood are determined by the socioeconomic situations of families and their locations on the residential terrain. In these respects, most mixed minority and white families resemble white families more than minority ones, with the principal exception of the families of black-white multiracials. As we have already seen, the starting point for many mixed children guarantees that they will grow up in a residential environment that, though often mixed, includes whites. Of course, childhood contact with whites does not imply that continued association with them, since these children could experience forms of exclusion on account of their nonwhite heritage.

The Pew surveys suggest that such exclusion is not a common experience for Asian-white and American Indian–white multiracials or for Anglo-Hispanics. These groups mostly feel accepted by whites—more so, in fact, than they feel in relation to those of their same minority ancestry. Sixty-two percent of Asian-whites feel "very" accepted by whites, compared to 47 percent who say the same about Asians, and 72 percent of Anglo-Hispanics feel very accepted by the white majority, compared to 49 percent who say the same about Latines. For American Indian–white multiracials, the perception of acceptance is even more lopsided in favor of whites. The perceptions of black-white multiracials are quite different: only one-quarter of them feel very accepted by whites, but nearly 60 percent feel that way about blacks.

The Pew surveys, including the survey on Hispanic identity, are informative about social interaction partners—about friends and neighbors in particular—and thus describe an important portion of the social milieus with which nonwhites and mixed minority-whites live. We can think of these social milieus as encompassing the everyday, amicable contacts of individuals outside of work. These contacts span a range from "greeting" relationships that do not go beyond saying "hello" in a friendly way to other relationships that involve deeper familiarity and perhaps semi-confidential discussions of personal issues.

Most individuals who are white and American Indian live in a white-dominated social world. Almost three-quarters say that all or most of their friends are white, and two-thirds live in largely white neighborhoods. Those who are white and Asian appear to inhabit more diverse worlds, but ones in which whites still are likely to be the majority. Nearly half say that most or all of their friends are white, compared to just 7 percent who say this about Asians. Nearly two-thirds say that all or most of their neighbors are white. The social milieus of Anglo-Hispanics also tilt white, but not as much: half say that all or most of their friends are whites, while one-quarter say this of Hispanics; the figures are very similar concerning their neighbors.

Individuals who are white and black are located in rather different spaces. Half of them say that all or most of their friends are black. However, just one-third claim to live in mostly black neighborhoods; this group is outnumbered by the more than 40 percent who live in mostly white neighborhoods.

Finally, and perhaps most tellingly, individuals from mixed minority and white family backgrounds appear mostly to marry whites. On the one hand, this marriage pattern supports the notion that whites make up disproportionate shares of their social milieus; on the other hand, it ensures that the next generation, their children, will grow up in heavily white, if still mixed, family contexts. Most people choose a romantic partner from the people encountered in everyday social environments, such as individuals they meet at school or at work. A high probability of marrying a white person indicates that one's social milieu is preponderantly white, although we cannot discount the possibility that some mixed individuals seek out a white partner.

The evidence about intermarriage comes partly from a study of interracial marriage, based on the Census Bureau's American Community Survey from a period centered on 2010. It found that white–American Indian and white-Asian individuals have high rates

TABLE 5.1. Marriage Rates to Key Groups for Mixed Minority-White Categories (Expanded), by Gender for Persons Aged 19–39

	% white	% same minority	% same mixed
		MEN	
American Indian-white	72.8	0.6	18.9
Asian-white	64.0	11.5	6.9
Black-white	43.3	18.6	14.9
Hispanic-Anglo	56.9	18.4	13.9
Other white mixed	44.8	—	16.8
		WOMEN	
American Indian-white	74.8	0.6	16.7
Asian-white	72.1	5.0	5.1
Black-white	35.4	35.8	15.6
Hispanic-Anglo	60.3	17.8	12.5
Other white mixed	42.9	—	16.1

Note: Percentages need not add to 100% (across each row) because marriages involving other than the specified categories are not reported. Expanded categories of mixture take into account responses to the ancestry question on the ACS, as well as race and Hispanic-origin data (see text).
Source: 2017 American Community Survey data, provided by IPUMS (Ruggles et al. 2019).

of marriage to whites: around 70 percent.[33] This research also found that a majority of white-black persons are married to whites. In all cases, the rates of marriage to someone from their same minority background are much lower.

My own tabulation from the 2017 American Community Survey (see table 5.1), using expanded categories of mixture for both partners and restricted to men and women under the age of forty to capture relatively recent marriage patterns, arrives at largely similar findings. More than 70 percent of American Indian–white men and women have taken a white partner, and the figure is similar for Asian-white women. It is a bit lower for Asian-white men, at 64 percent.

The big difference from the earlier study involves black-white men and women. With an expanded definition of the black-white category, the marriage rate to whites is substantially lower than that study found: 43 percent of men, and 35 percent of women. It seems plausible that the higher rates in the earlier study are connected with the selective reporting of a multiracial background; that is, marriage to a white person makes white ancestry more salient to an individual from a mixed black-white background, encouraging its reporting. The expansion of the black-white category through ancestry reporting is dominated by individuals who reported as exclusively black on the race question (but indicated some white or European ancestry). Nevertheless, we have to be careful not to exaggerate the significance of this difference in the studies. Individuals from a black-white background (expanded) have much higher rates of marriage to whites than do black-only individuals (11 percent for men and just 4 percent for women). Despite the orientation of many black-white individuals toward African American social milieus, because of discrimination, they have a distinct proclivity to choose white partners.

Nevertheless, for their marriage partners, black-white individuals are clearly more poised between white and minority groups than are other mixed majority-minority categories. The tendencies of some other mixed groups to take partners with whom they share a minority origin are at least worthy of note. American Indian–whites marry others from the same mixed category at substantial rates: 19 percent for men and 17 percent for women. Twelve percent of Asian-white men have an Asian-only spouse, and 7 percent have an Asian-white spouse. (Asian-white women are less likely to choose spouses of Asian descent.) Individuals in the "other white mixes" category, who come from complex mixed backgrounds, are also frequently paired with others from this category (16 to 17 percent). However, they much more frequently have a white partner (43 to 45 percent).

Multiple, mutually supportive studies describe marriage patterns among those who are mixed Latine and Anglo. Table 5.1 shows that, in the 2017 American Community Survey, majorities of Anglo-Hispanic men and women have a non-Hispanic white spouse (57 percent for men and 60 percent for women). However, sizable proportions also marry Latines or mixed Anglo-Latines. The figures are very similar for men and women: 18 percent have chosen a Latine partner, and 13 to 14 percent have a partner from a mixed Anglo-Latine background.

The strong tendency among individuals with mixed Anglo-Hispanic heritage to choose a white partner is confirmed by an important longitudinal study of Mexican American families, which collected data originally in 1965 and then followed up with the children of the interviewed families in the 1990s.[34] Hence, it is insightful about the marriage patterns of mixed Anglo-Mexicans in the latter part of the twentieth century. This study found that, compared to a Mexican American from an unmixed family, an individual who came from a mixed family had five times the odds of partnering with a white person.

More recent evidence adds to this picture, by extending it to other Hispanics. In particular, the Pew survey on Hispanic identity included a sizable subsample of Hispanics from mixed family backgrounds. The data from this subsample come broken down by whether the respondent identifies as Hispanic or not, and they distinguish only whether the partner is Hispanic or not. The recent data are quite consistent with the older Mexican American study. For those Hispanics who come from unmixed family backgrounds, the rate of partnering with other Hispanics is very high, at 87 percent. For Hispanic-identifying individuals from mixed families, however, the rate is substantially lower, 56 percent. For individuals from mixed backgrounds who do not identify as Hispanic, the rate plummets to 15 percent.[35]

IDENTITY

Identity—including some of its manifestations such as political preferences and opinions on what to tell children about their background—is often seen as the key to understanding the implications of ethno-racial mixing.[36] This emphasis, I think, is misplaced. Identity is itself the outcome of many experiences and social locations, from family narratives heard in childhood to the social milieus where one feels comfortable as an adult. Identity, moreover, is not only shaped by social milieus but takes on specific meanings within them. That is, identity can often be construed as positioning within a social context and is sometimes an assertion of individual distinction relative to the background social "color" of a milieu.

Ethno-racial identity is more complex than is often recognized. One way of looking at this kind of identity comes from social identity theory in social psychology. According to Henri Tajfel, one of the founders of the theory, a "social identity" can be defined as "that part of an individual's self-concept which derives from his knowledge of his membership of a social group (or groups) together with the value and emotional significance attached to that membership."[37] An identity in these terms involves an attachment to or orientation toward a group seen as one's own that may or may not exert a major influence on many life choices. Another way of looking at identity, which is perhaps not inherently in contradiction with Tajfel's definition but certainly in tension with it, sees identity as a way of distinguishing oneself from others. This view of identity involves not so much the group to which the identity refers as it does others who are not members of the group, the audience for what we might call an "identity performance."

Moreover, ethno-racial identity should not be understood, as it too often is, as just the *label* one applies to oneself, such as "Italian" or "Chinese." Such labels can be constructed in order to have ready answers to the "What are you?" question. Identity also involves what could be described as the *salience* of these tags: in what situations are they activated, and how intense is their relevance? The past research on ethnic differences among whites has revealed a great deal of variation in salience and shown that one's identity-as-label can be largely irrelevant to everyday life, becoming activated in mainly symbolic fashion as a means to distinguish oneself in interesting ways from others or to participate more fully in special occasions like family gatherings. Identity in this sense was aptly named "symbolic ethnicity" by the sociologist Herbert Gans. There is no reason a priori to rule out a similar phenomenon for some nonwhites and Hispanics; the sociologist Jessica Vasquez-Tokos notes, for instance, what she describes as the "thin" identities claimed by some of the subjects in her study of Mexican American intermarriages.[38]

One thing is certainly clear about identities-as-labels for individuals from mixed backgrounds. These identities are much less stable than the identity labels of individuals from unmixed family

TABLE 5.2. Identity Shifts of Asian-White (A & W) Individuals between the 2000 and 2010 Censuses

Identities		
2000	2010	% of total
Stable identity		
A & W	A & W	34.5
Alternate identity is white		
A & W	W	12.7
W	A & W	23.0
Alternate identity is Asian		
A & W	A	10.7
A	A & W	11.5
Any other switch		
A & W	Other	3.7
Other	A & W	4.0

Note: Only individuals who identified as Asian and white on at least one of the two censuses are included. The notation is: A = Asian; W = white.

Source: Liebler et al (2017): Table 4.

backgrounds; they are fluid and probably contingent on context.[39] One compelling demonstration of this fluidity comes from census data in fact. A research team based largely at the Census Bureau matched individuals in the 2000 and 2010 censuses, and they were able to locate the same individuals in both censuses for about 50 percent of the US population.[40] They then compared the ethno-racial responses across censuses for these individuals and—lo and behold!—they were sometimes different. Specifically, individuals of mixed heritage, but rarely the unmixed, answered these questions differently. (The usual caveat applies: we do not know that the individuals themselves answered the questions. Census forms are often filled out by a single member of a family or household. But whoever was reporting presumably had intimate knowledge of the backgrounds and identities of other household members.)

Identity fluidity is very evident in table 5.2, which shows the tabulation involving non-Hispanics who reported on either census as both white and Asian on the race question. Only 35 percent reported this way in both 2000 and 2010; in other words, about two-thirds were inconsistent, mostly reporting only one of the races on the other census. This inconsistency has a bias, however, one that is consistent with the high frequency of whites among the social affiliations of Asian-whites: white-only responses outnumbered Asian-only ones by a substantial margin (about 60 percent).

The lean toward whiteness in the identities of Asian-whites is confirmed by another study using a different census data set. The monthly survey required for employment statistics, the Current Population Survey, has a question on the birthplaces of parents, which the American Community Survey does not. The economists Brian Duncan and Stephen Trejo have examined the ethno-racial identities of adults with foreign-born parents.[41] They find that more than one-third of individuals with one Asian-born parent and one parent not born in Asia do not identify as Asian. Presumably, the bulk of this group has mixed Asian ancestry, but it is nevertheless quite remarkable that so many adults with Asian immigrant parents do not check "Asian," since the CPS race question, like the ACS one, allows multiple responses. Of those who do not identify as Asian, nearly 90 percent say that they are non-Hispanic and white.[42]

Black-white individuals also display a pattern of identity fluidity on the census, but it is one—again, consistent with the bulk of their social affiliations—that leans heavily toward blackness. More than 60 percent are inconsistent in their replies on the 2000 and 2010 censuses (see table 5.3). Among them, black identities outnumber white ones by a two-to-one margin. In strong contrast, individuals who are mixed American Indian and white lean extremely toward whiteness. Of those recorded as white and American Indian in either the 2000 or 2010 census, almost 90 percent appear as single race on the other, and white identities outnumber American Indian identities by a margin of four-to-one.

There is also considerable flux in Hispanic identities, as revealed by a second Census Bureau analysis, which matched across three time points for every individual.[43] The matched records include not only the 2000 and 2010 censuses but also an American Community Survey conducted between 2006 and 2010. This study examined individuals who appear to be Hispanic according to any of the three

TABLE 5.3. Identity Shifts of Black-White (B & W) Individuals between the 2000 and 2010 Censuses

Identities		
2000	2010	% of total
Stable identity		
B & W	B & W	37.4
Alternate identity is white		
B & W	W	5.4
W	B & W	10.2
Alternate identity is black		
B & W	B	13.5
B	B & W	19.6
Any other switch		
B & W	Other	6.3
Other	B & W	7.6

Note: Only individuals who identified as black and white on at least one of the two censuses are included. The notation is: B = black; W = white.
Source: Liebler et at (2017): Table 3.

surveys. This could mean that they answer positively at least once to the Hispanic-origin question (which appears on all census surveys and is the main way of identifying Hispanics, as discussed in chapter 4). Or it could mean that they cite a Latine ancestry (such as Salvadoran) on the ancestry question (which appears only in the ACS), even if they do not report themselves as Hispanic on the Hispanic-origin question. It may seem surprising, even incomprehensible, that respondents are this inconsistent, but we know that they are from prior research, and that inconsistent responses such as these are associated with a high level of education and other markers of social distance from the Hispanic population.[44]

The second Census Bureau analysis indicates that, of all individuals who can be identified as Latine at any of the three time points, 14 percent do not consistently check "Hispanic, Latino, or Spanish origin." If this number looks smaller than the ones cited earlier, it is because the base includes all Hispanics, including the population's large percentage of immigrants, who are rarely inconsistent. In other words, unlike the data discussed earlier, the Hispanic data are not limited to those from mixed backgrounds. A fairer comparison is to the overall percentage of inconsistent reports in the first Census Bureau study cited, which was just 6 percent of the total. By this measure, the instability of Hispanic reports is sizable.

Moreover, the study indicates that inconsistency in Hispanic reporting in census surveys is associated with a mixed Anglo-Hispanic family background. For instance, 2.6 percent of the Hispanics *never* report themselves this way on the Hispanic-origin question; their Hispanic ancestry can only be detected on the ancestry question. Nearly 90 percent of them present themselves as non-Hispanic whites, and 75 percent indicate having a non-Hispanic ancestry on the ACS ancestry question. Of the remaining inconsistent individuals—those who sometimes claim a Hispanic origin and sometimes do not and who amount to about 11 percent of Hispanics, or one of every nine—the majority report some non-Hispanic ancestry, and a sizable majority indicate "white only" on the race question. In other words, these are individuals who mostly appear as non-Hispanic whites in the census surveys in which they do not indicate Hispanic origin, but many of them come from mixed backgrounds.

This identity fluidity has big implications for census data. For one thing, it demonstrates conclusively that the mixed majority-minority group as counted by a single census is only the visible part of a larger, partly submerged population, since not all mixed-race individuals will report themselves that way (and partly Hispanic individuals are not identifiable in the decennial census because of the two-question format for ethno-racial background).

The consequences for the Census Bureau's population projections are damaging. Recall from the last chapter that the projections fix the ethno-racial categories of individuals when they are first encountered—either in the data that form the base for the projections or at the moment of their projected "birth" in the future. Once fixed, the categories do not change: an individual who is encountered as Asian-white, say, stays that way throughout a projection and is classified consistently on the minority side of the minority-white ledger. The great majority of mixed majority-minority individuals are encountered as children, when their ethno-racial origins are

reported by parents. (For the individuals "born" during the projection, their ethno-racial assignment is inferred from contemporary
parental patterns of reporting.) That means that the large majority
will appear in the projections as mixed or as solely minority—hence,
not white—and will remain that way until the end of the projection.
This implies that the projections are highly likely, if patterns of identity fluidity hold, to exaggerate the decline of the white population
(or more precisely, the population reporting as white) on any given
census.

Since the identities of mixed individuals are so fluid, it should not
come as a surprise that research findings are themselves variable;
expressions of identity depend on the questions asked and perhaps
on who is doing the asking. The Pew multiracial survey found, in a
bit of a contrast to the census comparison just described, that most
Asian-whites (70 percent) and black-whites (61 percent) consider
themselves to be "mixed race or multiracial." However, most American Indian–whites do not.[45] An analysis of a large-scale survey of
college freshmen arrived at a similar finding about Asian- and black-
whites, although with the order of the groups reversed: 71 percent of
black-whites opted for a multiracial label for themselves, compared
to a bare majority (54 percent) of Asian-whites. (American Indian–
whites were not analyzed separately.)[46] This survey also revealed
that the first-year students who did not identify as multiracial pre-
ferred a minority self-label to a white one by large margins. The
experiences of these survey respondents within the educational
system may account for the differences from other studies. A number of features of educational curricula, college campuses, and the
application process tend to emphasize minority experiences and
identities, such as the perceived impact of ethno-racial background
on one's chances of admission to selective colleges. And most college
campuses host a wealth of clubs organized around minority identities. The minority strands of mixed family origins are probably more
salient during schooling than at other points in the lives of mixed
majority-minority Americans.

The results in this section accord in broad strokes with the in-depth
interviews conducted by Strmic-Pawl. Although her respondents,

both Asian-white and black-white, respond with multiracial labels to a question about how they identify, the Asian-whites indicate in other ways that they feel more white than Asian and the black-whites reveal that they feel more black. In explaining, for example, why they mostly choose whites as romantic partners, about half of the Asian-whites indicate that they do not perceive such relationships to be "interracial." In fact, about 40 percent of them report thinking that marriage to an Asian partner would feel "interracial." For example, a Chinese-white woman addresses how it would feel to date an Asian: "It would feel weird, I think. Because I don't feel like I have much [of an] Asian culture. And I feel like my culture is a lot more White."[47] Unsurprisingly, black-whites feel very differently. For them, black culture and black social worlds feel like "home," as one respondent put it, and the white world seems unfriendly and unaccepting.

The complexities of identity are better illustrated by in-depth interviews than by survey data, especially surveys that present questions with a small set of options from which to choose an answer ("forced-choice" questions). For example, among Strmic-Pawl's respondents, we meet individuals like Michelle, a Filipina-white who "believes her phenotype approximates more the look of Asians than Whites, but she still 'feels' White. She joked that she is 'Whitewashed' and that applying the term 'Twinkie' to herself does make sense as she looks Asian on the outside but feels White on the inside." And there is Dan, who is Chinese and white: he "identifies as Asian in order not to be seen as plain or regular but identifies more with Whites." And Dana, who is also Chinese and white, has a white boyfriend plus white friends, but has a special relationship to a Chinese friend with whom she shops for clothing because "we have the same problems. We have the same body type, and we'll discuss it in detail."[48]

Strmic-Pawl's summary characterization of the identities of her Asian-white interviewees is that they mostly feel "white enough." The implication is that they do not feel only white, but do feel sufficiently white to be "immersed in White networks." And feeling "white enough" is quite important in another way: it allows

Asian-whites to shrug off occasional micro-aggressions, such as when they receive compliments on how well they speak English or are interrogated about where they are "really" from. In comparison, her black-white subjects see racism as a major part of their lives: "Their stories about racial discrimination did not center on jokes or moments of racist actions; rather their stories were about how life is lived as a Black-White multiracial person who spends significant time and energy managing racial discrimination."[49]

Hispanic-whites, like Asian-whites, also reveal an attenuated minority identity. Some of the best evidence we possess about them comes from the Pew Survey of Hispanic Identity. This survey, conducted by telephone in 2015–2016, included both individuals who identify as "Hispanic or Latino" and some who do not but who acknowledge having some Hispanic ancestry.[50] Pew estimated from the survey that 11 percent of all Americans with Latine ancestors do not identify as Hispanic or in terms of a Latine national identity, such as Mexican or Peruvian. Virtually all of these individuals have mixed family backgrounds, including both Latine and non-Latine parents or grandparents. The survey does not tell us how they identify, but 60 percent of them say that passersby on the street would probably see them as white. Reflecting, however, the degree of Hispanic mixing with nonwhites as well as whites (noted in the last chapter), about 20 percent believe that they would be seen as black.[51]

For many others, the salience of a Hispanic identity has declined. These individuals identified themselves as Hispanic to the interviewers, but say that this is not the most common label they use to describe themselves. Of the Hispanic identifiers who come from mixed family backgrounds, more than 40 percent say that they usually describe themselves as "American" (compared to 13 percent of those from unmixed backgrounds), and 60 percent regard themselves as "typical Americans."[52]

The intergenerational study of Mexican Americans by Edward Telles and Vilma Ortiz also finds that adults of Anglo-Mexican parentage have attenuated Mexican or Latine identities. Their concise summary of their findings on the children of intermarriages is on point (note that the non-Hispanic parents to whom they refer are mostly whites):

> Intermarriage was particularly powerful for Mexican Americans in its effect on the children of intermarried couples. The 9 percent of children with a non-Hispanic parent were less likely to know Spanish, were more likely to intermarry themselves, identified less with their Mexican origin, and were more likely to call themselves American. Such children were often perceived as and understood themselves as less Mexican.[53]

A reanalysis of the data finds in fact that mixed Anglo-Mexican ancestry substantially increases the likelihood that individuals "hardly ever" or "never" think of themselves as Chicano or of Mexican origin.[54] Complementing this picture is an analysis of census data that finds a significant group of individuals who are non-Hispanic whites according to the race and Hispanic-origin questions but who indicate on a separate ancestry question that they have some Mexican ancestry. They are, paradoxically, non-Hispanics of Mexican descent![55]

In sum, the overall picture of the identities of mixed majority-minority Americans is not a simple one. Of course, the complexity results in part from the fluidity and contingency of these identities: even the labels that mixed individuals use to describe themselves can vary from one situation to another, in contrast to the consistency to be observed among individuals of unmixed heritage. Yet, depending on the minority origin involved, many mixed individuals could be described as "leaning" in a particular direction. At one end of the spectrum, individuals with American Indian and white parentage think of themselves mainly as whites, while at the other end those with both black and white parentage mostly think of themselves as black. Asian-whites and Hispanic-whites are somewhere in the middle. When it comes to labeling themselves, Asian-whites state a preference for mixed identities, although their behavior on census surveys indicates some degree of lean toward whiteness. And they often feel similar to whites. It's harder to be certain about Anglo-Latines because the data about their identities are more sparse.

However, both the Pew study of Hispanic identity and the Mexican-American study suggest that they lean moderately in the direction of feeling like an "ordinary" American, which to most Americans is equivalent to being "white" at this moment in history.[56]

Conclusion

Let me start with the caveat that, at this point, there is a lot we do not know about individuals from majority-minority family backgrounds. The accumulated research to date could be described in terms of the familiar metaphor of multiple blindfolded investigators stationed at different parts of an elephant and describing what they can feel. They can surely arrive at some valid conclusions—it's very big! it has tusks!—but much about the animal remains out of reach, so to speak. There are similarly huge gaps in our knowledge. Perhaps most important, we lack any sound basis for drawing precise conclusions about how the phenotype, or bodily appearance, of mixed individuals affects their acceptance by others, their social locations, and their identities. While important regardless of the minority origin involved, it seems especially critical for Hispanic-white individuals, because the range of phenotypes among Hispanics is so great, given the variable mixing of Africans, Europeans, and indigenes that began hundreds of years ago with European colonization of the Americas.

Moreover, our studies of mixed individuals and their experiences are biased in ways that are not fully acknowledged because they are often framed in terms of broad, internally heterogeneous ethno-racial categories, like Asian or Hispanic. "Asian" is clearly a very diverse category. Because some Asian groups, especially East Asians and Filipinos, have a longer history in the United States and have intermarried with whites far more often, studies of Asian-whites tell us more about the mixing of these Asian groups with whites than they do about the mixing of South Asians.

During the next quarter-century, one consequential gap will prove to be our ignorance about ethno-racial mixing that does not involve a white parent. We have very little knowledge at this point about individuals with mixed, mainly minority family backgrounds.

The data that we can glean from demographic data sets, as presented in this chapter, are not very consistent. Overall, infants from mixed minority backgrounds generally start life in more disadvantaged family situations than other mixed infants. Yet their educational record is on a par with that of most mixed minority-white young adults. It may be that better data could easily resolve this apparent inconsistency. But the categories of minority mixture, encompassing about one-quarter of all mixed infants, are certain to grow in importance in the future. Not only will the overall size of the mixed population grow, but the relative sizes of the mixed minority groups will too, in tandem with the diversity of the young adults who are forming families. Although the interest of researchers in mixing that crosses the majority-minority division is understandable, much more attention needs to be paid to other forms of mixing.

When we turn to the mixing that is the main focus of this book, which involves the children of minority and white parents, we can see a reasonably clear picture emerging after the jigsaw-like pieces of knowledge, especially those confirmed by multiple studies, have been assembled, even if holes remain. That picture does not resolve one essential ambiguity in the social positioning of individuals with minority-white backgrounds—they remain individuals who span salient societal boundaries because they have connections on both sides from birth. But it does firmly contradict the demographic practice of assigning individuals with reported ethno-racially mixed origins to the nonwhite, or minority, side of a binary divide.

The majority of mixed majority-minority Americans appear to be integrated in social worlds that also contain many whites. They have grown up with whites and count whites among their close childhood and adult friends. Their educational attainment is higher on average than would be the case if it was determined mainly by their minority origin. Though they often are exposed to prejudice and discrimination, these experiences do not usually seem to harm their perceptions of acceptance by whites or their ability to mix with them in friendship circles and neighborhoods. Most tellingly, they have high rates of marriage with whites.[57]

The contradiction to the classification of mixed minority-white individuals as minorities is very evident in terms of identity because of the fluidity evident in their ethno-racial self-labeling. That fluidity moves more in the direction of a white label than a nonwhite label for many of them—especially American Indian–whites, Asian-whites, Hispanic-whites, and those with one parent of mixed, partly white race and another who is exclusively white (this last being a category about which, even with no direct observations, we can reasonably make inferences). Moreover, the evidence shows that many of the individuals in these categories feel white in important ways. Strmic-Pawl's characterization of Asian-whites as feeling "white enough" seems right for these other categories too: their members are not exclusively white, and they have not merged seamlessly into the white population, but on a practical, day-to-day level, they can function like whites much of the time.

One aspect of the identities described by Strmic-Pawl seems quite revealing: most of her Asian-white interviewees describe both sides of their background in terms of ethnic, rather than racial, labels. That is, rather than labeling themselves as "Asian" and "white," they say, for instance, that they are Korean on one side and German and Italian on the other.[58] (Given the extensive ethnic mixing among whites, ethnically mixed ancestry is common among the white parents of Strmic-Pawl's interviewees.) This way of labeling themselves creates an equivalence between the white and nonwhite ancestries: it makes the Asian origin into an ethnic origin rather than a racial one. In other words, individuals who are partly nonwhite may be assimilating to the forms of identity found among many whites thereby attaching their personal story to the narrative of immigrant-group assimilation.

To be sure, that the identities of many mixed individuals lean toward whiteness does not mean that they are passing as whites. Not at all. They still may assert the nonwhite side of their background and undoubtedly (though we know little about this) find ways to express it in their lives.[59] But we encounter the limits of viewing the significance of mixing mainly in terms of identity when we remember that their embeddedness in families and other social milieus that include many whites is likely to constrain their expression of ethno-racial identity (unless they are able to tolerate a great deal of strain in their relationships to those closest to them). They may tend to channel their identity into modes of expression that can be appreciated by those who do not share that identity. For example, expression through cooking or tourism is compatible with daily lives spent in the midst of others who do not share the same identity.

Multiracials with black and white parentage are the huge exception to this pattern, and their experience is quite distinct. They grow up in less affluent circumstances and are exposed to much more severe discrimination, as evidenced by their frequent complaints of mistreatment at the hands of the police. They are more comfortable with blacks than with whites and usually identify with the black side of their family heritage. The racism of American society has a greater impact on their lives than on the lives of most other multiracials. Yet they too exhibit a level of integration with whites that exceeds that of other African Americans, as reflected in the relative frequency with which they marry whites. Racism is not an absolute bar to the same processes of integration evident among other mixed minority-white Americans, but it is a major impediment.

What are we to make of larger significance in the surge of young people from mixed minority-white families, both for them and for the society? The question is especially challenging because, unlike in the past, when the racial divisions of American society generally forced mixed individuals to incorporate with one or the other side of their background, mixing today is more recognized and appreciated. To understand these developments, we turn in the next chapter to some ideas and some reminders about assimilation history.

6

Some Ideas and History for Understanding Today's Ethno-Racial Mixing

The number of youngsters from mixed majority-minority families has been surging for several decades; today more than 10 percent of the infants born in the United States every year have one white and one minority parent. An examination of the family circumstances of these infants indicates that on the whole they are like neither minority nor white families. Some are certainly close to whites in their economic and residential situation—or, in the case of Asian-whites, even more favorably positioned—while others are closer to minorities, as is true of black-white infants. On average, they are in between.

Although in some respects this in-between state continues as mixed majority-minority children grow into adulthood, in other ways their lives often reflect increasing integration with the white majority. For instance, their identities are unusually fluid and appear capable of presenting as mixed, white, or minority, depending on the circumstances and their own combination of origins. Yet for some important mixed categories, such as Asian-white and Hispanic-white, these identities lean white: when asked to choose between white and minority, they more often choose white. Black-white individuals are the striking exception. A second critical aspect of how mixed individuals have integrated with the white majority is social. Going along with their fairly frequent feelings of closeness to and acceptance by whites are mixed individuals' robust rates of participation in social milieus, such as neighborhoods and friendship circles, where whites are present in substantial numbers, if they are not the dominant presence. This social integration is sealed by the relatively high rates at which most mixed groups, including black-white men, marry whites.

The population projections that undergird the widespread belief in the arrival of a majority-minority society in the next few decades are based on the classification of the great majority of mixed majority-minority individuals as "not white," and hence as "minority." The evidence so far strongly contradicts this classification but does not of itself lead to a convincing way of understanding the broader societal significance of mixed family origins. Such an understanding appears all the more necessary given the virtual certainty of the growth of the mixed group in the near future. This chapter begins the work of forging that understanding, which continues into the next chapter.

As part of this work, I develop two kinds of tools in this chapter. One tool is theoretical: broadly put, it involves important ideas about processes that produce ethno-racial stability and change. Two bodies of ideas that have informed most social-science research in the United States on this subject are race theory and assimilation theory. The other tool is a more sophisticated understanding of history, especially the history of the mass assimilation of the descendants of the immigrants of the late nineteenth and early twentieth centuries. The focus here on deepening our understanding of that history is in no way to imagine that the near future is likely to replicate it; for reasons I will provide later, that is extremely unlikely. Nevertheless, a more nuanced understanding of that history provides clues about what we should look for today.

Theories

RACE THEORY

Race theory (or critical race theory) posits that the cardinal features of race as a social characteristic arise from the positioning of groups within a hierarchical power structure involving white domination of minorities.[1] So stated, the theory has a worldwide significance, as expressed by the memorable formulation of W. E. B. Du Bois: "The problem of the twentieth century is the problem of the color line—the relation of the darker to the lighter races of men in Asia and Africa, in America and the islands of the sea."[2] In this perspective, as Du Bois implies here, Hispanics are viewed as one of the subordinate races subject to white domination. There is no need for the prefix "ethno-," nor any need, for that matter, to see the problem as restricted to the past century.

Domination of one group by another has, of course, been a central feature of human history, but a brilliant insight of race theory is that race per se is a relatively modern concept. Racial domination and subordination arose from the European waves of exploration, conquest, colonization, and enslavement that started in the fifteenth century. According to the historian George Frederickson, this domination ironically gained additional potency from the ideas of the Enlightenment, which posited a fundamental human equality and undermined the taken-for-granted naturalness of hierarchy.[3] Once Enlightenment ideas had taken hold, white Europeans had to justify intellectually their domination of nonwhites. The development of racist ideologies, which assert inherent white superiority and non-white inferiority, dates to the eighteenth century.[4] These ideas have had long-lasting effects, even if today they are almost universally rejected except by white supremacists.

Another compelling insight of race theory is that forms of racial domination can evolve—racism is shape-shifting and therefore hard to eradicate. African American history shows repeatedly that what appeared to be major steps toward equality were subsequently whittled down by white resistance or revealed to be less powerful than they initially seemed. Emancipation at the end of the Civil War was initially followed by the period of Reconstruction (1865–1877), which saw major black gains in the formerly Confederate states. But barely more than a decade after the war ended, white domination was reestablished in the South, aided by political understandings among elite whites, both North and South, and by organized violence intended to reverse black advances. During the ensuing decades of the nineteenth century, Southern states erected a legal and social edifice, Jim Crow, to establish racial segregation and suppress black political power. This institutional regime of strict segregation received constitutional sanction in the 1896 *Plessy v. Ferguson* decision of the US Supreme Court. Then, nearly a century after the end of the Civil War, the civil rights movement achieved major legal and legislative gains, starting with the 1954 Supreme Court decision *Brown v. the Board of Education of Topeka*, which held that the racial segregation of children in public schools is unconstitutional, and ending with the multiple civil rights acts of the 1960s, which dismantled the remnants of the Jim Crow system of segregation and outlawed various forms of discrimination. Yet, as many have noted since, movement toward equality of situation between whites and blacks—as opposed to legal equality in principle—has been glacially slow. More than a half-century after the *Brown* decision, the high level of school segregation that continues to prevail is but one indicator.[5]

The adaptability of racial domination to meliorative change can be seen in terms of its capacities as a system. Racial domination, as the recent literature properly emphasizes, does not depend as much as is often imagined on widespread prejudice or discrimination by racist individuals. Rather, it is embedded in the normal functioning of many societal institutions, such as education and policing. Institutional racism is much more important in the contemporary era than are racist individuals, though they have certainly not disappeared, as the rise of political white nationalism indicates. Moreover, institutional racism demonstrates a capacity for innovation in the face of change as whites strive to preserve their privileges or their sense of group position vis-à-vis minorities.[6]

When the civil rights legislation dismantled the legal basis of Jim Crow segregation, other parts of the system of racial domination took up the slack, and a major innovation solidified African American disadvantage. After passage of the Fair Housing Act of 1968, the residential segregation of whites and blacks remained at extremely high levels in many regions of black concentration, especially in the North, bolstered by the practices of the real estate industry and by whites' fear that black entry into their neighborhoods would lead to lower property values, higher crime levels, and general deterioration in the neighborhood environment. In some metropolitan regions like Chicago and New York, segregation was so extensive, or "hyper-segregated" in the characterization of sociologists Douglas Massey and Nancy Denton, that many African Americans had little or no everyday contact with whites outside of certain institutional contexts, like schools and the police.[7] Black-white segregation, though slowly easing, remains at high levels in much of the United States today.

A major innovation in racism as a system appeared in the form of mass incarceration, which began during the 1970s, soon after the civil-rights period, as part of the "war on drugs." Its devastating effects on African American men and communities led the legal scholar Michelle Alexander to characterize it as the "new Jim Crow."[8] Mass incarceration has also had a significant impact, though not as great, on Latine communities. A combination of forces produced these disproportionate, deleterious effects, including more intensive policing of minority communities; the use of bail to hold poor people in jail, which often forces innocent people to accept plea bargains; and much more punitive treatment of drug infractions by minorities. Recent research finds that as many as one-third of black men have felony convictions, and rigorous field studies have demonstrated very negative consequences for their subsequent employment.[9] The effects of mass incarceration on African American families and communities are widespread and profound as a consequence of the absence of many men when they are in prison and their economic precarity after they are released. Reflecting these negative effects on black communities are low rates of marriage and high rates of single-parent families and of children growing up in poverty.[10]

A system that buttresses white advantages over minorities—frequently labeled as "white supremacy" by race theorists—can too easily be seen as operating in a color-blind way or, even if minority disadvantages are recognized, as not redounding to an unearned advantage for whites. This is all the more true when the processes involved, like those of the criminal justice system, are remote from the everyday lives of whites (another consequence of residential segregation). Indeed, as we saw earlier, many whites today believe that they are the victims of racial discrimination.

It is in the general nature of systems of privilege that a social boundary separates the more privileged from the less privileged and that the more privileged seek to achieve what is often called "social closure" to prevent, as much as possible, less privileged individuals from crossing that boundary. That is to say, powerful groups usually try to "hoard" opportunities and resources, and consequently they "patrol" boundaries to keep them intact and as impermeable as possible.[11] This pattern has a correlate in the social psychology of group membership. Ethno-racial self-categorizations reflect a balance between internal self-assessments (how do I think of myself?) and external labels imposed by others (how do others see me?). Race theory, in particular with respect to minorities, attributes much greater weight to the external classification. Racial labels are imposed by the more powerful white group, and the individual on whom they are imposed cannot easily forge an alternative social definition of self. As we saw with black-white individuals, they have experiences, such as mistreatment at the hands of the police, that "tell" them they are socially black.

Race theory suffers, however, from a critical limitation: it has been elaborated mostly in terms of the African American experience.[12] Its fit there unfortunately is all too obvious, but its applicability to some other nonwhite minorities is more questionable. Certainly, one can see how it could apply to American Indians living on reservations, but it is arguably less applicable to American Indians living elsewhere, many of whom also have white ancestry and mix easily with whites. One can also see its relevance for a portion of the Hispanic population, such as Puerto Ricans, who come from an island that entered the United States through conquest and remains a territory, not a state. Moreover, many Puerto Ricans as well as Dominicans are distinguished from other Hispanics by having visible African ancestry. In addition, many Mexican immigrant families are hampered, despite long residence in the United States, by lack of legal status, a problem that the white-dominated political system refuses to resolve.

A corollary weakness of race theory is its tendency to subsume other nonwhite minorities under the conceptualizations that fit the African American (and American Indian) experience. This leads to such common designations as "peoples of color," which suggests that these groups are all subject to a similar degree to racial subjugation. Yet the broad-gauge application of race theory to immigrant groups coming from Africa, Asia, and Latin America remains at issue. One attempt to cope with this problem from a race-theory perspective has been made by the sociologist Eduardo Bonilla-Silva, who has proposed the eventual emergence of a three-tier racial system with an intermediate tier for the "honorary" whites in many of these immigrant groups.[13] Yet, in light of the social integration that, as we have already observed, often results from family mixing, it is not clear how the distinction between whites and "honorary" whites can be maintained in everyday social intercourse.

We should not assume a priori that immigrant groups that are phenotypically distinctive from white Americans of European descent are destined to become racial minorities in the US social system. Because they are immigrant groups, they may also benefit from the processes of inclusion that have historically benefited immigrant groups in the American context.[14]

ASSIMILATION THEORY

Assimilation theory is often wrongly positioned in opposition to race theory. The relationship between them needs more considered reflection, which I will defer for a moment. Assimilation theory in fact shares with race theory the core assumption that ethno-racial groups are situated within a hierarchy, with whites at the top, but it does not envision as rigid a hierarchy as race theory does. The group at the top, the most socially powerful group, is the majority; the others are minority groups. In principle, these terms by definition refer to placement within a societal hierarchy and not to size. (Thus whites in South Africa, a small minority of the population, were the "majority" group under apartheid.) However, unlike race theory, which tends toward a bipolar division—whites versus groups of color—assimilation theory rests on an underlying conception that allows more differentiation among groups along different dimensions. Indeed, in its nomenclature, assimilation theory speaks more frequently about "ethnic" groups than "racial" groups, subtly adding an element of elective membership to the emphasis on social exclusion in race theory. (Max Weber's famous definition of an ethnic group as one whose members share "a subjective belief in their common descent" underscores the role of personal identity in ethnic attachment.[15]) Accordingly, individuals, even groups, can move within the group hierarchy through boundary processes, such as boundary crossing and boundary blurring.[16]

Assimilation theory arose in the United States in the encounter between immigrants and urban environments, which was intensively studied by early American sociologists such as Robert E. Park and W. I. Thomas in Chicago in the early twentieth century. Reflecting on the question of how immigrants and their children moved from being outsiders to becoming, if not quite insiders, at least a part of American life, Park and E. W. Burgess formulated an early definition of assimilation as "a process of interpenetration and fusion in which persons and groups acquire the memory, sentiments, and attitudes of other persons and groups and, by sharing their experience and history, are incorporated with them in a common historical life."[17] This definition does not imply that assimilation eradicates all traces of ethnic difference.

The precise conceptualization of assimilation, however, remained in flux. Milton Gordon's treatment of it in his mid-century classic *Assimilation in American Life* (1964) accounts for some of the vicissitudes of assimilation theory. Gordon, unlike Park and Burgess, posited that assimilation is the absorption of the minority group into the majority group.[18] Part of his theory—in fact, its major contribution—was a recognition that assimilation is inherently multidimensional. One dimension is acculturation, which he envisioned as a one-way process: the immigrant minority acculturates by acquiring all of the cultural patterns of the majority, explicitly identified by Gordon as middle-class white Protestants of largely British ancestry, while the majority remains unaffected. Translated into the twenty-first-century United States, Gordon's conception of assimilation is basically a whitening process. Minority groups or their members can assimilate by becoming, and being accepted as, white. This conception has been the source of much justified criticism and is far too limited to grasp the realities of assimilation in multiracial America.

The latest version of assimilation theory, often dubbed "neo-assimilation" theory, was developed by Victor Nee and myself in order to overcome the major limitations of prior assimilation ideas.[19] We believed that a viable assimilation theory must: (1) demonstrate how assimilation can occur without nonwhite minorities becoming whites; (2) acknowledge that assimilation can involve two-way changes, that is, that there can be some degree of mutual influence between majority and minorities (the degree of mutuality being an issue to be settled empirically, not theoretically); (3) avoid implying, as earlier theories had, that assimilation is inevitable and develops in a linear, irreversible fashion; and (4) recognize that assimilation often leaves considerable room for the expression of distinct identities and cultural differences within the mainstream society.

Crafted with these aims in view, our definition of assimilation is

the decline of an ethnic [or racial] distinction and its corollary cultural and social differences. "Decline" means in this context that a distinction attenuates in salience, that the occurrences for which it is relevant diminish in number and contract to fewer and fewer domains of social life. Individuals' ethnic origins become less and less relevant in relation to the members of another ethnic group (typically, but not necessarily, the ethnic majority group): individuals from both sides of the boundary see themselves more and more as alike, assuming they are similar in terms of some other critical factors such as social class; in other words, they mutually perceive themselves with less and less frequency in terms of ethnic categories and increasingly only under specific circumstances.[20]

Another way of putting this last point is to say that assimilation involves "decategorization": individuals coming originally from different sides of an ethno-racial boundary—one majority, one minority—no longer commonly think about each other, or treat each other, based on their category memberships but as individuals.[21]

Because this definition is agnostic about how the perceived similarity between individuals on the two sides of a boundary grows, it allows for similarity arising because of changes that take place on both sides as a result of mutual influence. It also indicates that assimilation is a matter of degree, not an all-or-nothing proposition. Assimilation can be significant without eradicating the ethno-racial differences and distinctions between the two sides, though it does entail the decline of their social significance.

Studying the interactions between new immigrant groups and established ones in the communities of Silicon Valley, the sociologist Tomás Jiménez has elaborated on the "relational assimilation" that arises from interactions across such dividing lines.[22] He describes a proliferation of cross-group relationships that develop between neighbors, coworkers, and students in the same school. These relationships generally go beyond merely civil interactions in mutually shared public spaces and develop, through considerable give-and-take, into mutual understanding. Moreover, they are hardly one-sided: they are not dominated by the members of the established groups. In some respects, in fact, these relationships have a considerable impact on the established groups. For example, interactions with immigrants and the second generation made Silicon Valley whites more conscious of their whiteness, and not necessarily in a good way: whiteness, by comparison with the cultural richness of immigrant families, seemed for many a vacuous identity.

Yet examining assimilation in terms of interactions between individuals across a boundary does not provide the whole picture, because these interactions generally take place within the carapace of mainstream society and its culture and institutions. The idea of the mainstream is central to neo-assimilation theory. Assimilation, in this theory, does not require minorities to join the dominant group (whites) but rather to participate in a societal mainstream. Nevertheless, the concept of the mainstream reflects the social power of the white majority, which effectively controls the institutional and social spaces that offer the most desirable and abundant opportunities for social advancement. Therefore, the mainstream is attractive to many minority individuals. Jan-Willem Duyvendak and I have described the mainstream in the following way:

> Two interlocking aspects of the mainstream reveal the power of the native majority. One is institutional: The mainstream encompasses a core set of societal institutions, such as the education system, the economy, the polity, and the media, whose leading positions are occupied by members of the native majority or by others who have met their standards for acceptance (Alba and Nee 2003: 12). These institutions broadcast mainstream standards and values to all parts of the society, and they also possess a critical gatekeeping role. Thus, the gatekeeping that controls access to improvements in educational credentials and jobs for immigrants and the second generation is generally in the hands of individuals who employ mainstream criteria, as it occurs through institutions such as schools that reflect the mainstream's culture and standards. (The exception—a rare case—is when a minority group has successfully established its own sub-economy; and usually this offers just truncated ladders of mobility.) For this reason one can speak of "dominant formal and informal ways of doing and thinking" in a society, which reflect the most consequential parts of the mainstream.

Another aspect of the mainstream consists of the social and cultural settings—not just formal institutions—where the members of the native majority, even when they are working class, feel "at home" (Alba 2009). This aspect emphasizes the more subjective and emotional side of being part of the mainstream. Feeling at home not only means that the setting is familiar, safe and predictable but that one feels in control as well: one belongs, and one believes (perhaps incorrectly) one has the power to define who else belongs (Duyvendak 2011). This conception highlights also that the use of the singular "mainstream" is a matter of convenience because the mainstream can be itself internally diverse, differentiated by region, religion and social class, to name but a few dimensions. Moreover, although the presence of the native majority identifies the settings that are part of the mainstream, these milieus need not be ethno-racially exclusive (though, obviously, some may be). That is, members of immigrant minorities can and do participate in them also, whether in work environments, neighborhoods, or sports teams; and the interaction across boundaries is greater when some degree of social compatibility exists. In the usual case, such compatibility requires more adjustment, whether achieved by past assimilation or present efforts, by individuals from minority backgrounds than by those in the majority. This asymmetry reflects differences in social power, especially the potential for exclusion by the majority.

This more social-demographic aspect of the mainstream is the more encompassing: it overlaps with the institutional one insofar as institutions can be constituted by assemblages of social settings, such as offices and social relations among personnel (institutions also require rules and procedures, which are not implied). Nevertheless, any operationalization of the socio-demographic conception demands recognition of certain practical limits that are hard to specify with complete precision. There has to be a socioeconomic floor to the mainstream—for instance, we should not count the homeless or desperately poor in it, even if they belong to the native majority. And some in this majority—such as the adherents of certain religious groups, such as the Amish and Ultra-orthodox Jews—shun the mainstream society and should also not be reckoned as part of it. But we believe that the native-majority working class belongs in it because integration, which often requires multiple generations to run its course, can begin with integration with the working-class part of the mainstream.[23]

Neo-assimilation theory points to a number of mechanisms that promote assimilation for a substantial portion of minority groups. The single most important is the intersection of the aspirations of many minority group members with the social structures through which they can realize them. The theory posits, in other words, that most individuals of whatever origins seek to improve their lives materially and socially. They pursue practical strategies in search of a better job, a better place to live, and interesting social milieus—social mobility, in the broadest sense of the term. Since whites and their cultural standards still dominate the institutions that control access to most socioeconomic opportunities, such as educational systems, and predominate among the occupants of the most valued social milieus, minority individuals and families almost invariably must make adjustments, whether by learning a different accent in speech or by encouraging their children to learn a new sport, in order to achieve social mobility and improve the chances that their children can do so also. In this sense, assimilation can be unintentional, a by-product of social mobility strategies. As Victor Nee and I put it, assimilation frequently happens while minority individuals "are making other plans."[24]

An anecdote from my own recent experience may convey some nuances of the institutional aspect of the mainstream better than an abstract discussion. I was attending the wake for a cousin, which took place in an inner suburb of New York City, whose residents a few decades ago were mostly white ethnics but are now a mix of whites, blacks, and Hispanics. When I arrived, the room was filled with white ethnics (to judge by appearances and the names I heard as I was introduced) who were relatives, neighbors, and parishioners from the local Catholic church. A few nonwhites seemed to be former coworkers. (My cousin had been retired for a few years at the time of her death.)

Then the volunteer fire department showed up. Her son, my second cousin, is a captain. The fifty to sixty members, all dressed in uniforms that appeared to vary in accordance with rank (and visibly correlated with age), lined all the walls of the room. They included men and women, whites, blacks, and Latines. Surrounding the seated mourners, they removed their caps more or less in unison on command from the chief, an older white man, and listened to a prayer from the chaplain. Then came the most impressive part: they proceeded two-by-two to the bier to show their respect and individually turned to embrace my cousin's son, their fellow firefighter; many of the women—again, white, black, and Latina—exchanged kisses on the cheek with him. Then they left. When I discussed the fire department's appearance later with my cousin, he said that it was almost time for his twenty-fifth anniversary as a member, an anniversary celebrated with a roast of the member ("that's the way we do it"). His mother had hoped to live to see it.

How does this episode illustrate the sort of integration through mainstream institutions that I am pointing to as a form of assimilation? To begin with, there is an incentive to join a volunteer fire department, apart from the social respect that may be acquired: in New York State, volunteer firefighters can earn pensions. Surely, for members, who spend a fair amount of time with each other, there is also an incentive to rise through the ranks, especially since rank is so visibly marked by uniform and insignia. Membership, especially coupled with the ambition to rise, involves "buying into" the rules and culture of an organization. And as the ceremony at the wake exemplified, membership involves some degree of the relational assimilation described by Tomás Jiménez—mutual respect and even affection that crosses ethno-racial lines.[25] Indeed, the celebration of a membership anniversary with a roast implies more than respect: it assumes enough acquaintance with the other that acerbic good-natured remarks can be delivered at a formal public event. My cousin explained to me later that, though the chief may still be white, the assistant chiefs are diverse, and presumably the speakers at the roast would be too.

Of course, minority individuals should not be deemed to be assimilated per se just because they belong to a volunteer fire department. They may go back to otherwise segregated lives at their jobs and in their families and neighborhoods. However, if they participate in such a mainstream institution, they are assimilated to some degree. And if they are similarly integrated in their lives away from the fire station, at work and at home, then they are assimilated according to the Alba and Nee conception.

Organizations also feature mechanisms that can promote mobility and assimilation. The antidiscrimination laws forged during the civil rights era have had long-lasting effects in the workplace, even though their legal impact has been weakened over time by a more conservative turn in national politics and in the judicial philosophies reigning in the federal courts. For instance, prominent race discrimination lawsuits settled for large amounts, such as those in 1996 against Texaco and in 2000 against Coca-Cola, reaffirmed for many companies and nonprofit organizations the need for policies to protect themselves from the potential harms of their own discrimination. In turn, they became more attentive to the issue, instituted diversity and multicultural training workshops for managers and employees, and developed internal rules and procedures to reduce discrimination. "Diversity" became a mantra in hiring and promotion decisions as corporations and nonprofits have striven to, at a minimum, present a face that is not exclusively white to the public. To be sure, these facts do not mean that equal opportunity reigns; however, workplaces have become far more integrated at multiple levels than could have been imagined in the middle of the twentieth century.[26]

Some mechanisms that promote assimilation do so by sanctioning bad behavior, but others encourage "good" behavior. Affirmative action or positive discrimination, though legally challenged, still operates in many organizational contexts. Thus, elite private universities still pursue affirmative action strategies in their admissions in order to ensure that their student bodies are "diverse," although their admission policies have disproportionately benefited the children of nonwhite immigrants rather than those coming from native minority families.[27] A *New York Times* analysis of elite college enrollments in 2015 found that only about half of the student bodies at the eight Ivy League schools was white, and that Asians and Hispanics made up the largest shares among the nonwhite students.[28] Adding to the momentum of these policies are cultural shifts among college-educated whites in favor of the greater inclusion of minorities. For many whites, overt expressions of crude ethno-racial prejudice have become taboo. They have not, of course, disappeared. But overall, despite their resurgence in the Trump era, they have become more covert and weakened to the extent that their public expression is sanctioned.[29]

Other conceptualizations that are helpful in thinking about assimilation processes have to do with social boundaries. A social boundary is a distinction that individuals make in their everyday lives between those who are "like me" and those who are not. This distinction shapes mental orientations and actions toward others. By definition, assimilation involves boundary change, but boundary changes are not all the same. Roughly speaking, the contrast between bright and blurred boundaries identifies a critical difference shaping assimilation.[30] Bright boundaries draw unambiguous distinctions, so that individuals know at all times which side of the boundary they are on. Blurred boundaries allow for modes of self-presentation and social representation that open up zones of ambiguity.

In the case of a bright boundary, assimilation generally takes the form of boundary crossing by individuals. Crossing a boundary is likely to be experienced as something akin to a conversion: an individual departs from one group and abandons signs of membership in it in an attempt to enter into another group, taking on all of the conversion's social and psychic burdens—growing distance from peers, feelings of disloyalty, and anxieties about acceptance. The epitome of this process is racial "passing." Boundary crossing, by its nature, is a fraught process that not everyone will be willing to undertake.

A blurred boundary, by contrast, enables individuals to be seen as members of the groups on both sides of the boundary, either simultaneously or sequentially. Where boundaries are blurred, assimilation may be psychologically eased insofar as the individuals undergoing it do not sense a rupture between their participation in mainstream institutions and their familiar social and cultural practices and identities; consequently, they do not feel forced to choose between the mainstream and their group of origin. Assimilation of this type takes place in intermediate, or hyphenated stages that allow individuals to feel simultaneously like members of a minority and members of the mainstream. Boundary blurring makes assimilation less individualistic and more open to minority group cohorts who recognize similarities in their experiences. This depiction of boundary blurring suggests that it is central to an understanding of the significance of ethno-racially mixed backgrounds.

Similar to race theory, assimilation theory has a major limitation in its range of applicability. It has proven, in both the past and the present, to fit the experiences of immigrant groups and their descendants, but not those of groups like Native and African Americans, who entered American society through conquest or enslavement.[31] These two bodies of ideas about race and ethnicity in American society are often presumed to be contradictory, as if only one can be true, but in fact there have been attempts to combine them. The most serious such attempt is "segmented assimilation" theory, proposed by sociologists Alejandro Portes and Min Zhou. In opposition to the focus of assimilation theory on the pathways that lead to the mainstream, Portes and Zhou argue that there are several distinct trajectories into different "segments" of American society, and that race in the form of the white versus nonwhite distinction plays a central role in the specific trajectory of individuals and groups. One of the key trajectories is a classic form of assimilation: "growing acculturation and parallel integration into the white middle-class." Another, however, can be characterized as "downward assimilation" into an extremely disadvantaged minority status; the theory posits that nonwhites from weak immigrant communities with low average levels of human capital are at risk of following this trajectory. The third involves resistance to mainstream assimilation: selective acculturation and embeddedness in an ethnic community support socioeconomic mobility within the confines of an ethnic economy.[32]

Segmented assimilation theory has been a valuable source of ideas about the life routes pursued by the contemporary second generation.[33] The theory, however, takes mainstream assimilation largely for granted, viewing it simply as the outcome of racial acceptability (to whites) and favorable socioeconomic position. Its analytical energies are concentrated on the other two trajectories. But there is not convincing evidence of downward assimilation as a major route; that is, the data we have do not demonstrate, as the theory posits, the failure on a large scale of the second generation to advance socioeconomically beyond the immigrant one.[34] The third pathway, involving upward mobility within an ethnic world, is mainly open to groups that arrive with substantial human and/or financial capital, such as the Cubans. And then it may last only a generation or two, after which successful group members scatter into the mainstream.

The most serious problem for this theory is its assumption that the key racial distinction, between whites and everyone else, is exogenous—not mutable within the conceptual system but a determinant of almost everything else. Accordingly, segmented assimilation theory cannot help in the development of insights into how racial distinctions are affected by assimilation processes. This assumption is not such a problem for analyses of contemporaneous social processes or, as is common in social science, for ones observed in the recent past (recorded in, say, survey data), because the American racial system looks stable in the short term. However, it is a decided weakness when thinking about several decades in the future, especially in the early twenty-first century, when ethno-racial mixing in families is beginning to soar.

In the end, as sociologists Zulema Valdez and Tanya Golash-Boza have argued, we need the two theories, of race and of assimilation.[35] They provide two different lenses for looking at the societal landscape, each bringing into sharp focus some distinctive features and processes. If we are going to achieve a realistic, comprehensive analysis of race and ethnicity in the present and near future, the theories are complementary, not antagonistic. To some extent they apply to distinct groups; to some extent they apply to distinct aspects of the experiences or different parts of the same groups.

HOW THE TWO THEORIES UNDERSTAND MIXED FAMILY ORIGINS

The research findings of the last chapter already show the relevance of both race theory and assimilation theory to individuals coming from mixed majority-minority family backgrounds. Individuals with black-white parentage have experiences of racialization, such as harsher treatment by the police, that incline them in the direction of black identities and affiliations. Individuals from other mixed nonwhite-white backgrounds, including American Indian–whites, Anglo-Hispanics, Asian-whites, and those with one mixed-race parent and one white parent, also have some of these experiences, such as micro-aggressions like slurs and jokes at their expense. Nevertheless, most of them appear to integrate into social milieus where whites are numerous, many can identify some of the time as whites, and many marry whites. One unknown is the impact of phenotype: how does the spectrum of appearance associated with mixed backgrounds, ranging from light-skinned with European features to dark-skinned with an indigenous or other non-European physiognomy, affect the ethno-racial orientation of mixed individuals? The evidence that Asian-whites, for example, are often comfortable in milieus with many whites can hide the very different experiences and self-understandings of a minority within this group.

The findings for mixed minority-white Americans are problematic for the majority-minority narrative, which portrays society as rigidly divided between whites and everyone else, because they point to a rapidly growing part of the population that is anchored, through kinship at a minimum, on both sides of the ethno-racial divide. The findings are also problematic for the census classification of most mixed individuals as minorities.

Mixed individuals who are integrating into often diverse milieus that contain whites are likely to play a pivotal role in the near future in defining the ethno-racial contours of the United States. Race theory at this point lacks the conceptual apparatus to adequately address the twenty-first-century significance of this new and largely unheralded force. It remains under the spell of historical experiences of racial domination, especially of African Americans. Many African Americans have some degree of white European ancestry, often dating back to slavery, when white masters could impose their will on female slaves. The "one-drop" rule that emerged from this biological mixing lasted long after emancipation, consigned partly black Americans to the African American group, and arguably still affects perceptions of mixed, partly black individuals, such as former president Barack Obama. Vilna Bashi Treitler observes that, in this country, "ethnicity and race are so related that a racially black person identifying himself as German, for example, will be treated as if his listeners had misheard."[36] However, the generalization that the one-drop rule is still in effect—that whites uniformly impose a minority status on mixed individuals—does not square with the present-day evidence.

A related way in which race theorists have tried to conceptually align ethno-racial mixing with exclusive white racial domination is through positing the emergence of an in-between racial tier to contain most mixed individuals. As mentioned earlier in this chapter, the sociologist Eduardo Bonilla-Silva's Latin Americanization thesis is the preeminent example.[37] Labeling this intermediate tier "honorary whites," Bonilla-Silva describes it as akin to the "coloured" category during South African apartheid. He hypothesizes that this tier would be constituted out of a diverse set of not fully white groups and categories, such as Chinese and other Asian groups, light-skinned Latines, and the majority of mixed persons. However, unlike the coloured group in South Africa, which was anchored in a legally defined category, or the *mestizo* group in Latin America, the functioning of such a diverse tier as a social group or formation is questionable, at the very least. There is no evidence that the members of the different groups and social categories located in this hypothesized tier recognize a shared common situation or feel any special orientation toward one another as a consequence. No term for this tier has arisen in popular discourse. At this point, the "honorary white" tier remains a hypothesis in search of empirical realization.

Inevitably, then, the discussion of the larger significance of mixing today must involve assimilation theory. Assimilation ideas raise certain questions: Should we understand mixed family backgrounds as in general a step toward ultimate absorption into whiteness? Or could the growing presence of mixed individuals in white social milieus change the self-definition of the mainstream part of American society? To address these questions, we must take a detour into the American history of assimilation and specifically into the mass assimilation of the so-called white ethnics in the quarter-century following World War II. This was the paradigmatic experience for assimilation theory, the empirical reality from which it was abstracted by mid-twentieth-century theorists like Milton Gordon and the more recent historians of whiteness such as David Roediger. However, I will argue that certain features are missing from the way this history is commonly understood today. Exploring it in a more nuanced fashion suggests unforeseen possibilities for the near future. This is in no way to say that the near future will replicate the past—it will not, and for reasons I will also try to bring out.

Takeaways from Assimilation History

THE PUZZLE OF POST-WORLD WAR II
MASS ASSIMILATION

The quarter-century following World War II was the key period for the assimilation—the full incorporation into the mainstream—of the so-called white ethnics: the second- and third-generation descendants of Catholic, Jewish, and Orthodox immigrants who arrived in the United States in the late nineteenth and early twentieth centuries. We will look specifically at Italians and eastern European Jews to illustrate the main patterns of mass assimilation.

Italians, coming mainly from the poor southern regions of Italy, were the largest group of immigrants in the early part of the twentieth century. These immigrants were often illiterate and possessed few skills that could serve them well in an industrializing economy. Settling in cities, many entered urban economies on their lowest rungs, in the ranks of unskilled labor, by taking jobs such as ditch digging. Their children did not perform well in schools and were widely regarded in the 1930s as a source of social problems such as truancy, school dropout, and gang membership. Early on, Italian immigrants had acquired a reputation for crime, especially organized crime, and were stigmatized with an epithet, "guinea," that, in referring to Africa, demeaned their claim on whiteness.[38]

Eastern European Jews presented a strong contrast to the Italians in many respects, yet they too were excluded from the mainstream before the 1950s. These immigrants brought entrepreneurial experience and an abundance of relevant occupational skills. Their children frequently racked up exemplary school records and began to climb the educational ramparts and compete for entry into elite colleges and universities that had been the preserve of the children of white Protestants. Quotas limiting their entry followed in the 1920s. Moreover, the second generation, even after achieving unusually high levels of education, often met with anti-Semitism when searching for appropriate jobs. In law, for example, the elite "white shoe" firms were closed to Jews.[39]

Much changed—and rapidly—after World War II. Italian American college attendance and graduation rates rose steeply among those educated in the 1950s and 1960s, and by about 1970 there was no longer a difference between the young adults of Italian descent and other whites. Social integration accompanied socioeconomic uplift. The urban residential concentrations of Italians weakened as many of the socially mobile moved to ethnically integrated but heavily white suburbs. An additional indicator of social integration was intermarriage: a quarter-century after the war, the intermarriage rate in the third generation was on the order of 70 percent, and many Italian Americans were marrying non-Catholics.

Anti-Semitism was discredited for many white Americans by the war and the revelations about Nazi genocide, and attitudes toward

Jews became more sympathetic as a result. Jewish organizations mounted challenges to exclusionary institutions such as elite colleges, which began to dismantle their quota systems. By 1970, Jews were the most successful of the white ethnic groups by the standard measures of socioeconomic situation, including occupational position and income. Intermarriage on a large scale did not come as quickly as it did for the Italians. Jews, as the bearers of a unique religious heritage and a history of persecution and worse at the hands of Christians, were not all that eager to marry non-Jews. But come it did as the social and cultural differences between Jews and other highly educated whites diminished. In the 1950s, about 10 percent of Jews married out, but by the 1980s the figure was around 50 percent (and, in a sign of group ambivalence, disputed).[40]

Race theory has an answer for why this mass assimilation happened. Developed by historians such as Noel Ignatiev, Matthew Frye Jacobson, and David Roediger and the anthropologist Karen Brodkin, it has been dubbed "whiteness theory" and is probably the most widely accepted view today among academics and intellectuals. This historical narrative is ultimately rather straightforward and intellectually satisfying in some respects. Some of the European immigrant groups, it begins, were not perceived as fully white when they arrived in the United States.[41] Their problematic position in the racial order was compounded by their initially humble position in the labor market: the work they did at first was not seen as fitting for native whites. And they often lived near and intermingled with African Americans. The challenge they faced was to gain acceptance as members of the dominant race. This they did partly through their own efforts, as they struggled upwards by putting distance between themselves and blacks. The Irish, it is often noted, bore an intense hostility toward African Americans, which climaxed in the New York draft riots of 1863, when mobs including many Irish immigrants attacked blacks. On a more day-to-day basis, the Irish often refused to work alongside blacks, leading to the exclusion of African American workers from some occupations in Northern cities.

The European immigrants and their descendants were also more favorably treated by the state. For one thing, they were legally "white," a status that gave them a variety of rights and privileges that were denied to nonwhites. Unlike Asian immigrants, who were barred from naturalization until the mid-twentieth century, the European immigrants could become American citizens and thus gain access to the ballot box. They and the second generation were in fact courted for their votes by politicians in Northern cities and thereby gained numerous tangible benefits, such as municipal jobs and representation in elected and appointed positions. And because they were not subject to antimiscegenation laws, they were candidates for marriage with other whites, which promoted their social integration.

They were also on the right side of the color line when it came to the racially differentiated consequences of New and Fair Deal policies, exemplified by the Federal Housing Authority, the Social Security Act, and the GI Bill, all of which gave critical advantages to ethnic whites that were withheld from most African Americans. The original Social Security Act of 1935 had pernicious consequences for blacks because its pension provisions left out agricultural work and domestic service, where many of them but few whites labored.[42] And New Deal housing policy, a Depression-era attempt to spur economic activity, ultimately contributed to the growth of racial inequality. Most important, the policies of the Federal Housing Authority, by guaranteeing mortgages, ignited an expansion of homeownership among whites, including the ethnic whites. This postwar expansion enabled upwardly mobile ethnics to leave urban enclaves and to participate in the Euro-American mixing occurring in the newly developing suburbs. At the same time, by redlining areas that were occupied by African Americans or that might be occupied by them, these policies reinforced residential segregation. Ultimately, they contributed mightily to the huge present-day wealth discrepancies between whites and blacks because of the large role played by homeownership in the intergenerational wealth accumulation of many whites.[43]

This is all true, although casting the Irish and the southern and eastern Europeans as nonwhites exaggerates their racial distance from other whites. They are better understood as inferior whites, who were nevertheless seen as racially superior to nonwhites.[44] In any event, there is a huge hole in the logic underpinning whiteness theory, rendering it inadequate as an explanation of post–World War II mass assimilation. In addition, whiteness theory is a one-dimensional account that, by ignoring other critical dimensions of difference, misleads about this assimilation and the mainstream it produced.

The explanatory inadequacy of whiteness theory lies in an unresolved contradiction: Race theory rests on the strongly justified proposition that a privileged group (such as American whites) is always prepared to defend its privileges and engages in various forms of social closure to exclude outsiders from sharing in the bounty. This assumption is key to the claims that whites work to maintain and shore up a societal system that keeps nonwhites in positions of inferiority. The assumption is consistent with an enormous body of social-science research, such as social identity theory, which demonstrates the investment that humans have in core identities. Social identity theory is the source of the recent experimental research, cited in chapter 2, showing that whites adopt more conservative political stances when confronted with demographic scenarios leading to a majority-minority America.

Yet, according to the whiteness explanation, white Protestants of predominantly northwest European ancestry (for example, English, Scots, Dutch) were prepared to treat the descendants of Catholic and Jewish immigrants from such places as Ireland, southern Italy, and Russia as equals once their whiteness was confirmed. This would be amazing if true because it would mean that an economically, politically, and socially dominant group was willing all of a sudden to share its privileges with very large groups of previous outsiders. What heightens the amazement is that other social distinctions apart from race were available to white Protestants in the middle of the twentieth century in order to continue to exclude the newly minted whites: namely, religion and ethnic or national origin.

Religion, ignored by whiteness theory, was especially potent as a social and political distinction through much of American history. Religious divisions, especially between Catholics and Protestants, were of long standing, going back to the colonial period, and intensely felt. During the nineteenth and early twentieth centuries, anti-Catholicism was a major political, cultural, and intellectual force in American life, as white Protestant Americans feared that their society and its democratic institutions would be submerged under the flood of largely Catholic immigrants, coming first from Ireland and Germany and later from Italy, the Catholic parts of the Austro-Hungarian and Russian empires, and Mexico. In the middle of the nineteenth century, an anti-Catholic, anti-immigrant political party, the Know Nothings, won numerous local and state elections and some congressional ones. Anti-Catholicism as a political force was resurrected in the late nineteenth century by the American Protective Association (APA), a secret society and political movement that sought to oppose what it construed as Catholic electoral power. The APA and anti-Catholic sentiments more generally contributed importantly to the decades-long drive to restrict immigration, which succeeded in the 1920s and imposed discriminatory national-origins quotas on the southern and eastern Europeans, and to the resurrection of the Ku Klux Klan during the 1920s.[45] Politically, anti-Catholicism flared again when Al Smith, the first Catholic to be nominated for president by a major political party, campaigned in 1928. Protestant ministers in many parts of the country thundered against his candidacy and exhorted their congregations to vote for his Republican opponent. Smith lost in a landslide.

Such ethnic and religious distinctions (the two overlapped extensively until midway into the second half of the twentieth century) could have formed the basis for an enduring social cleavage. Into the 1960s, when the election of John F. Kennedy as president placed beyond doubt the mainstream acceptability of Catholics, most Catholic children received some or all of their education in a separate parochial system (which had emerged in the mid-nineteenth century to remove them from the Protestant influences perceived to operate in public schools). This separation of children into distinct schools left no doubt in communities about who was Catholic and who was not, and school records further identified many Catholic youth to others, such as employers. Since different schools had their own sports teams and other extracurricular activities, this separation in effect also promoted a social distance between Catholics and non-Catholic youth, who were less like to encounter each other outside of the school day. The political scientist Robert Putnam observes that, in his Ohio hometown during the 1950s, everyone knew who was Catholic and who was Protestant. The religious distinction became therefore a major divide when it came to friendship, dating, and marriage.[46] With their names, social networks, and other characteristics, Jews were equally identifiable in mid-twentieth-century America and were excluded from many Christian-dominated social settings.

Jews have always been a small part of the American population and were about 3 percent at the middle of the twentieth century. Catholics, however, amount to a much larger proportion. In 1957, when the Census Bureau's Current Population Survey included a question on religion—the only time that a Census Bureau survey has asked about it—Catholics, the vast majority of them descended from nineteenth- and twentieth-century European immigrants, formed one-quarter of the population, while white Protestants were just under 60 percent.[47] Adding Jews and Catholics to the dominant group expanded it by almost 50 percent. One would think that the prospect of such an expansion would have made the average white Protestant blanch and resist the newcomers. What then made them acceptable?

A NON-ZERO-SUM ASSIMILATION THEORY TO EXPLAIN THE PUZZLE

Any complex historical process involves a variety of unique factors that contribute to the outcome and cannot easily be disentangled from it. One factor often cited as a cause of the mass assimilation of white ethnics is the four-decade hiatus in mass immigration starting in the mid-1920s. Undoubtedly, this hiatus weakened ethnic communities by depriving them of steady inflows of newcomers and contributed to the cultural assimilation of the southern and eastern Europeans. However, the notion that an immigration halt could render lower-status immigrant-origin groups much more acceptable to a dominant native one is very questionable. At a minimum, religion created a bright boundary separating white Protestants from Catholics and Jews. Thus, the downturn in immigration during World War I due to the interruption of transatlantic ship traffic did not lead to a decline in stereotypes and prejudice; in fact, the wartime period and the few years afterwards produced some of the worst xenophobia the United States has ever seen.

An explanation of mass assimilation has to account for the relaxation of the ethno-religious boundaries that plainly divided the pre–World War II white population into what one sociologist described at the time as the "Triple Melting Pot": three distinct subsocieties that each enclosed family and other close relations.[48] My proposal is a non-zero-sum assimilation theory that presumes changes in social structures that open up space for formerly marginalized minorities to enter the mainstream without appearing to threaten the status of established groups. This theory pinpoints three critical, generalizable processes at the core of this assimilation that are thus logically sufficient to generate the outcome:

1. *Status uplift*: The processes that raised numerous white ethnics to socioeconomic parity with middle-class white Protestants, without appearing to intensify competition along ethno-religious lines, can be conceived as a "non-zero-sum mobility"; that is, downward mobility by members of more privileged groups was not required in order for upward mobility by members of less privileged groups to take place. The status uplift for white ethnics such as the Italians was very much a matter of socioeconomic ascent in the sense of advancing educational and occupational status. However, the concept can be applied even to groups with high levels of human capital, such as today's Asian Indians, who arrive as highly educated immigrants. Non-zero-sum mobility can advance them and their children in status—broadly construed to include, for example, relative positioning within work organizations and professions—to parity with otherwise similar whites.[49]

2. *Social proximity*: The proliferation of amicable relationships across boundaries brought upwardly mobile white ethnics into close, regular contact with their socioeconomic peers in the dominant group. These processes helped convert socioeconomic advance into social proximity to the dominant group and set up the conditions for the operation of the "contact hypothesis."[50]

3. *Moral elevation or destigmatization*: The ideological or symbolic underpinnings of a boundary were revised to acknowledge that many members of the minority had the same moral worth as the members of the majority. Such a revision in the beliefs held by at least a portion of the majority (it is typical that an enlightened vanguard accepts moral equality with the minority well ahead of the majority's mass) makes the arrival of upwardly striving ethnic-minority members more acceptable than it would have previously been.

These three conditions became abundant during the quarter-century following World War II, a period when younger, later-generation Irish, Italians, Jews, and other white ethnics were able to enter the mainstream en masse. During this period, the social boundaries that had previously excluded these groups from the mainstream blurred and eventually receded in salience. Non-zero-sum mobility was associated with the burgeoning prosperity of the immediate postwar period, itself a by-product of the paramount position of the United States in the world economy, given that it was one of the few industrial economies to escape massive wartime destruction. In 1950, the United States accounted for more than one-quarter of the world's total economic output.[51]

This prosperity allowed enormous public investment in education, which was spurred in part by the educational grants provided to returning veterans in the GI Bill (1944) and in part by Cold War competition with the Soviet Union. In just three decades, 1940 to 1970, the country's college and university system quintupled in size, allowing a much higher fraction of high school graduates than ever before to continue their education. In 1940, a mere 9 percent of eighteen- to twenty-four-year-olds were enrolled in a college or university. By 1970, that fraction had exploded to nearly one-third. In a single generation, higher education had become a mass system, no longer just the preserve of an elite.[52] The resulting transformation, funded mainly by a huge government investment in state and municipal institutions, produced a paragon of non-zero-sum mobility, for it was not just the white ethnics who were advancing but also many white Protestants, who took advantage of educational opportunities that would not have been available before the war.

The expansion of the higher educational system prepared many more young Americans, including white ethnics, to take advantage of the proliferating postwar opportunities to obtain middle-class jobs, including new ones such as computer programmer. The advancing ethnics and other whites experienced, in other words, a substantial uplift in socioeconomic status compared to their parents' generation. A more analytic way of putting this is that the US economy generated abundant occupational mobility. This mobility was itself a product of a far-reaching transformation of the American workforce: over time, economic opportunity was reshaped as some occupational slots expanded and others shrank. Between 1930 and 1970, the percentage of Americans working in agriculture fell sharply, forcing many grandchildren and great-grandchildren of earlier immigrants who settled on the prairies to seek jobs in cities. The unskilled portion of the blue-collar workforce also declined precipitously; many in the immigrant generation, like the Italians, had found employment in these jobs. White-collar occupations, however, expanded robustly, especially jobs in the professional and technical categories, which were generally high in status and well remunerated.

Such massive shifts are associated with structurally engendered mobility: that is, a large part of each new birth cohort entering the workforce is constrained by a rearranged regime of opportunities to take jobs very different from those held by its parents. The period from 1930 to 1970, which runs from the economic extremes of the Great Depression to post–World War II prosperity, also spans immigrant generations—from the work lives of southern and eastern European immigrants to those of their children and grandchildren. For the latter, occupational transformation entailed a sharp contraction at the lower end of the workforce, where many of their immigrant forebears had found jobs, matched with an expansion in its middle and upper reaches. Even had they wanted, most of them could not have followed their immigrant parents and grandparents into similar occupations because those jobs, such as Italians unloading on the docks, were growing scarcer. The choice for ethnic youth was clear: either get the education required to obtain the white-collar jobs that were proliferating or find a place, frequently through kin connections, in one of the skilled trades. Otherwise, they faced reduced economic prospects.

The second condition—the blooming of amicable relationships across ethno-religious boundaries—was in its way also a by-product of non-zero-sum mobility in the middle of the twentieth century. That is, it was associated with profound shifts in residence as a result of the rapid postwar development of the suburbs as the desired residential space for middle-class white families. The suburb became a melting pot for whites as families from diverse ethnic and religious origins bought homes and neighborhoods became mixed. As Herbert Gans describes the residents of one of these early new suburbs in his classic, *The Levittowners*, "thirty-seven percent reported being of Northern European origin (English, German, or Scandinavian); 17 percent were eastern European (mostly Russian Jewish with a scattering of Poles); 10 percent, Irish; 9 percent, Southern European (mainly Italian), and the remainder a heady mixture of all of these backgrounds."[53]

African Americans were excluded from the suburban melting pot by federal policies that greatly restricted home loans to blacks and by the white-only policies of many developers. (Developers claimed to be constrained by the prejudices of white buyers; Mr. Levitt of the Levittowns famously declared, "We can solve a housing problem, or we can try to solve a racial problem, but we cannot combine the two."[54]) But for whites the suburb was a crucible for mixing, especially since so many suburban whites were married couples raising

children. Second- and third-generation ethnics came into contact in
schools and neighborhoods with a variety of others, some of them
ethnics from other groups and some of them native white Protestants. As a consequence, white ethnics were thoroughly integrated
into the white mainstream, as signaled by the rising rates of intermarriage among whites of diverse ethnic backgrounds.

The third condition, the destigmatization of white ethnics by
elevating their perceived moral worth, began during the war and
flourished afterwards. This moral elevation was crucial because it
made it much easier for native-born white Protestants to accept
the growing numbers of upwardly mobile white ethnics who were
showing up in jobs and neighborhoods where they had been rare
before. In effect, this elevation made the ethnics seem worthy of
the opportunities that the established members of the mainstream
took for granted as their birthright, as part of the American Way. At
the same time, most whites accepted as a matter of course that these
opportunities were not available to nonwhites.

The process was encapsulated in what amounts to a metaphor: a
fighting unit of the American military seen as a microcosm of a "melting pot" society. The mass mobilization necessary during the war
produced a general awareness of the understandable family attachments to European countries, particularly to the enemy powers Germany and Italy, felt by a sizable part of the population within a few
generations of immigration. It seemed critical to the war effort therefore to inspire a sense of national solidarity that could embrace these
white ethnic Americans. The result was a self-conscious attempt to
highlight the ethnics' contributions to the fight, the blood they were
shedding on the nation's behalf. Films made for domestic consump-
tion more or less deliberately portrayed the American military as a
national cross-section of the white population. Wartime journalism, like the reports from the front by the famous reporter Ernie
Pyle, worked the same vein of ethnic iconography. This carefully
cultivated wartime solidarity presaged a different vision of America, one that for the first time included white ethnic Americans as
members of the charmed circle of full-fledged Americans. Nonwhite
Americans, however, remained outside that circle. Their men fought

in segregated military units (typically led by white officers), and their accomplishments usually were not recorded by the mainstream press—with perhaps the exception of the Japanese American 442nd Brigade, the most decorated unit of the US Army.

The iconography of the fighting unit as a representation in miniature of white ethnic diversity permeated the popular novels and films created toward the end of the war and in the next few decades. John Hersey's *A Bell for Adano* (1944), Norman Mailer's *The Naked and the Dead* (1948), and James Jones's *From Here to Eternity* (1951) were all published to critical acclaim, achieved wide readership, and were made into successful films. They and others like them interpreted the World War II experience for a large segment of the American population and the generations that followed.[55] This narrative has not lost its imaginative power, as illustrated by the 1998 film *Saving Private Ryan*, which recapitulates it. Although these works presented ethnic Americans as the moral equals of other white Americans, showing them as contributing to American victory with everyday heroism and sacrifice, they were open about the prejudices present in American society, including those felt by ethnic Americans toward one another. Nevertheless, their vision was triumphant in lifting the curtain of stereotypes from the ethnics.

The emergence of television as a mass medium in the 1950s also played a pivotal role in the symbolic uplift of white ethnics, with eponymous shows like *The Jackie Gleason Show*, *The Milton Berle Show*, and *The Perry Como Show*. These enormously popular shows brought sympathetic, ethnically tinged stars weekly into homes throughout the country. Gleason, the child of an Irish American father and an Irish immigrant mother, was a comedian with a repertoire of regularly appearing characters, most famously, the Brooklyn bus driver Ralph Kramden in the multi-character skit *The Honeymooners*. Como, the child of Italian immigrants, was a singer whose show competed in a ratings battle with Jackie Gleason's in the mid-1950s. The most popular of all in the early 1950s was Milton Berle, born Mendel Berlinger, whose show at one point achieved almost universal coverage on existing television sets. Berle was given the sobriquet "Mr. Television" and fondly known by many children as "Uncle Miltie."[56]

To be sure, resistance by native white Protestants to the rising white ethnics did not simply melt away in the postwar period. The social ascent of massive numbers of ethnics was contested, but not successfully blocked, as it would have been earlier in the century. Large-scale assimilation is compatible, at least for a time, with resistance by some members of the majority and their reassertion of claims of moral superiority. The strength of the resistance is illustrated by the experiences of Jews and Italians, the two largest ethnic groups derived from the massive southern and eastern European immigration. In the very postwar decades when the assimilation of these groups was intensifying, they became, one after the other, the focus of widespread public suspicions that they held beliefs and were engaged in activities that were harmful to the United States. As a result, their communities and many individuals were the subjects of state surveillance, and some were stigmatized, if not penalized, by institutions and public opinion.

Jews were ensnared by the Red Scare of the 1950s. The anti-Communist fervor whipped up by Senator Joseph McCarthy and his supporters and the investigative activities of the House Un-American Activities Committee targeted especially the industries and professions, such as entertainment and teaching, where Jews were numerous. The FBI under Director J. Edgar Hoover carried out extensive surveillance of many Jewish (and other) Americans in search of links to the Communist Party. Children often learned decades later, through Freedom Of Information Act (FOIA) applications, how closely their parents were observed by FBI agents and how many of their friends, neighbors, and coworkers of that time informed on them.[57] The era produced many victims, and Jews were prominent among the blacklisted figures in entertainment who could not find work and the university faculty who were dismissed from tenured positions. Leonard Bernstein, Aaron Copland, Howard Fast, Lillian Hellman, Arthur Miller, Zero Mostel, and Edward G. Robinson, all from Jewish backgrounds, were among the blacklisted.[58] The execution of Julius and Ethel Rosenberg in 1953 by electrocution, on the charge of giving American atomic secrets to the Soviet Union, undoubtedly strengthened in the minds of many Americans the association between Jewishness and Communist and other left-wing leanings.

In the next decade, the focus of suspicion gravitated to the Italians. The nature of this suspicion was very different: Italians were suspected of criminal rather than subversive political activity. Effectively, the group was singled out by government policy as the major source of the nation's organized crime problem. The association of organized crime with southern Italians, especially Sicilians, and their culture has a lengthy history in the United States, dating back to the Black Hand activities of the immigration period. But after the sensational 1963 congressional testimony of Joseph Valachi, a one-time Cosa Nostra insider, this association became an identification. That identification was cemented into place by the 1968 *Report of the President's Crime Commission*, which claimed that the "core" of organized crime in the United States was constituted by the Mafia, a national network of Italian American crime families. Moreover, this structure, it declared, "resembles that of the Mafia groups that have operated for almost a century on the island of Sicily."[59]

The involvement of some Jews and Italians in communism and organized crime, respectively, is not in doubt. But each of these episodes is revealing about a perennial American response to immigration and its aftermath, one that is still evident today. The response to a perceived threat was a veritable crusade by parts of the American establishment against an "enemy" that was defined—to a significant extent in one case (communism) and entirely in the other (organized crime)—in terms of a historically recent immigrant group, one seen earlier in the century as outside of the American mainstream. The dangers posed by this "enemy" were depicted as extreme, potentially threatening the nature of American society as it then existed. Domestic communism was believed to have the potential to subvert American democracy. The Mafia (or La Cosa Nostra) was seen as penetrating and exploiting important economic and political institutions, from unions to certain urban industries, to local and even national politics. Political radicalism and crime, in fact, were threats that Americans had historically identified with foreign and immigrant influences.[60] Anxieties about damage to American institutions inflicted by new, unassimilable immigrant groups had contributed to the restriction legislation of the 1920s.

These suspicions were not without consequences for the mobility and integration of the members of the affected groups. The suspicions had ethnic dimensions that inevitably allowed them to spread beyond the small group of Communist Party members, in the one case, or the initiates of Cosa Nostra families, in the other. Especially for those with a career in the public eye, the mere suggestion of an association with the wrong person or group could be stigmatizing. As late as the 1990s, hints of Mafia family connections ruined the attempts of some prominent Italian American politicians to reach higher elective office.[61]

Another indicator of some degree of continuing resistance to the arrival of previously marginal groups in the mainstream part of society is how strenuously the groups themselves had to work to remove remaining barriers in the immediate postwar years. Jews, a group with a legacy of enduring anti-Semitism in Christian-dominated societies, supported an unusually robust set of organizations concerned with their welfare and were notable in this respect. Their legal and political successes paved the way for others—in their campaigns, for example, against the use of religious and racial criteria in admissions to elite universities and professional schools.[62] In short, the mainstream entry of the white ethnics was not accomplished in the fashion of an upbeat Hollywood ending: the already privileged did not have an epiphany and welcome the once scorned newcomers into their midst. Instead, the previously marginal groups to an important extent had to fight their way in. And this time their efforts bore fruit.

In closing out this part of the argument, I want to acknowledge again the enormous complexity of the mass assimilation following World War II. Like any historical shift of this magnitude, many forces can be argued to have contributed to it. My claim is that, in terms of social-psychological principles such as the contact hypothesis, the three processes I have singled out are sufficient to account for mass assimilation and that, when they are present, we should expect to find ongoing assimilation.

However, race theory points to another feature of US society that could have been *essential* to the mass assimilation of white ethnics—namely, the existence of a stigmatized out-group. African Americans, as a group, could serve as a negative point of reference to anchor the status elevation of rising whites.[63] Certainly, it was the case that some disparaged groups concentrated in the urban working class at midcentury, exemplified by Italian Americans, strove to separate themselves in status terms from African Americans, expressing vehement race prejudice and attacking some blacks who entered their neighborhoods.[64] Moreover, there was a tight temporal interweave between the assimilation of white ethnics, which included their socioeconomic ascent and mobility out of urban enclaves, and the surge in the numbers of northern urban African Americans as part of the Second Great Migration, which took place during the same period. The upswing in the numbers of nonwhite minorities, which also included Puerto Ricans in some East Coast cities, made a workforce available to take the jobs at the bottom tiers of the urban economy that were being vacated by the ethnics. Neighborhoods that could house the newcomers were also becoming available.

The question of whether assimilation in the United States requires a permanently excluded group or whether the exclusion of African Americans, Puerto Ricans, and some other nonwhites has so far been an incidental feature of assimilation, a product of more durable but ultimately surmountable disadvantage, seems to me the most fundamental question about the ethno-racial construction of American society. An implicit assumption about the answer has led some social scientists to speculate that, in the new era of mass assimilation, the United States is gravitating toward a black-nonblack cleavage as its most consequential ethno-racial divide.[65] To that point, one can observe that the new immigrant groups are to some extent leapfrogging over African Americans—a pattern implied in the differences found in earlier chapters among mixed minority-white individuals according to their nonwhite origin—just as white ethnics did more than half a century ago.[66]

Yet I believe that the question should be held open. I confess to shrinking from the pessimism implied by a positive answer to the question of a permanently excluded group.[67] Such pessimism further implies that full African American inclusion requires a profound, even revolutionary, transformation of American society, and it is difficult to imagine how such a transformation could take place. But another reason is that the evidence that the mass assimilation of the white ethnics necessitated the continuing exclusion of African Americans is not clear-cut. In the postwar period, white ethnic groups seemed to have entered the mainstream everywhere there were sizable communities of these groups, as far as we can tell.[68] The arrival of large numbers of Southern-born African Americans in those decades was more variable, with small impacts in some medium-sized Northern cities with many ethnics, like Erie, Pennsylvania.[69]

Also important is that African American advance was itself a prominent feature of the postwar period. A period of great prosperity, accompanied by massive socioeconomic uplift and ethnic inclusion, made whites more generous. Some of the earliest fair employment laws that barred racial discrimination were passed in states that had large white ethnic populations, like Massachusetts and New York, and black workers were notable among the beneficiaries of these laws.[70] Moreover, at the same time as white ethnics were advancing in the North, the civil rights movement was gaining moral momentum in the South and heading toward its greatest successes. These came from legislation at the national level during the 1960s that depended on the support of Northern congressional members, many of whom had substantial numbers of white ethnic constituents but were also enthusiastic backers of civil rights. In this sense, there appears to have been a relaxation of the tensions between two types of boundary change—change at the boundaries between white ethnic populations and the mainstream and change between racial minorities and whites.

THE IMPACTS OF ASSIMILATION ON THE MAINSTREAM

Another big takeaway from the history of assimilation is that the mainstream is not a static end zone to which minorities must adjust as they make their way toward it and eventually into it. Of course, the white ethnics did adjust in many respects. But the mainstream was changed too by their arrival. In 1970, the mainstream, especially in the regions where the earlier European immigrants and their descendants were numerous, did not look like it had looked in 1940. In this respect, race theory is fundamentally misleading about the outcome of assimilation. It casts the process as a homogenizing one: the ethnics were problematic whites early in the twentieth century, but they succeeded in removing the question mark from their whiteness. Their assimilation did not alter the racial character of the mainstream.

In fact, the mass assimilation of the white ethnics made the mainstream much more diverse. The characteristics that defined the white ethnic groups as outsiders were primarily ethnic and religious—especially the latter—rather than racial. Even as late as the 1940s, President Franklin Roosevelt could openly express a genteel version of white Protestant dominance when he told Leo Crowley, an Irish Catholic New Deal official, "Leo, you know this is a Protestant country, and the Catholics and Jews are here under sufferance. It is up to you to go along with anything I want."[71]

When the mainstream expanded at midcentury to include the white ethnics, it became religiously more diverse as a consequence. To be sure, Jewish and Catholic ethnics modified their religious behavior and beliefs as they assimilated, in tandem with their experiences of growing compatibility in the frequent social encounters across ethnic and religious lines within the mainstream. Thus, many Catholics developed individualized forms of faith that allowed them to dissent from specific Church teachings, such as on birth control, that seemed incompatible with their lives in mainstream milieus.[72] But importantly, Catholics and Jews did not cease to be Catholics and Jews; assimilation did not require them to convert to a form of the dominant religious grouping, post-Reformation Christianity. And these religions received their mainstream charters, as it were, and became accepted as thoroughly American, an incorporation celebrated in a famous book of the mid-1950s, Will Herberg's *Protestant-Catholic-Jew*.[73] The identity of the mainstream society evolved accordingly—from the Christian America upheld by Protestant whites prior to midcentury to "Judeo-Christian" America, a term that in fact appears to have been invented in the early 1940s.[74] It became an identity that has stuck.

A greater degree of ethnic variation in the mainstream also became acceptable as part of the postwar expansion, as signaled by the much more frequent use of hyphenated identities, like Irish- or Polish-American. Earlier in the century, hyphenated identities were frowned upon; in denouncing them, Theodore Roosevelt famously called upon white Americans to "swat" the hyphen and think of themselves as exclusively American.[75] Hyphenated identities came into common usage in the postwar period, especially after 1970 when ethnic Americans felt more secure in their place in the mainstream. A swath of essays and books mistook the popularity of this ethnic self-expression for a "resurgence" of ethnicity, which it was not, given the steady weakening of ethnic communities and the rise in intermarriage.[76] A better conception of it was as a "symbolic" form of ethnicity that allowed whites to connect with their immigrant ancestral origins without demanding too much of them in their everyday lives, which were more and more carried out in ethnically mixed, though racially segregated, social milieus.

This is not to deny that some cultural differentiation by ethnic origin continued among whites. Political orientations and affiliations offer an intriguing example. On the whole, Catholics and Jews of recent immigrant origins had strong connections to the Democratic Party, which in many Northern cities was led by Irish Catholic-dominated machines into the 1960s. The machines offered various forms of support, including government attention to community needs and access to municipal employment and even to elected office, in return for votes. But this bargain fell apart as more and more ethnics were incorporated into the mainstream and their mobility to the suburbs became a potent centrifugal force. A curious divergence took place between Catholic and Jewish ethnics. By and large, the political behavior of the Catholic ethnics converged with that of white Protestants who were similar to them in social class, residence, and so forth. In other words, the political distinctiveness of religious and ethnic factors declined for them.[77] Jews, on the other hand, remained resolutely left of center in their politics, even if most of them no longer espoused the socialism of the immigrant generation.

Jews have retained a distinctive profile in other ways that seem to reflect cultural difference. They continue to attain very high levels of education, leading to remarkable concentrations employed in professional and entrepreneurial occupations. One might ask: are Jews really assimilating? According to the equation of assimilation with integration into the mainstream, they are certainly doing so. Here the recognition that the mainstream is not a uniform sociological entity is especially relevant. The mainstream is highly variegated along such lines as age, region, political orientation, social class, and the urban versus rural divide. Jews have integrated into those parts of the mainstream that are appropriate given their individual characteristics. And they have not simply adapted to fit into the mainstream; they have also had a discernible impact on it, as is evident in American intellectual life.[78] In the process, their perceptions of differences between themselves and the non-Jews they encounter as peers have declined; the boundary between them has blurred. Accordingly, intermarriage has risen sharply and become commonplace.

Conclusion

Different conceptions of American society have been vying for attention in recent decades, both in the public arena and in the academic literature. According to one, the United States is a white supremacist society where nonwhites, with rare exceptions such as sports and entertainment stars, are prevented from attaining the same status as whites. According to another conception, the United States is dominated by a mainstream society that, while the preserve in the past of white Protestants and today of whites, is open to the influences of new groups and therefore exhibits considerable fluidity and expansion of membership over time.

Strange as it may seem, both of these conceptions can be true in the sense that they correspond with the rigidity or malleability of specific ethno-racial distinctions and with the relationships of different minority populations to the mainstream. The race conception applies most clearly to groups that originally entered American society through conquest or enslavement, and it has been most thoroughly demonstrated for African Americans. Race theory is applied to powerful effect when it is used to identify and explicate the evolving mechanisms of racial oppression, such as mass incarceration.

The assimilation perspective applies most clearly to groups that came to the United States as immigrants and, most obviously, to the ethno-religiously distinct Irish, Italian, and eastern European Jewish groups that came during the nineteenth and early twentieth centuries. Indeed, one could say that the perspective developed as a reflection on their experience of eventual inclusion. Much evidence indicates that it applies also to substantial portions of the post-1965 groups from Africa, Asia, the Caribbean, and Latin America. The striking contrast in the past experiences of Asian immigrants and their children, when they were racially excluded from the mainstream society, and those of today underscores the relevance of the assimilation perspective. Yet there is no basis for a conclusion that the assimilation perspective applies uniformly throughout today's immigration-derived groups. The extent to which race theory may apply to those in these groups who are phenotypically most different from white norms of appearance remains an urgent question.

The surge of young Americans from mixed minority-white family backgrounds, with its echoes of the historic role of intermarriage and mixed ancestry in eroding ethno-religious distinctions among whites, might seem an easy fit to assimilation ideas. However, the distinct experiences of individuals with black and white parentage evoke another echo of the past—namely, the racist "one-drop" rule—and show that race theory is relevant as well, at least to some in the growing mixed group. Nevertheless, for the most part, what we know about individuals from mixed families, as synthesized in the last chapter, conforms to what we would expect based on the assimilation perspective.

The value of reexamining the experiences of European-American assimilation, which took off in the quarter-century following World War II, lies in its revealing picture of assimilation processes "on the ground." This picture debunks some of the simplistic and misleading myths about assimilation, such as the idea that assimilation must mean the eradication of all signs of distinctive origins and the wholesale adoption of the mainstream culture and identity. In contrast to the race theory conception of white ethnic assimilation, which is limited to the elevation of groups to full whiteness, the examination of assimilation in the past reveals that one by-product was substantially more visible diversity in the mainstream society than had been the case before and a greater spectrum of cultural variation aligned with ethnic origins.

Invoking assimilation ideas in relation to the growing significance of mixed minority-white family backgrounds still leaves us with a major puzzle. The unique societal circumstances that produced the mass assimilation of the white ethnics—extraordinary postwar prosperity, large-scale investment in the expansion of public higher education, the exodus en masse of many urban dwellers to the suburbs, and the moral revaluation of ethnics emerging from their wartime role—might seem to make that assimilation a one-off, not to be repeated. How can we understand the assimilation reflected in the rise of mixing in families, which has happened, moreover, during a time of greatly heightened economic inequality? The next chapter provides an answer.

7

Assimilation in the Early Twenty-First Century

The rising prevalence and average social characteristics of individuals with mixed majority-minority family backgrounds appear much more compatible with assimilation than with race theory. The hugely important, if partial, exception to this generalization is the group with mixed white and black origins, whose members encounter racist barriers like those confronting African Americans and who identify mostly with blacks. However, mixed black and white individuals also advance educationally beyond black-only Americans and marry whites at higher rates.

Yet the question lingers: what is prompting the assimilation of mixed individuals? In other words, what does it tell us about processes occurring in the contemporary United States and their potential ramifications? The last chapter's review of mass assimilation history highlighted a set of dynamics—such as massive structural, or non-zero-sum, mobility and a moral uplift of white ethnics resulting from understandings of the wartime experience disseminated through mass culture. That review could easily make the postwar period of assimilation seem unique, not to be repeated. To comprehend assimilation in the early twenty-first century, we must determine whether similar forces are at work in the contemporary United States or whether other processes are fostering it.

The Demographic Background to Non-Zero-Sum Mobility

An obviously critical dynamic in the mass assimilation of the mid-twentieth century arose from the rapid, massive expansion of mobility opportunities, in both the postsecondary educational system and the labor market, where the supply of jobs suited to college-educated labor market entrants grew robustly. As I noted, this expansion, which depended on postwar prosperity, was associated with the paramount position of the United States in the world economy just after the war. The postwar decades were also unusual in their low overall level of economic inequality.

My argument is that expansions of opportunity facilitate upward mobility by minorities because of their "non-zero-sum" character; that is, their upward mobility does not require downward mobility by some in the dominant majority. In the postwar period, both white ethnics and many working-class native white Protestants encountered an abundance of opportunity unknown to their parents. Consequently, ethnic mobility could occur without intensifying perceived competition along ethno-racial lines, which would have provoked stronger defensive reactions by the more powerful white Protestant group than occurred.

On the face of things, the non-zero-sum situation in post–World War II America would not seem like a pattern that could be found in the early twenty-first century. The contemporary situation presents a strong contrast in economic terms to the 1945–1970 period: economic growth is generally modest today, and income and wealth inequality is extremely high, higher than has been seen since the 1920s. There is persuasive evidence that the extreme inequality is inhibiting social mobility, especially from the lowest income tiers, where many minority families, black and Hispanic most notably, can be found.[1] Without opportunities to move upwards, many minorities lack the social status to interact on a basis of parity with whites, a prerequisite for the decategorization I described as tantamount to assimilation into the mainstream. In the absence of substantial economic expansion and the presence of overall inequality, where can non-zero-sum mobility be generated?

The answer is in demographic shift and its ramifications. In a process that is being repeated throughout the economically advanced societies of North America and Western Europe, a transition to a more diverse population (also called "a third demographic transition"[2]) is taking place. This transition is being accomplished largely through birth-cohort replacement, since everywhere younger cohorts are far more diverse than older ones. The current period is especially momentous because of the synchronization of this process to another demographic phenomenon: the aging of the baby boomers. The large cohorts born in the decades just after World War II but before the onset of renewed mass immigration are already leaving the ages of economic and civic activity. Generally speaking, the members of these cohorts belong overwhelmingly to the native white majority group. In the United States, the youngest baby boomers were born in 1964, putting them in their midfifties in 2020, when the oldest baby boomers are just reaching their midseventies. These cohorts, it should be noted, enjoyed an unusual degree of opportunity to obtain university degrees and occupy favorable positions in the labor market. As they depart, the transition is accelerating: the workforce is becoming more diverse.[3] This implies in particular that the demographic reservoir that historically has staffed the upper ranks of the workforce, well-educated native-born white men, is shrinking. It cannot supply enough workers of the same quality to replace those leaving the labor market. This is a non-zero-sum situation par excellence.

THE CHANGING COMPOSITION OF THE LABOR MARKET'S UPPER STRATA

The next question is obvious: is there evidence of economic mobility by minorities? There is—a look at the top of the occupational hierarchy, at positions that were once monopolized by whites, reveals growing ethno-racial diversity. With Guillermo Yrizar Barbosa and

TABLE 7.1. Non-Hispanic White Percentage in the Top Quartile of Jobs, by Birth Cohort and Year of Data, 2000–15

		Baby boom cohorts			
Ages:					
2000	56–65	46–55	36–45	26–35	
2010		56–65	46–55	36–45	26–35
2015			51–60	41–50	31–40	26–30
Percentages:					
2000	88.3	86.0	82.2	77.0	
2010		85.3	80.9	72.8	69.4
2015			80.4	71.2	66.7	68.0

Source: Calculations from the 2000 Census PUMS and 2009–11 and 2015 ACS data sets, provided by IPUMS (Ruggles et al. 2019).

Brenden Beck, I have analyzed that hierarchy in terms of occupational tiers, using the large samples of the Census Bureau's American Community Survey.[4] We have ranked occupations in terms of their median earnings and then assembled the top-ranked occupations sufficient to account for one-quarter of the full-time workforce. By examining the ethno-racial composition of this top quartile across birth cohorts and across census samples (that is, over time), we find unmistakable signs of change. The key results, reported in terms of the percentage of whites occupying the top quartile, are shown in table 7.1.

For much of the second half of the twentieth century, whites held a virtual monopoly on these positions. That is shown by the very high white percentage, nearly 90 percent, among the late-middle-age workers (ages fifty-six to sixty-five) of 2000. They represent the workers who would have reached prime working age in the 1960s. The top-quartile workers of the baby boom, ages thirty-six to fifty-five in 2000, were still heavily white, between 82 and 86 percent, but were more diverse than the oldest group. Ethno-racial diversity reached more substantial levels in the birth cohorts that followed, as the percentage of whites dropped below 80 percent in the youngest cohort (ages twenty-six to thirty-five) of 2000 and then below 70 percent in the youngest workers of 2010. That level continued in the youngest group of 2015. Moreover, in each cohort, diversity

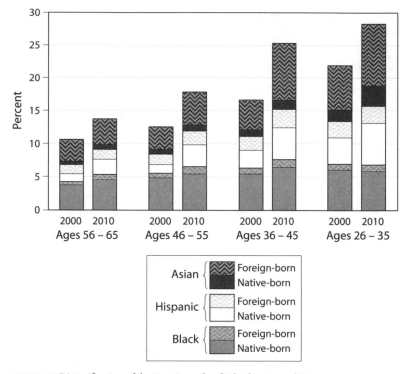

FIGURE 7.1 Diversification of the Top Quartile of Jobs, by Age and Year
Source: Calculations from the 2000 Census PUMS and the 2009–2011 American Community Survey; see Alba and Yrizar Barbosa 2016.

increased over time, no doubt as minorities, who perhaps start lower and/or rise more slowly than whites, were promoted into top-quartile jobs. In 2015, among top-quartile workers under fifty years of age, more than 30 percent were minorities.

The groups that are benefiting from this diversification in the top quartile of the workforce are principally those of the immigrant-origin population; African Americans are gaining only modestly. This conclusion is exemplified by a comparison of the compositions of this tier by age in 2000 and 2010 (see figure 7.1). US-born blacks represented about 6 percent of younger cohorts in both years; this represented an increase from their 4 percent share in older cohorts, but fell well below the increases that appeared among the immigrant-origin groups. The groups whose numbers surged included Asians, both foreign and US-born, and US-born Hispanics.

Increasing rapidly at the top of the occupational hierarchy, Asians constituted just 4 percent of the oldest top-quartile workers in 2000 but were almost 13 percent of the youngest workers in 2010. The role of Asian immigrants is predominant so far in these changes, but the share of the US-born is growing, reflecting a generational shift among Asian adults (who are still mainly immigrants).

Native-born Hispanics can now be found throughout all the tiers of the workforce, though they historically have been concentrated in the bottom half of jobs (but not nearly as much as immigrant Hispanics). However, their numbers are growing rapidly at the top: in the top quartile, they go from 1.2 percent to 6.3 percent when the oldest cohort of 2000 is compared to the youngest of 2010. An equally dramatic increase is found just below, in the second quartile, where the equivalent rise is from 2.1 percent to 9.2 percent. For this research, my collaborators and I did not seek to identify the role of the mixed Hispanic and white group. But it is logical to view it as playing an important part, since chapter 5 showed its members to be disproportionately represented among Hispanics with college degrees, especially from selective colleges. Moreover, while Asians are increasing their numbers at the top primarily by entering professional and scientific occupations, Hispanics tend more toward the managerial domain. Higher percentages of Hispanics in the top quartile occupy managerial positions than is the case for whites of the same age group.[5]

The surge of minorities at the top of the occupational structure is largely a function at this point of the demographic shifts across cohorts rather than increases in the probabilities of minority representation. That is, population-based probabilities—the percentages in the top tier of the labor force based on the number in the underlying population—have mostly held quite steady.[6] These probabilities still favor whites, or at least individuals with a strong claim on whiteness through family background and phenotype. But as top-tier positions become occupied increasingly by individuals from mixed or unmixed nonwhite family backgrounds, we can expect hiring and promotion decisions to favor minorities more than they do now. Then the probabilities are likely to change.[7] Quantitative shift eventually brings qualitative change.

THE RISING DIVERSITY OF HIGHER EDUCATION

The recent educational records of young minorities, especially Asians and Hispanics, also indicate that the representation of minorities in the higher echelons of the workforce is very likely to increase further, as the baby boom completes its departure. The Asian record of educational achievement is so well known as to need little evidence: Asians are overrepresented in all of the country's elite universities by large margins compared to their overall population percentage.[8]

The improvements in Hispanic educational achievements are less well known. In the recent past, Hispanics were characterized by relatively high rates of dropout from high school, but this is less and less the case. The disparity in high school graduation rates has narrowed since 2000 as the rates have climbed for all major ethno-racial groups, but especially for Hispanics.[9] Moreover, among high school graduates, Hispanics now have a rate of continuing into the post-secondary system no different from that of whites as a consequence of a sharp rise in their college-going since the mid-1990s. According to a 2019 report of the American Council on Education (ACE), "the growing Hispanic population . . . is seeking higher education at levels not seen before."[10] To be sure, the US higher educational system is very stratified, and Hispanics still are relatively concentrated in community colleges and less selective four-year schools in its lower strata.

Nevertheless, the number of young Hispanics who are graduating with baccalaureate degrees is soaring. In just the ten-year period between 2004 and 2014, that number more than doubled. No other group saw an increase anywhere near as large; in the same period, the number of BAs earned by non-Hispanic whites rose by just 15 percent. In the later year, Hispanics made up 11 percent of graduates. Because the numbers of all minority groups (except Native Americans) earning BA degrees are increasing more rapidly than for whites, the share of whites among new graduates is falling: it was 64 percent in 2014, down from 73 percent ten years earlier.[11]

Whites are also declining among the ranks of those earning post-baccalaureate degrees. According to the ACE, whites with

TABLE 7.2. Rates (%) of College Graduation and Post-Graduate Education for 25–26 year-old Whites and Hispanics, 2000 and 2017

	2000			2017		
	BA	Post-grad	Cohort size (thousands)	BA	Post-grad	Cohort size (thousands)
			MEN			
Whites	24.3	3.3	2,128.2	28.3	4.9	2,501.7
Unmixed Hispanics	8.5	1.6	274.3	13.2	1.6	670.8
Anglo-Hispanics	19.9	3.2	31.8	24.9	2.9	84.1
			WOMEN			
Whites	29.0	5.3	2,098.2	34.0	9.0	2,394.9
Unmixed Hispanics	12.3	2.5	268.4	18.4	3.5	641.8
Anglo-Hispanics	24.8	3.9	34.3	28.7	6.8	76.5

Note: The "post-graduate" category includes individuals who are continuing their education as well as those who have earned a postgraduate degree.
Source: 2000 Census PUMS and 2017 American Community Survey, provided by IPUMS (Ruggles et al. 2019).

baccalaureate degrees are substantially less likely than their Asian, black, and Hispanic peers to enter graduate school. It follows that the newest earners of graduate degrees are more diverse than before. For instance, in 2016 the white share of those earning a professional degree, such as the JD or MD, fell to 61 percent from 76 percent twenty years earlier; the equivalent decline among doctoral degree earners was from 59 percent in 1996 to 48 percent in 2016.[12]

The data in table 7.2 help to clarify the nature of some of these changes. The table shows the baccalaureate and post-baccalaureate education rates for white, Hispanic, and mixed Anglo-Hispanic young adults in 2000 and 2017. (The Anglo-Hispanic category here is the same "expanded" category, identified by taking account of responses to the ancestry question, discussed in chapter 5.) The purpose of looking at a narrow age cohort (twenty-five- to twenty-six-year-olds) in each group is to measure educational life chances at a specific recent moment in time and then, through the comparison between 2000 and 2017, to capture the changes identified by the ACE. (The comparison is between individuals who would have attended college in the mid-1990s and the early 2010s.) The table shows percentages of postsecondary attainment but also the sizes of the cohorts in order to sort out to what degree the changes reflect improvements in educational life chances and to what degree they involve greater ethno-racial diversity in the younger cohort.

The table indicates a remarkable increase in the chances of college graduation and postgraduate education for all three groups in less than two decades. Even among whites, the rates have risen notably—for the twenty-five- to twenty-six-year-olds of 2017, one-third of the men and more than 40 percent of the women held at least the baccalaureate—and show no sign of decline in entrance to postgraduate education. The educational rise is the strongest for the unmixed Hispanic category: the men in this category improved their rate of baccalaureate attainment by 50 percent (from approximately 10 to 15 percent). Nevertheless, the continuing inequality among the categories is also striking. In 2017, the highest graduation rates are found among whites, the lowest among the unmixed Hispanics. The Anglo-Hispanics are in between but are clearly closer to whites.[13]

The swing over time in the ethno-racial composition of baccalaureate and post-baccalaureate degree holders turns out to be a function of changes in birth cohorts more than of changes in rates of educational attainment, despite the obvious importance of the latter. Among all the twenty-five- to twenty-six-year-olds of 2000 (born in 1974–1975), whites outnumbered individuals with any Hispanic heritage by almost seven-to-one. However, among the twenty-five- to twenty-six-year-olds of 2017 (born in 1991–1992), the white edge had slipped to three-to-one. Combined with the improvements in graduation rates, the demographic shift brought about a marked change in the composition of the pool of college graduates in less than two decades. Among the baccalaureate earners in the earlier cohort, whites overwhelmingly outnumbered Hispanics (including mixed ones) by a margin of fifteen-to-one; in the later cohort, the margin had fallen to six-to-one. Today whites are still preponderant, but the Hispanic portion of the highly educated is no longer negligible.

The ethno-racial diversity of students has also climbed steeply in the elite sectors of the higher educational system, including the Ivy

League and other elite private colleges and universities, as well as the more selective campuses of public higher education. Asians and Hispanics have been central to this increasing diversity, but the role of Hispanic students is again the more remarkable. Research by the *New York Times* shows that the Latine percentage of students entering elite colleges and universities has grown very substantially since 1980, to about 13 percent of first-year students.[14] This number still lags behind their share of the college-age population. However, their proportional representation is increasing: their share of the first-year class at elite schools is now about two-thirds of their share of the age group (properly discounted to remove recent immigrants). The story is not as positive for black students, whose representation at elite schools has not changed since 1980; it remains stuck at about 6 percent of the entering group, even though the fraction of blacks in the age group has been rising and is now about 15 percent. Moreover, the black students at many private elite schools come disproportionately from immigrant families rather than African American ones.[15]

As noted in chapter 5, the CIRP Freshman Survey data, collected by UCLA's Higher Education Research Institute, show that mixed white-Hispanic individuals were important to the growth of the Hispanic student body at more selective colleges and universities in the early years of the century. It is possible that the relative advantage of mixed white-Hispanic students has eroded over time as the overall numbers of Hispanic students entering higher education have surged. There is no way for us to tell given the existing data.

In sum, students in higher education are rapidly becoming more diverse, but this does not mean that the educational system has reached a state of equity with respect to the nation's major ethnoracial groups—not at all. Much of the increasing representation of Asians and Hispanics and of the declining representation of whites (as conventionally defined) is driven by demographic change in the college-age group. However, there has been some improvement in the chances of Hispanic students to earn a baccalaureate and enter the most selective colleges and universities. The role of mixed Anglo-Hispanic youth is salient in both respects.

The disturbing note is the stagnation in the overall situation of black students. The ACE report observes that black students are disadvantaged because they have relatively high rates of dropout from baccalaureate programs and relatively high levels of student indebtedness.[16] They also exhibit the most skewed gender distribution among college students: fewer than 40 percent of black students are men. Problems like these offset the rise in black participation in higher education that has taken place since the mid-1990s. Even the most positive news for black students has to be qualified: the black share of doctoral degrees awarded each year has doubled in two decades, to 7.6 percent, but half of all black doctoral students are at for-profit institutions, a far higher percentage than for any other group. This gain, in other words, is likely to be accompanied by increasing indebtedness and a more uncertain labor market payoff for an advanced credential. At a time of rapidly growing diversity among the nation's college students, the stagnating fortunes of black students could fairly be called an unacknowledged crisis.

The growing numbers of what amounts to immigrant-origin minorities in the pool of highly educated Americans carry major implications for the upper tiers of the workforce. The graduating classes of the near future, including those of elite colleges and universities, whose alumni frequently ascend to powerful and remunerative positions in the economy, will have relatively fewer whites and many more Asians and Latines. The share of jobs in the top tiers held by these children and grandchildren of post-1965 immigrants will continue its increase. Again, this will not demonstrate in and of itself that the system has become much more equitable; indeed, recent research suggests that highly educated Asians still face some degree of ethno-racial penalty in the labor market, and the same surely holds for Hispanics.[17] Nevertheless, as the share of these immigrant-origin minorities in positions of authority grows, the system will likely tilt toward greater fairness because they will be making more of the hiring and promotion decisions and can act as a check on biased decisions by their white colleagues. Whether greater equity will include African Americans, given their continuing stark underrepresentation among graduates, is an obvious question.

Increasing Social Proximity to Whites for Some

An important mechanism in the mass assimilation of the mid-twentieth century was the proliferation of informal social interactions by many second- and third-generation ethnics that crossed ethno-religious lines and, perhaps especially, connected them to members of the "native" white group, Protestants with ancestry from northern and western Europe. These interactions were spurred enormously by the suburbanization of whites starting in the 1950s, which brought whites of different backgrounds together in many new communities and drained urban ethnic communities of socially mobile young adults, who were seeking residential surroundings for their families that corresponded to their own rising socioeconomic status. Since the suburban communities were racially exclusive and concentrated many whites who were in the same family stages, suburbanization facilitated social interactions between whites that often gave little attention to their ethnic and religious origins, exemplified in the familiarity between families that arises from friendships between their children.

This mechanism is not being replicated in the same way in the early twenty-first century. Moreover, the United States today is still a highly segregated society when it comes to where people live and with whom their children go to school, as an extensive research record demonstrates.[18] Nevertheless, on a smaller scale, some minorities are being integrated into mainstream communities with many white residents and also some minority ones—even though the attention paid in both research and media reports to segregation and the processes that sustain it has obscured this quieter integration process.

Minority families have powerful incentives to attempt to enter neighborhoods with many white residents, if they have the financial ability and are not blocked from entry by discrimination or white hostility. (Of course, this claim also assumes that white neighbors will be sufficiently accepting of their presence that the newcomers will not subsequently be driven away by extreme discomfort.) Various forms of place-linked advantage, such as good schools and low levels of poverty and crime, are concentrated in white-dominated neighborhoods. The sociologist Patrick Sharkey, in an analysis that examined the characteristics of census tracts and those of their neighbors, found that in 2000 two-thirds (68 percent) of white-majority tracts were advantaged and surrounded by other advantaged tracts.[19] (Relative tract advantage was defined in terms of such variables as the percentages of residents who were receiving welfare or were unemployed, for which the advantaged tracts had below-average values.) Not only were the immediate surroundings of the residents of advantaged neighborhoods (census tracts) relatively benign, but they did not live close to sources of social problems. In sharp contrast, very few black-majority or Hispanic-majority tracts were advantaged in this spatial sense—just 4 and 5 percent, respectively. Instead, the tracts of minority concentration exhibited spatially extensive disadvantage: very high percentages of tract residents were disadvantaged, and they were surrounded by other tracts with high levels of disadvantage. This was true of 87 percent of black-majority tracts and 83 percent of Hispanic-majority ones.

The organization of residential space in the United States in terms of a correspondence between advantages and amenities, on the one hand, and ethno-racial concentrations, on the other, presents a clear set of incentives for socially mobile minority families attempting to gain the best environment for their children: living in neighborhoods with many whites is the best bet. To be sure, there are plenty of minority families who believe that their children are best off when surrounded by other children like themselves. And it is also the case that some whites will move away from their neighborhood as its residents become more diverse.[20] But in a momentous change from the situation prevailing a half-century ago, metropolitan regions that have welcomed significant numbers of immigrants in recent decades have few neighborhoods with many white residents that have remained racially exclusive. Whites who insist on living in all-white surroundings can find such places in small towns and rural areas, especially in the Midwest; the hitch is that economic opportunities may be scarce and many of the younger residents may be leaving.[21]

If we are to make sense of the patterns of segregation *and* integration, we need to distinguish, as we have been forced so often to do, between the situation of African Americans and the situation of Asians and Hispanics, the ethno-racial groups growing rapidly through immigration. (The black American group is also growing through immigration, but it remains the case that most of its members are descendants of forebears who were enslaved at some point in the United States.[22]) Both the levels and dynamics of integration differ between these groups. A point often made about all three of these populations is that their levels of segregation appear stable across decades, implying that their residential integration with whites is stagnant. This point is misleading because of the large scale of the immigration feeding into the Asian and Hispanic groups.

According to the standard indicator of segregation, the so-called index of dissimilarity, there has indeed been little change in the *overall* segregation of Asians and Hispanics from whites. For Latines, the national average of the index of dissimilarity (in relation to whites) has hovered around the value .50 since 1980.* This Latine-white value is below the level of segregation from whites observed for black Americans, which is close to .60, but the value is still quite high, indicating that half of the Latine group would have to move in order to match the residential locations of whites. For Asians, the value of the index is more moderate, around .40 since 1980.[23]

For groups that have grown during the decades since 1980 owing to large-scale immigration, the stability of the dissimilarity measure is deceptive. New immigrants typically head on arrival to ethnic enclaves, where they often have friends and relatives and where they can find the needed social support in a new and unfamiliar situation. In other words, immigration by itself involves a residential dynamic that should lift the value of the segregation measure. However, for

---

*A value of the index of dissimilarity can be given a specific interpretation: The index measures the proportion of one group (a minority, say) that would have to shift residentially to match the spatial distribution of another (whites, say). The index value is typically calculated for each metropolitan region, and the national value is usually a weighted average, reflecting the relative sizes of the minority population in different regions.

Asians and Hispanics, that value has been stable for decades. This can only be true if there has been a counterbalancing outflow from ethnic enclaves.

These inflow-outflow dynamics are especially apparent for Latines, the more critical of the two major immigration-linked populations because of its large size and the typically humble position of the immigrant generation. Immigrant enclaves are established in most areas of the country where immigrants from Latin America have settled. However, these enclaves offer very limited possibilities for Latine families to improve their residential environment as their economic circumstances improve.[24] The native-born generations show a pronounced tendency to move away from these enclaves and into neighborhoods with more whites. Part of this story is increased movement to suburbs, where segregation levels are more moderate. In addition, social mobility leads to integration, since income and other socioeconomic variables, as well as measures of acculturation such as English language use, are related to residential integration. In other words, the higher the values of these variables for Latines, the higher tends to be the percentage of the white majority in the neighborhoods where they live. And it is not just a matter of residential exposure to whites but also of other improvements in residential context, such as having more affluent neighbors.[25] The families of children with mixed Hispanic-white heritage are an important component of residential integration, according to the data presented in chapter 5. Those data showed that the distribution of Hispanic-white infants across major types of residential space is more like that of infants in exclusively white families than that of infants in Hispanic-only families.

The integration-segregation story for Asians is quite different because they are simply not as segregated from whites to begin with. Although there are Asian enclaves—often in suburban settings ("ethnoburbs"), as exemplified by the well-known Los Angeles suburb Monterey Park—most Asians do not live in such enclaves but rather in neighborhoods that include a mix of groups, including most often whites and other Asians.[26] This is revealed by another index of segregation, the so-called isolation index, whose value indicates the percentage of Asians in the neighborhood where the average Asian lives in a specific metropolitan region. In 2010, only in the Honolulu area did Asians tend to live in majority-Asian neighborhoods, and only in two other metropolitan regions (San Jose and San Francisco) was the average percentage of Asian neighbors above 40 percent. By contrast, in that same year, there were nineteen metropolitan areas where Hispanics on average resided in majority-Hispanic neighborhoods, and in another ten the average Hispanic was located in a neighborhood where at least 40 percent of residents were also Hispanic. In 2010, the largest group in the neighborhood of the average Asian in the nation was not Asian but white.[27] The rising percentage of Asians in the nation's population may modify these patterns somewhat, because the isolation index value tracks the overall size of a group. Although we will have to await the 2020 Census results to see how this turns out, the tendency of many Asian families, especially affluent ones, to reside in areas with many whites along with a significant presence of Asian immigrant families indicates that the overall segregation of Asians from whites is highly likely to remain modest.

Moreover, for Asians as for Hispanics, intermarriage and hence children of mixed background are associated with living in more heavily white neighborhoods, as demonstrated once again by the data presented in chapter 5. These show that families raising Asian-white infants are concentrated to an unusual degree among the homeowners in outer-city and suburban spaces, where whites tend to be preponderant. Since these data are quite recent, they suggest a pattern of integration that will not be altered by the 2020 Census.

African Americans also are becoming more integrated with whites, but the mechanisms of integration are different because the residential dynamics associated with immigration such as generational shift are not as relevant for blacks as a group. African Americans remain the most segregated minority group. (Whites are the most segregated of all groups.) However, the average level of black segregation, as indicated by the index of dissimilarity, has been slowly declining for half a century. In 1970, the value of the black-white dissimilarity index was .79—almost 80 percent of either group would have had to move to match the residential distribution of the other. By 2010, that value had declined to .59, descending just below the .60 threshold, which is widely regarded as the marker of very high segregation. Nevertheless, the rate of decline has been glacially slow; if it continues, segregation will not reach the level regarded as "moderate" until late in the second half of the century. Moreover, in some of the most segregated metropolitan regions— counterintuitively, these are politically liberal areas in the Northeast and Midwest, such as Chicago and New York—the level of segregation has not decreased much over several decades and remains close to .80, its national average in 1970.[28]

The decline of black-white segregation is at least partly due to the movement of many middle-class blacks out of black-majority neighborhoods and away from areas of concentrated disadvantage. This is a new development in the awful history of racial segregation, for outside the South blacks until recently were largely confined to black-majority areas by white discrimination and hostility. The sociologist who identified this new pattern, Patrick Sharkey, has found that, since 1970, the percentage of middle- and upper-income black households living outside of black-majority neighborhoods has almost doubled, going from 33 percent to nearly 60 percent.[29] It appears from the data in chapter 5 that mixed-race families are playing some role in this development, since the distribution across different types of residential space of the families with black-white infants lies in-between those of the families of black-only infants and of the families of white-only infants. But black-white families are not as proximate to the distribution of the white-only families as other mixed minority-white families are.

An important issue, still unresolved, is whether the increasing residential integration of middle-class blacks with whites is enabled in part by the growing presence in former white-dominated neighborhoods of some nonwhite immigrants and their descendants. This idea is often described as the "buffering" hypothesis. In effect, the argument is that neighborhoods that are increasingly diverse—or "global," as some authors describe them—create opportunities for African Americans to participate in their diversity because the growing presence of other nonwhites (Asians and Latines) shields blacks from the white hostility that would greet them if they were the sole integrating minority. Perhaps another way of putting this is also fair: whites with a low tolerance for minorities tend to leave diversifying neighborhoods, and the whites who remain are more open to having nonwhites as neighbors. There is definitely evidence to support the buffering hypothesis, but as the notion of a variable tolerance for diversity implies, the most diverse areas in the United States are also losing some of their white population.[30]

Whites' residential integration with minorities should not be overlooked. It plays a key role in the story. Those who write about residential segregation often complain that the frequently extreme segregation of the ethno-racial majority is not viewed as problematic, only the segregation of minority groups is. Yet, though whites in the United States do succeed sometimes in segregating themselves, as in gated communities, immigration has had a large impact in diversifying the communities where most of them live. The average white in a metropolitan region resides in a neighborhood that is 75 percent white.[31] In other words, on average, one in four neighbors of whites belongs to a minority group. This is obviously the other side of rising minority integration with whites: if minorities, especially those of immigrant background, are living increasingly in communities with many whites, it follows that many whites are living with them. In 2010, 11 percent of the neighbors of the average metropolitan white were Hispanic, 8 percent were black, and 5 percent were Asian.

An average can conceal a lot of variation, and this is true when it comes to whites' residential situations, which correspond to a large degree with the overall ethno-racial diversity of the region in which they are located. There are still some regions that are not very diverse. For example, the population of the Pittsburgh metropolitan region was 89 percent white in 2010. The average white resident of the region lived in a neighborhood that was 90 percent white. Nevertheless, this degree of homogeneity on a regional scale is unusual. In many neighborhoods throughout America, the increasing ethno-racial diversity of the society, largely a result of the post-1965 immigration, is unavoidable, if only because of the diversity visible in encounters on the street or in public places.

Elevating Moral Worthiness

The third leg of the assimilation stool for white ethnics in the mid-twentieth century was a cultural transmutation—the upgrading of their moral worth through the representation of the World War II experience in journalism, literature, and film. This was a powerful shift in the iconography for such groups as Italians and Jews, who, for different reasons, had been denigrated by ordinary white Americans for their perceived moral unworthiness in the prewar period (Italians as criminal, Jews as mercenary or, paradoxically, too left-wing). The advent of television after the war made stars of individuals who crafted personas in part based on their ethnic origins, such as Milton Berle and Perry Como.

Once again, it is hard to see a precise replication of this experience in the present, but that is not to deny the important and visible mutations in cultural realms. As in the earlier period, literature and, probably more important, television, film, and music are shifting in ways that highlight persons of minority origins and emphasize themes connected with nonwhite groups and their experiences.

Growing diversity has been evident in literature for some time, with writers like Toni Morrison, Oscar Hijuelos, and Amy Tan rising to prominence in the 1980s and 1990s. The early twenty-first century has introduced an abundance of original voices from nonwhite groups, such as Junot Díaz, Jhumpa Lahiri, and Colson Whitehead. Unsurprisingly, movies have been slower to swing into line, since the investment that films typically require increases their dependence for commercial success on broad audience appeal. Nevertheless, the last few years have brought to prominence films that have been made by minority directors with minority casts about minority themes, such as *Moonlight* (Academy Award for Best Picture in 2016), *Black Panther* (2018), and *Crazy Rich Asians* (2018). *Coco* (2017), an animated film from Disney and Pixar about the

Mexican Day of the Dead, had a white codirector but otherwise exemplifies the new trend. There is every reason to think that the minority presence on the big screen will be sustained, for these films were commercial successes: *Black Panther* is among the ten highest-grossing films on a worldwide basis.[32] According to the *Hollywood Diversity* report on films from 2015–2016, "films with casts that were from 21 percent to 30 percent minority enjoyed the highest median box office receipts and the highest median return on investment."[33]

In addition, the #OscarsSoWhite movement has had an impact in broadening the candidate field for these highly recognized awards to include more members of the film industry from nonwhite backgrounds. In 2019, minority actors for the first time won the majority of acting awards. The Academy of Motion Picture Arts and Sciences, whose members determine the Oscar winners, has committed to diversifying a membership that still reflects the historical white dominance of the industry. Diversity is also increasing on the film lot, though slowly and with a substantial distance to go to reach parity. The greatest progress in recent years has come in cast diversity: between 2011 and 2016, the percentage of films with casts that were 90 percent or more white fell from about half to a little more than one-third. Still, in 2016, only African Americans among minorities on screen approached their representation in the population; Latines, with just 2.7 percent of film roles, were strikingly underrepresented.[34]

Television and popular music are also participating in the increasing ethno-racial variegation of American culture in ways that have no precise parallel to the mid-twentieth-century changes. Television, with its profusion of cable channels and numerous shows, has become a very different medium from what it was in the 1950s, when the viewing audience had just a few channels to choose from. Its current format would appear to offer more latitude for diversity, and the data bear this out. For instance, the percentage of leads on broadcast and cable shows that went to minority actors in 2016—19 and 20 percent, respectively—exceeded the equivalent figure in film, which was just 14 percent. To be sure, the numerous viewing options in any one time slot present a potential downside: these minority leads could be playing to audiences made up of largely minority viewers. However, the data do not support this idea. In fact, white audiences seem to prefer shows with a strong minority presence: white households in 2016 gave their highest ratings to shows whose casts included at least 40 percent minority actors.[35]

American popular music has long reflected the influence of minority genres and artists, especially African American ones, but until the later part of the twentieth century, this influence was all too frequently channeled through white artists, such as Elvis Presley, who then reaped the lion's share of the rewards. This changed with the arrival of Motown on the popular music scene. Hip-hop's breakthrough into the mainstream music scene in the 1990s solidified the prominence of African American artists. Latine artists such as Jennifer Lopez, Bruno Mars, and Ricky Martin also became mega-stars. The importance of minority artists to the music industry is confirmed by a recent USC Annenberg study of seven hundred songs on the *Billboard* charts between 2012 and 2018.[36] Not only were 44 percent of all the singers from minority backgrounds, but the analysis revealed that, even in this brief period, the percentage of minorities among the hit-makers climbed sharply, reaching 57 percent in 2018. However, the study did not provide a breakdown by ethno-racial group of the minority artists.

The stage, once in the vanguard due to productions in the 1950s like *West Side Story* and *A Raisin in the Sun*, has lately appeared to lag behind other cultural media in giving prominence to minority performers and themes. But this may be changing with the sensational success on Broadway of *Hamilton*, created by Lin-Manuel Miranda, a New Yorker of mainly Mexican and Puerto Rican descent. This musical about a Founding Father subverts audience expectations with minority actors performing as such iconic American figures as George Washington, Thomas Jefferson, James Madison, and of course Hamilton himself. The play's musical numbers, which feature hip-hop as well as R&B, continue the subversion of audience associations with the Founding Fathers of the eighteenth century. The plan for a movie featuring the show's original cast to appear in 2021 promises to bring the work to a mass audience.

These increases in the visibility of minorities and the themes associated with them correspond directly to changes in mainstream cultural venues. When it comes to US cultural production, Broadway, Hollywood, and the Oscars epitomize the mainstream. The changes imply that it is harder and harder for whites to avoid exposure to diversity, whether on movie and television screens or in music. Whether the exposure to diversity in the early twenty-first century has the same humanizing impact that exposure to European-American diversity had after World War II remains to be seen.

The Expansion of the Mainstream

Taken as a whole, the evidence of minority socioeconomic mobility and entry into mixed families with white partners, combined with the patterns of integration so apparent for many of the children from mixed families, suggests strongly that we are witnessing processes of mainstream inclusion that have parallels in the American past. The main motor for growing integration in the early twenty-first century is different—demographic shift rather than economic expansion— but the integration seems similar in key respects. The top tiers of the workforce are becoming more diverse as more minorities, especially Asians and Hispanics, are placed in positions of greater prestige and remuneration as well as greater authority. The shifts in the pool of highly educated young Americans, including those with degrees from elite colleges and universities, appear to guarantee that the transition away from exclusive white domination of the highest tiers of the workforce will continue. Of course, this leaves a question: will minorities begin to gain substantially greater representation at the very top, in positions such as the CEOs of large corporations, and thereby achieve a significant presence in what C. Wright Mills famously labeled "the power elite"?[37]

These developments suggest some acceleration of mainstream inclusion. Minority students, Asians and now Hispanics, are surging among college-goers, including at elite campuses, where the numerical presence of whites is weakening. Seeking to improve the residential environments of their families, more and more socially mobile minorities are moving to—and by their presence integrating—what had been largely white neighborhoods. On a more intimate plane, more are joining white family networks through intermarriage, and reciprocally, whites are increasingly included in minority family networks. Many in the next generation, the children of mixed families, are growing up in circumstances that guarantee contact from early ages with white peers.

As this description implies, the mainstream expansion is not restricted to the individuals, mostly young, who have grown up in minority-white families. Minority individuals married to whites and upwardly mobile individuals in largely white work and residential contexts are also entering the mainstream in significant numbers. But it is the children of mixed minority-majority unions who offer the most convincing evidence of mainstream expansion, at least in part because, by virtue of their family origins, they straddle very visible societal boundaries. As a result, they attract the attention of researchers, and hence we have accumulated an incomplete but significant body of data and research about them.

The contemporary mainstream integration is allowing *some* individuals with minority origins, especially the descendants of immigrants, to enter social spaces shared with many whites and find acceptance there. Acceptance, I want to emphasize, does not erase all aspects of ethno-racial distinction. It needs to be thought of in relative rather than absolute terms: minority or part-minority individuals in mainstream settings generally are much more accepted by mainstream whites than they would be otherwise, but their ethno-racial differences are still noticed some of the time and may be remarked upon in ways that are offensive. It is useful to remember that, despite the more than half a century that has elapsed since post–World War II mass assimilation, the US populace still includes anti-Semites, and stereotypes about Italian Americans and organized crime have not disappeared.[38] Invidious ethno-racial distinctions are anchored in cultural tropes that can survive for a long time, even as their relevance to the everyday lives of their targets dissipates.

Yet there is every reason to think that now, as in the past, mainstream entry is connected with what I earlier called "decategorization"—interactions between whites and minorities becoming determined less by their ethno-racial social identities and more by other personal characteristics than they would have been in the absence of this inclusion. But decategorization is not usually completed in the short term; like other assimilation processes, it may unfold intergenerationally, as suggested by the greater integration of individuals growing up in mixed families. It is not essential to this process that minority individuals want to assimilate or think of themselves as doing so. It is sufficient that they want to improve their lives or the lives of their children; because of the ethno-racial stratification of American society, this intention usually requires greater commitments to mainstream institutions and greater exposure to, and interaction with, whites.

One way to bring out the character of the contemporary mainstream expansion is to compare its similarities to and differences with the expansion of the mid-twentieth century. Several features stand out: two are similarities and one a difference.

First, like the mass assimilation of the mid-twentieth century, early twenty-first-century assimilation is engendering new diversity within the mainstream. The assimilation of the white ethnics expanded the mainstream such that it could no longer be comprehended under its previous identity as "white Christian America" (post-Reformation implied). This new diversity was, moreover, not just a matter of religion—the inclusion en masse of Catholics and Jews in the mainstream—but also of ethnic identities, such as Irish and Italian, that had been previously marginalized. The identity of the mainstream shifted to "Judeo-Christian" to encompass the new charter religions, and hyphenated identities, such as Polish-American, gained a new acceptability. The idea that assimilation meant becoming "American" and nothing else lost its legitimacy.[39]

The mainstream today is becoming more visibly nonwhite in many parts of the United States where the population is already very diverse as a result of large immigrant inflows, as evidenced by the diversity of the neighborhoods in which many whites now live. The mainstream popular culture, as represented in movies and music, is undergoing similar changes, as I have noted. The identities of integrating nonwhites are not fading to the degree that is to be expected if assimilation means the eradication of ethno-racial distinctions. Even the more fluid identities of individuals from mixed minority-white backgrounds often stress the minority component, either by itself or in combination with white. Since whites themselves have accepted hyphenated ethnic identities and some continue to use them, the assertion of new identities involving non-European or nonwhite elements is unlikely to be successfully challenged in mainstream settings.

Will the identity of the mainstream evolve in tandem with its growing diversity, as it did in the mid-twentieth century? A possible mutation is implied by analogy with the changes of mid-twentieth-century America. Some observers have argued, however, that contemporary assimilation "whitens" nonwhite entrants to the mainstream.[40] The implication is that the mainstream will remain a white bastion of domination. Surely, mainstream integration for those with nonwhite family origins entails whitening in the sense that they must become like whites to some degree if they are to have amicable or even civil interactions with them. In the long run, if we assume multiple generations of marriage with whites, identification with the white group could be the end result. But the maintenance of the exclusively white identity of the mainstream seems unlikely in the foreseeable future, if only because a new diversity—for example, in mainstream cultural production—seems already to be a hallmark of the early twenty-first century. And unlike the mid-twentieth century, this era has seen immigration continuing on a sizable scale, fortifying immigrant enclaves and guaranteeing a supply of vital cultural and identificational elements for later generations to deploy.[41]

These observations suggest that the mainstream could evolve in the direction of a more multicultural identity. At least, it might do so in those parts of the United States where diversity is abundant and becoming woven into the social fabric through numerous encounters across ethno-racial boundaries. In these areas, epitomized by the regions of long-standing immigrant settlement, such as Los Angeles and New York, the presence of individuals with nonwhite or Hispanic ancestry in positions of leadership usually evinces no surprise from most whites. In other areas of the country, where diversity is minimal or comes in the form of a sharply defined stratification between whites and nonwhites, as in rural areas where recent Hispanic immigrants make up a low-wage workforce, the mainstream remains decidedly white in character.[42] Probably most whites in these areas would reject the addition of nonwhite elements to it. In this respect, as in the political domain, the United States is dividing along geographic lines, in part because the white population has over time sorted itself by migration between those who are comfortable with diversity and those who are not.[43]

A second similarity, and a much more disturbing one, is the advantage that immigrant-origin groups, especially the US-born generations of Asians and Hispanics, appear to have over African Americans in terms of mainstream acceptability. This advantage is reflected in the very different experiences of black-white individuals that lead them to claim exclusively minority identities much more often than is the case for other individuals with mixed minority-white parentage. The post–World War II mass assimilation also involved groups of recent immigrant vintage, and though it began when the bulk of the African American population was concentrated in the South and held in the shackles of Jim Crow, it also largely bypassed the African Americans in Northern cities. Indeed, mid-century assimilation may have been built in part on the ability of the new groups to distinguish themselves from blacks.

This consistent disparity between immigrant groups and African Americans (and Native Americans living on or near reservations) suggests deeply rooted preferences among whites for immigrants over other minorities. In any event, the immigration-assimilation narrative is a familiar one to whites, lodged in many family memories and therefore easily extended to new groups. Aspects of this narrative encourage native whites to value immigrants and their children for their moral virtue as individuals who have chosen to come to the United States to advance themselves and their families and who work hard to overcome initial disadvantages. Their appearance in large numbers in mainstream settings is thus seen as a reflection of their ambition, talent, and just plain grit, as implied by the stereotype of Asians as "model" minorities. By contrast, the immigrant experience in the family background of most whites provides no basis for understanding the very different experiences of African Americans, whose ancestors were brought to the country in chains and who, even after emancipation, have been prevented from experiencing social mobility and assimilation by Jim Crow, institutionalized racism, and ferocious prejudice and discrimination. Only a minority of white Americans—though this is also true of black Americans—disagree with the statement that "Irish, Italians, Jewish and many other minorities overcame their prejudice and worked their way up. Blacks should do the same without special favors."[44] White Americans' thinking about minority disadvantage has been dominated by the immigrant analogy.

The children of immigrants also have social-psychological advantages over the descendants of native minorities. They are the beneficiaries of a "second-generation advantage," in the words of one study of the children of immigrants.[45] One reason is that the children of immigrants, like their parents, tend to see prejudice and discrimination as obstacles that can be overcome through effort and intelligence. Their immigrant parents frequently tell them that they will have to work much harder than native whites to obtain the same status and rewards, but these lessons need not be discouraging because they also teach that high goals are attainable. Studies find that the children of immigrants are unusually optimistic.[46] By contrast, the lessons taught in African American families often have more to do with protecting oneself from the injuries of white racism. Such lessons are likely to produce a guardedness that contrasts with the optimism of the immigrant second generation.

And yet there are hints that this may be changing for African Americans. One hint lies in the new pattern of residential integration for many middle-class African Americans, who for the first time are able to leave neighborhoods that expose them and their children to severe place-linked disadvantages, such as nearby poverty and crime. Another hint lies in the prominence of African Americans in the burgeoning diversity of the mainstream popular culture. Linked to these hints is the idea that ethno-racial diversity in general could provide openings for African Americans to enter the mainstream alongside Asians and Hispanics. Studies of residential integration offer qualified support for this so-called buffering hypothesis.[47]

Moreover, the role of African immigrants has grown rapidly since 2000. A growing part of the African-descent population now has immigrant origins; the figure was about 10 percent in 2017. Many of the African immigrants, such as the Nigerians, who have been the object of the most social-science attention, bring high levels of educational and professional attainment, and their children therefore begin life in unusually favorable circumstances compared to other black Americans.[48] If these groups are able to enter the mainstream to the degree that other nonwhite immigrant groups have done so—something I must underscore remains to be demonstrated—then they will contribute to an expansion of the black presence there and possibly ease the way for more African Americans with non-immigrant backgrounds.

Yet today's assimilation and that of the mid-twentieth century differ in one major respect: the smaller magnitude of assimilation in the present. The non-zero-sum mobility associated with the demographic changes of the early twenty-first century is no match for that generated by the economic expansion of the mid-twentieth. As a result, the contemporary mainstream expansion is more selective, involving smaller portions of minority groups; and it is less inclusive of individuals with African ancestry, as I have repeatedly noted, than it is of those of Asian or Hispanic descent (though it leaves out many with these backgrounds as well). An unanswered question for immigrant-origin groups is whether this selectivity is connected with sources of disadvantage that have yet to be identified and demonstrated. Among Latines, the groups where African descent is often visible in skin color and features—Dominicans and Puerto Ricans—are noticeably disadvantaged, as evidenced by high poverty rates.[49] And there could be other phenotype differences among Hispanics, connected with indigenous versus European ancestry, that lead to racial discrimination; some research suggests disadvantages of this sort, but the findings are not consistent.[50] In addition, having undocumented parents and siblings is surely linked to disadvantages for US-born youth, not least because these families have difficulty rising beyond very low income levels and are hesitant to leave the protection of immigrant enclaves. Disadvantages connected with lack of legal status could affect some in both the Asian and Hispanic populations, but the evidence we have pertains to the latter. The educational achievement of children coming from homes headed by undocumented immigrants is less than that of children from other immigrant homes.[51] Finally, we know that not all Asians are equally advantaged: some of the refugee groups that arrived several decades ago from Southeast Asia, such as the Cambodians and the Hmong, are very disadvantaged educationally. These disadvantages are masked, of course, when these small groups are merged into the broader Asian category, which is dominated by groups with very high second-generation educational attainment, such Chinese and Indians.[52]

The comparison of the contemporary mainstream expansion to that of the past also prompts questions for which we have no answers as yet but that point to possibilities to watch for in the near future. In contrast to the past, today's mainstream is expanding during a period of large-scale immigration, with much native-white scapegoating of immigrants and Hispanics. One question then concerns the impact on mainstream minorities of the apparent exclusion and disadvantage suffered by many individuals with similar nonwhite origins. The sociologist Tomás Jiménez has hypothesized that the scapegoating and precarious status of Mexican immigrants will affect the identities of later-generation and more assimilated Mexican Americans, preventing their identities from collapsing into the thin identities associated with symbolic ethnicity among European Americans.[53] The knowledge that individuals like oneself are in situations of exclusion and disadvantage could intensify one's ethnic identity and desire to assert it. Could this knowledge affect the fluid character of the identities of mixed individuals that we see in the evidence? There is no way to answer such a question at this point.

Another question involves the political consequences of mainstream integration. The previous wave of assimilation is often viewed as having converted many in the second and third generations, who grew up in Democratic families, into Republicans.[54] A more insightful way of understanding this shift is that the role of ethnic origins in determining political orientations and behavior declined as mainstream assimilation proceeded, while the roles of social class, residence, and other factors increased; this is political assimilation, by definition.[55] In this way, the ethnics' political behavior largely converged with that of white Protestants, covering the gamut from conservative Republican to liberal Democrat. This was particularly true for the Catholic ethnics, while Jews remained the exception.

It is reasonable to hypothesize that mainstream entry will also mean over time that the political orientations of many of the assimilating individuals of today will be determined less by their ethnoracial backgrounds and more by their other characteristics, such as residence and income. In other words, according to this hypothetical reasoning, they will vote more like similar whites. The extent to which this happens could vary considerably by the minority origin involved, just as the political assimilation of an earlier era differed by religion.

The resistance of Jews to political assimilation can be interpreted in terms of their collective understanding of their history of persecution. The members of a group whose historical memory is so threaded with themes related to the struggle against oppression are unlikely to put that memory aside when making political choices. This logic indicates that a similar resistance to political assimilation can be anticipated on the part of individuals of African descent who enter the mainstream. It seems ludicrous to envision African Americans voting in significant numbers like whites who are similar in social characteristics apart from race.

For the other groups with a substantial mainstream presence, Asians and Hispanics, the hypothesis of political assimilation has more potential. It is true that Asians can point to a history of racist discrimination and exclusion in the United States, exemplified in immigration and citizenship laws and in Japanese internment during

World War II. However, though Asian Americans lean in a liberal direction on numerous policy issues and supported Barack Obama in 2012 and Hillary Clinton in 2016 to a greater extent than whites did, they are more split when it comes to party affiliation than are African and Latine Americans.[56] This suggests that they may not have the collective adherence to a political perspective that would stiffen resistance to political assimilation. Nevertheless, the question remains open.

For Latines, there is already suggestive evidence of some political assimilation. In 2016, a substantial majority of the Latine electorate, 65 percent, supported Hillary Clinton, but a sizable minority, nearly 30 percent, voted for Donald Trump, despite the anti-immigrant, anti-Mexican nature of his campaign rhetoric. At least, these were the figures to emerge from the exit polling conducted on behalf of a consortium of news media.[57] This level of support for Trump was disputed by another survey group, Latino Decisions; its own polling of Latines, it claimed, showed that nearly 80 percent of Latines voted for Clinton. While the precise split in Latine voting is debatable, what the arguments on both sides appear to accept is an assimilation gradient in the Latine vote: more assimilated Latines have a greater tendency to support Republicans. That is, Latino Decisions made its case based on the claim that the exit polling for the media oversampled Hispanics who were monolingual English speakers or who lived outside of Hispanic residential concentrations. Its argument, in other words, was that the exit polling found more Trump voters because its sample overrepresented more assimilated Hispanics.[58]

Conclusion

Non-zero-sum assimilation, a largely unrecognized feature of American society in the early twenty-first century, occurs when large-scale structures of a society change in ways that create opportunities for members of marginalized or excluded groups to move up without compensating downward mobility by members of established groups. The key mechanism behind non-zero-sum assimilation today is demographic shift, a consequence in part of the resumption of immigration in the 1960s but also of the aging of the native white population. This is evidently a very different mechanism from the robust economic expansion of the post–World War II period, which allowed both previously marginalized ethnics and working-class white Protestants to enjoy new opportunities for higher education and movement into the middle class or higher.

Today's non-zero-sum assimilation processes arise chiefly through shifts across birth cohorts, as older ones leave the ages of economic and civic activity and younger ones enter them. At the upper end of the age distribution, the large, heavily native white cohorts of the baby boom are exiting the ages of labor market participation; at the lower end, each new cohort entering higher education and then the labor market is more diverse than its predecessors, with larger percentages of minorities and individuals from mixed backgrounds. The exit of the baby boomers is unleashing sequences of mobility: as individuals just below them move up, positions into which others can move are freed up. Among highly educated young adults starting their careers, demographic shift gradually fills these pools of talent with individuals who are not from exclusively white families. Inevitably, then, the top tiers of the workforce are becoming visibly more diverse, with an especially notable presence of immigrants and their descendants.

Non-zero-sum assimilation is furthered by the growing social proximity between portions of the white population and socially mobile minorities and mixed individuals. Not all whites are amenable to increasing diversity in their social environments, and not all nonwhites are able to enter milieus with many whites as their equals. Nevertheless, and despite the recognition that averages can conceal a lot of inequality, increasing proximity across the majority-minority divide is evident in the rising diversity of the residential environment of the *average* white. It is even more apparent in the increasing rates of intermarriage between whites and others. Intermarriage ramifies through kin networks; that is, at a stroke, intermarriage creates multiple cross-group kinship ties. Increasingly, Americans of all groups have family networks that include close kin from ethno-racial backgrounds different from their own. There is no reason to think that ethno-racial mixing in families will let up in the near future.

Finally, these assimilation processes are enhanced by the symbolic elevation of minority groups and their experiences as the mainstream culture has expanded to include them. This expansion is highly visible in Hollywood, the symbolic shrine of the mainstream. In recent years, films highlighting minority experiences and featuring minority actors have reached the apex of recognition, as reflected in box office receipts and awards won, including Oscars. Still missing from this symbolic diversification, however, are Latines, whose presence remains small and not commensurate with their status as the largest minority population.

Although history is not repeating itself exactly, there are some resemblances between the assimilation of white ethnics in the mid-twentieth century and the assimilation of nonwhites today. Those similarities justify viewing the non-zero-sum assimilation of the present as expanding the mainstream of American society, that part within which ethno-racial origins have only modest effects on individuals' social lives. At present, and probably in the future, that expansion is making the mainstream in some parts of the United States much more diverse.

But there is also a key difference between the two eras. The earlier period of assimilation was a much more prosperous time. Today, when macro-economic conditions are quite different, assimilation appears to be more restricted and hence more selective. This difference is apparent in overall group inequalities, which remain large, even among the younger cohorts who are benefiting the most from enhanced mobility opportunities. In the earlier period, by contrast, the younger cohorts caught up to other whites over a short time span in education and labor market position.[59] This contrast raises the question of whether constraints on today's mainstream expansion can be loosened. I attempt to answer that question in the next chapter.

8

Social Policies to Broaden Mainstream Assimilation

The argument so far has been that the surge of young people from mixed minority-white backgrounds is undeniable evidence of ongoing assimilation into the mainstream of society by a sizable group with some nonwhite parentage. This assimilation is not limited to the mixed group; it surely includes many of their minority parents, for example, as well as others. But it is difficult to put precise bounds around it statistically, in part because mainstream participation often is partial or incomplete and in part because the mainstream now cuts through the ethno-racial groups that are readily identifiable in data. Of the groups that we can identify in large-scale demographic data, mixed young Americans—in particular those with a white parent and another parent whose minority origins derive especially from the immigration of the last half-century—show the most unambiguous signs of assimilation, such as feeling socially comfortable with whites, frequently marrying whites, and identifying in flexible ways that include references to whiteness.

The expansion of the mainstream suggests that a societal majority may include most whites for the foreseeable future. For those in the mainstream, ethno-racial origins carry much diminished weight in determining life chances, social affiliations, and even identities. This reduced role of origins can be characterized as decategorization, which also entails interactions with others that are not fundamentally colored by ethno-racial categories. But to reiterate, the mainstream is itself internally diverse along such lines as region, religion, social class, and political affiliation. Entry into the mainstream enhances these dimensions as determinants of behavior while diminishing the importance of ethno-racial origins.

From the perspective of social justice, these observations may seem to have little significance. It appears possible that there will still be a powerful majority, whose members will enjoy advantages over other Americans in most social arenas, and that there will continue to be many Americans who are marginalized and who, because they are not white and may be poor, suffer disadvantages that are hard, or even impossible, to overcome. Of course, in all complex societies there are differences of power along multiple dimensions, from the ability to pave the way for one's children toward successful adulthood to the opportunity to see one's values validated by the culture and institutions of the mainstream. We should demand that such differences not be extreme and that everyone have a meaningful chance to obtain valued social goods, such as a decent place to live or a job that provides an adequate income, more than a modicum of social status, and a sense of purpose. We cannot realistically, however, expect to eliminate inequalities of power.

Yet that is where American society today seems to be failing most sharply by its own ideals. The distribution of social power is extremely unequal, a consequence of intensifying economic inequalities of wealth and income and of the increasing penetration of economic power into political arenas. The opportunities to become a part of the mainstream are very unequally distributed and very limited for those at the bottom of the class structure. Poverty is sticky in a way that makes it difficult for those who grow up in it to escape very far. Defective legal status is similar and its effects are intergenerational. Even when the children of undocumented immigrants are US-born, and hence citizens, their chances for mobility are restricted.

Opportunities are also constrained by institutionalized and individual racism. Even when they have a white parent, individuals with an African American heritage suffer various forms of exclusion that tell them they are still minority Americans. The impacts of racism are undoubtedly worse for those who have two black parents or who have very dark skin. Those impacts are also acute for many American Indians, especially those who live on or near reservations. And though our current state of knowledge makes it hard to know how much racism is endured by others, it seems certain that Hispanics who visibly have African ancestry and others with features associated with indigeneity, such as body shape, size, and skin tone, are affected by it.

As I have already observed, the assimilation of the early twenty-first century differs from that of the mid-twentieth century in its smaller magnitude and greater selectivity. Nevertheless, this chapter will ask how we can expand the reach of mainstream assimilation and enhance opportunities to enter the mainstream. The discussion is divided into three parts. The first part examines how the role of economic inequality in restricting assimilation can be reduced. The second part, speaking specifically to the case of African Americans, addresses the need to go beyond color-blind solutions in order to redress racist exclusion. Finally, I take up the handicaps imposed by defective legal status, not only for immigrants who lack a durable legal status to reside and work in the United States but also for their US-born or US-raised children.

Intense Economic Inequality and the Constriction of Non-Zero-Sum Mobility

Upward social mobility by minorities without compensating downward mobility by some in the white majority holds, I have argued throughout, a special significance for large-scale assimilation (as compared to assimilation by exceptional individuals). Non-zero-sum mobility, as I have called it, is less threatening to the majority group and therefore does not exacerbate ethno-racial competition in the way that would happen when visible minority upward mobility combines with downward mobility by whites (more precisely, downward mobility that is unexpected based on family experience and personal qualifications). The enormous mobility of the middle of the twentieth century was made possible by the unusual prosperity and low inequality in the United States in the immediate postwar period, when its economy was a global colossus. The more constrained upward movement in the early twenty-first century is enabled by a demographic transition, which is being accomplished at present and in the near future by a synchronized shift as the heavily white baby boom leaves the labor market and far more diverse cohorts of millennials and those born afterwards enter it. This shift is evident in the quiet expansion of ethno-racial diversity in the upper tiers of the workforce, spelling an end to white monopolization of the best jobs.

Yet the mobility that contributes to assimilation—the movement into mainly middle-class and upper-middle-class jobs where minority and whites work together as peers (under the conditions of the contact hypothesis)—is constrained today by the high levels of economic inequality in the United States. This inequality throws sand in the gears of mobility, retarding especially the upward movement of individuals whose starting point is in the lowest income tiers.

Economists like Raj Chetty, Miles Corak, and the late Alan Krueger have demonstrated that, whether the comparison is across time, to the US past, or across geography to other economically advanced countries in the present, the extent of economic mobility in the United States today is low. And low economic mobility is inextricably linked to high inequality. Krueger coined the phrase "the Great Gatsby Curve" to characterize the positive relationship between economic inequality and the transmission of economic status between generations (the inverse of economic mobility).[1] Corak has produced the empirical relationship at the international level between the two. This is an upwardly sloping shape of data points that can be approximated by a straight regression line.[2] At the top end, the most unequal and the least propitious for mobility, are the United States and the United Kingdom, with Italy hovering nearby. At the bottom end, where low inequality and high mobility are paired, are the Scandinavian countries.

In the United States, the stickiness of economic status—the tendency of the economic position of parents to be reproduced in a similar economic position for their children—is especially pronounced at the top and the bottom of the economic ladder. The children of parents who have very high income or wealth tend to stay close to their parents' position, and even if they fall, they generally do not fall far. For anyone living in the United States today, that observation does not seem very surprising. More disconcerting, however, is that the children of the poor have only a fifty-fifty chance of climbing out of the economic cellar. Corak validates these observations through a comparison to Canada, where, despite superficial similarities to its North American neighbor, inequality is substantially lower and economic mobility higher. According to Corak, because of lower economic mobility in the United States, "more than half of sons raised by top decile fathers fall no further than the 8th decile, and about half of those raised by bottom decile fathers rise no further than the third decile."[3]

The economist Raj Chetty, along with a team of researchers, has examined the changes over time in the likelihood that children will earn more than their parents, which is widely understood as "the American Dream." Their analysis is not just impressive but definitive because, taking advantage of new, "big data" opportunities, they have been able to examine tax records ("deidentified" so that the researchers cannot know who they belong to) linked to census records. They find that, since the middle of the twentieth century, the chance that children's earnings will surpass their parents' has fallen quite a bit. For children born in 1940, that likelihood was 90 percent; for those born in the 1980s, it had declined to 50 percent. Lest it be thought that the favorable estimate of upward earnings mobility for the older group is just a consequence of having been born in families still impacted by the Great Depression, they show that upward earnings mobility falls rather steadily, not sharply, across the birth cohorts from 1940 to 1980.[4]

This analysis of falling economic mobility also connects the decline to rising inequality. Chetty and his colleagues explore counterfactual scenarios with rather simple simulations to answer the question of what would have happened if macro economic conditions were different. One condition they consider is the slowing rise in US gross domestic product (GDP) over the period. If economic growth were higher, would this make much difference for the decline in mobility? The answer they come to is no. But what would make an appreciable difference is a more equitable distribution of economic growth. As they described the two conditions they tested, "The first scenario expands the size of the economic pie, dividing it in the proportions by which it is divided today. The second keeps the size of the pie fixed, but divides it more evenly than in the past."[5] The first scenario would reduce the mobility decline by only 29 percent, and the second by 71 percent. This is convincing evidence that high and rising inequality is constraining intergenerational economic mobility.

The extreme economic inequality of the United States in the early twenty-first century is implicated in multiple visible aspects of its ethno-racial and social class divisions. Since inequality constrains upward mobility from the bottom tiers, it also limits the ability of many descendants of recent immigrants, especially those from Latin America, to take large steps toward the mainstream. The chances of Americans born in recent decades to surpass the economic position of their parents have fallen, and many end up feeling that they have been left behind. Indeed, a sizable proportion have indeed been left behind: if only 50 percent of those born in the 1980s exceed the income of their parents, as Chetty and his team estimate, then a substantial group of Americans will in fact be less well off than their parents were.[6] The whites among these "left behinds," as they have been called, figure importantly in the politically expressed social resentments and anxieties that propelled Trump to victory in 2016 and have roiled national politics ever since.[7]

Extreme inequality has also stiffened the role of privilege near the top. Studies of changes in the income distribution over time have shown that those at the very top—the top 1 percent, even the top 0.1 percent—have benefited disproportionately from the gains from national economic growth in recent decades, while the share of total income going to the mass of the population, the bottom 90 percent, has stagnated.[8] A situation like this implies that parents at the top will do everything possible to ensure that their children remain at the top too, for any slide down the economic ladder, even by a few rungs, could have large consequences for their status as adults. For instance, affluent parents today spend much more on such educational enrichments for their children as private schools, tutoring, and summer camps than did equivalently affluent parents a half-century ago.[9] The goal of these expenditures is to give children an additional boost to secure their entry to the most selective colleges and universities, since these play a critical role in minting economic privilege in a new generation. Stories in the media in 2019 revealed the extreme lengths to which affluent parents are prepared to go, even paying for ringers to take standardized tests for their children or bribing sports coaches at elite schools to include their children as athletic recruits for sports they do not play.[10]

THE HIGHER-EDUCATION ESCALATOR

An important part of the story of economic inequality is the inequality of earnings according to educational credentials—in particular, the earnings differential between college and high school graduates. On an international plane, the size of that differential in a country correlates with its degree of income inequality; in the United States, the differential has grown since the 1980s in tandem with overall inequality.[11]

A college degree holds special importance for economic mobility, particularly to those from disadvantaged families seeking to rise substantially on the income ladder. Chetty and another team of collaborators have shown that the intergenerational persistence of economic status (the correlation between parents' and children's incomes) is much lower among college graduates than in the general population. This can only happen if children from lower-income families experience a sizable income gain from a college credential, so that the advantage of those from higher-income families is substantially reduced (but not necessarily eliminated).[12]

Despite the general equalizing effect of college, the specific college attended makes quite a difference, and the inequalities among college credentials are implicated in inequality overall and in the advantages of those from privileged backgrounds in particular. Very elite colleges, such as the Ivies and Stanford, offer streamlined access to the very top of the income distribution, the top 1 percent. This access is also available to students from lower-income families who attend these colleges; nonetheless, the schools are not much of a mobility motor for them because few students with these origins are admitted. The researchers note that at these colleges "more students come from the top 1% of the income distribution (14.5%) than from the bottom half of the income distribution (13.5 percent)."[13]

Far more important for the mobility of students from lower economic rungs are public universities, especially some mid-tier universities such as the City University of New York (CUNY). Chetty and his team construct mobility scores for colleges and universities by combining "access"—defined as "the fraction of students who come from families in the bottom quintile" of the income distribution—with the "success rate, the fraction of such students who reach the top quintile."[14] This scoring system may place too much emphasis on the chances of students coming from poor families, and it therefore highlights schools that give unusual access to such students, such as CUNY and some California State and Texas campuses.[15] But the larger point is that for students from less affluent families, the public universities play a more potent role as mobility escalators than do the privates, especially the elite privates. Looking at how access to these high-mobility schools has changed since 2000, Chetty and his team arrive at the disconcerting finding that students from low-income families have a decreasing likelihood of attending schools with the best mobility scores.[16] This decline compounds the difficulties encountered by youth from low-income families as they try to advance socioeconomically in the early twenty-first century.

ADDRESSING ECONOMIC INEQUALITY

To state the obvious: any strategy for addressing inequality must reduce the concentration of economic resources at the top. That concentration grows more extreme toward the economic pinnacle, the top 1 percent and the top 0.1 percent. The share of wealth possessed by the latter, a tiny sliver of the population, increased by one estimate from 7 percent in 1978 to 22 percent in 2012, while the share of wealth held by the bottom 90 percent declined.[17] The power of those at the pinnacle of the wealth distribution is revealed by their disproportionate income harvest from the recent economic growth: one estimate has it that the pretax income share of the top 1 percent of earners rose from 12 percent in the 1980s to 20 percent in 2014, while that of the bottom half of the income distribution stagnated.[18] According to this analysis, the tax and income redistribution policies of the government have so far not had much effect on this intensifying income inequality, which is increasingly driven by income derived from capital. The concentration of income gains from national economic growth is consistent with the much-observed flatness in the wages of the average worker, which, corrected for inflation, have not budged from their level in the early 1970s, nearly half a century ago.[19]

Increasing the taxes on high incomes and high wealth is an essential part of the strategy for reducing inequality. Many Americans are unaware that the US government imposed very high marginal tax rates on the largest incomes for much of the period after it introduced the federal income tax in 1913. The rate on top incomes climbed to 77 percent during World War I before declining. It then rose to 63 percent and 79 percent during the Depression. In the final years of World War II, it reached its zenith, 94 percent, but it did not fall appreciably once the war ended; it remained mostly above 90 percent until the 1960s and fell below 70 percent only with the presidency of Ronald Reagan.[20] There is a strong precedent, in other words, for marginal rates on high incomes that are much greater than those of today.

A new possibility in the political discussion is a tax on wealth in all its forms. Of course, one form of a wealth tax, the property tax on real estate, is a stalwart in the income generated by local governments, so a wealth tax is not unknown. The economists Emmanuel Saez and Gabriel Zucman have discussed how a broader federal wealth tax could be implemented in the United States.[21] To ensure that it burdens only the very wealthy, it should be applied annually to wealth above a high threshold, which would be taxed at a low rate. There are numerous uncertainties about a wealth tax, such as how nonfinancial forms of wealth could be valued and how serious is the risk of expatriation by the wealthy to avoid taxation, but Saez and Zucman suggest feasible ways of handling, if not solving, these questions. And as they point out, other countries, including France and Switzerland, impose taxes on wealth. In principle, then, a wealth tax is a potential tool for decelerating, if not reversing, the rapid buildup of wealth inequality in the United States.

The government income generated by additional taxes on income and wealth could be put to many purposes that would reduce inequality by directly and indirectly boosting the income and wealth of Americans in the bottom half. Measures to improve the country's deteriorating infrastructure, such as roads and bridges, would accomplish this in a collective sense (as well as generate a great deal of blue-collar employment). Obviously, much could be done to address inequality at the individual level, such as reducing student debt or implementing a full-employment program through a job guarantee by the federal government.

One potentially fruitful use of additional money would be to reduce the high level of child poverty. Based on the Supplemental Poverty Measure, which corrects the official poverty measure by taking into account government assistance to low-income families, the Census Bureau has estimated that one of every six children (15.6 percent) in the United States lives in poverty, and that nearly 5 percent are being raised in deep poverty, defined as family income below 50 percent of the poverty line.[22] Child poverty is unusually common in the United States compared to its economic peers. A UNICEF report from 2017 examining child well-being in the forty-one wealthiest countries found that the United States ranks seventh-worst in child poverty and among the five worst on an overall measure of child well-being.[23] A 2019 report from the National Academies of Sciences concluded, based on a comprehensive evaluation of relevant research, that growing up in poverty "compromises children's ability to grow and achieve success in adulthood."[24] This threat to healthy adulthood is especially dire for minority children, whether American Indian, black, or Hispanic.

The National Academies report provides a roadmap for investments to reduce child poverty, with a goal of halving its rate. The report offers alternative packages of investment that would achieve this goal or come close. The packages that cut the deepest into poverty combine programs that reward work—by, for example, expanding the Earned Income Tax Credit, which supplements the incomes of low-wage workers with children—with programs that directly support the incomes of families with children, such as instituting a universal child allowance, a program that has been implemented in other countries. The packages offering the greatest promise in alleviating child poverty are the most expensive, estimated to cost about $100 billion per year, or about 10 percent of the projected military spending in fiscal year 2020.[25] But reducing child poverty would also have substantial long-run macro-economic benefits by decreasing social expenditures and increasing the workforce and economic growth.[26]

The government income obtained from higher taxation of the affluent and wealthy could also be fruitfully invested to improve educational systems, at all levels. There are large inequalities in school-related skills among children when they enter school; reading levels and mathematics knowledge, for instance, correspond strongly to economic inequalities and hence are correlated with race and ethnicity and family composition.[27] Some school districts that have taken innovative approaches to remedying these school-entry inequalities appear to have met with some success, but on the whole the American K-12 system is not geared toward compensating for the systemic inequalities that children bring to school from their homes and communities. For one thing, very large inequalities in school financing are connected with the quality of school resources and the quality and training of the teacher corps. Since schools depend heavily on local financing in many states and there is substantial residential segregation by social class, inequalities in school financing correlate substantially with those in family socioeconomic status.[28] For another, children's exposure to the school environment, on an annual basis, is relatively short in the United States, and students from less well endowed family environments have been shown to lose some of their school-acquired skills during long periods out of school, such as summer vacations.[29]

It should be unsurprising, then, that the United States does not perform well on standardized international comparisons of academic skills, such as literacy and mathematics skills. The PISA program tests students' skills at age fifteen, when they are nearing the end of secondary school and hence are unlikely to substantially improve before completing their educational foundation (K-12 in the United States). In 2015, the PISA tests found that American students performed about average compared to those in other OECD countries, which is not as good as it might seem. American students' average performance did place the United States in a group with several other peer economies, such as France and Sweden, but behind many others, including all of the OECD Asian countries and numerous other western European peers, such as Germany, Ireland, the Netherlands, and the United Kingdom.[30] The US international position in education has slipped badly from the 1960s, when it still led the world in educational attainment.[31]

It's hard to imagine that the inequalities among schools can be reduced significantly without a much larger federal role. The existing inequalities, insofar as they can be traced to funding, are compounded by funding inequalities among and within the states. Currently, the federal government contributes only about 8 to 9 percent of K-12 financing. In a recent estimate, school districts serving large numbers of minority children receive about 13 percent less in state and local monies than those educating mostly white children; viewed in terms of family income, the gap is smaller—about 7 percent—between those districts that serve mostly students from low-income families and those that serve students from the most affluent families.[32] In considering these deficits, one should keep in mind that schools serving poor and heavily minority student bodies need *more* than the average resources in order to compensate for the skills gaps that students bring to school in the first place; instead, they are getting less. There is clearly a role for the federal government in moving the system toward a more equitable level of school financing. The existence of multiple federal school funding programs demonstrates that this could be done without violating the constitutional provision making education the responsibility of the states.[33]

Postsecondary education is another critical site to consider for the investment of tax dollars. The Chetty-led group's analysis makes clear the centrality of public colleges and universities to the social mobility of students from less advantaged family backgrounds. This has been the role of these institutions for a considerable period of American history: a crucial element in the post–World War II quarter-century of mass assimilation for white ethnics was the enormous, fivefold expansion of higher education, which was almost entirely due to public investment in state and municipal colleges and universities.[34] However, today the public sector is suffering from massive disinvestment: disinvestment by states has been the trend since 1980, and it has accelerated in the period since the 2008 recession.[35] It is virtually impossible to imagine much of this role being taken over by the private part of the higher educational system, especially its elite tier. The elite institutions have not grown in tandem with the expansion of the college-going population, and consequently the competition for places in their first-year classes has become fierce, with affluent parents resorting to corrupt and even illegal tactics to secure places for their children. In any event, the elite colleges are like Gulliver at the start of his visit among the Lilliputians—pinned down by numerous restraints, such as their commitment to favoring the children of alumni. They offer access to few children from the bottom half of the income distribution.

Public higher education is an appealing vehicle for investment to spur mobility by minorities and low-income students. Such investment could be directed toward improving the quality of education, especially in the lower-tier colleges and universities that do the most to advance students from disadvantaged backgrounds. It could also go toward tuition at public colleges and universities, making them more affordable for these students and limiting the student debt they accrue, which has been shown to affect decisions to continue in school and also to put a brake on the economic progress of these students once they leave school.

Addressing Racism

Efforts to lower the extremely high level of economic inequality in the United States today would expand avenues of social mobility and widen access to the mainstream for the children and grandchildren of immigrants from Asia, the Caribbean, and Latin America. But the benefits, as we have seen throughout, would not be equally shared across all groups. A complex system of racism, operating at multiple levels from institutions to individuals, holds back African American mobility. As demonstrated in the last chapter, black workers have not gained as much traction in the top tiers of the workforce as a result of the ongoing demographic transition to diversity as have Asians and Hispanics. When I first wrote in *Blurring the Color Line* (2009) about the demographic transition, then just at its beginning given the ages of the baby boomers, I held out the hope that African Americans could benefit as much as Latines and other immigration-origin groups.[36] I was wrong, but I would like to think that my mistake was instructive because it was based on the assumption that African Americans and immigrants and their children would benefit more or less equally from non-zero-sum mobility, a color-blind process of social change.

My mistake was in not realizing that the racism afflicting African Americans is as severe and as deeply embedded as it is. Its severity is manifested in the disproportionate impact of the criminal justice system on African American men, about one-third of whom will be convicted of felonies, and on black families and communities.[37] Whether racism will hold back the newest waves of black immigrants, many of whom have come from Africa with high levels of education, and their children is a question yet to be answered authoritatively.[38]

Racism also damages the lives of others, including many American Indians, especially those who live on or near reservations, Afro-Latines, and probably Latines who have an indigenous appearance.

Quite possibly, it also affects some Asians. The specific mechanisms through which racism operates cannot be assumed to be the same for different groups. The literature and research on those mechanisms has delved most deeply into the African-American case, since they are the largest group to be profoundly affected by racism. The discussion of remedies for anti-black racism has recently been reinvigorated by increasing attention to reparations. For these reasons, I also concentrate my discussion on them.

One starting point for thinking about how to address racism is another analysis by Chetty and his collaborators, in this case of the intergenerational reproduction of racial income inequalities.[39] This analysis links parents and their children born between 1978 and 1983, who were therefore in their thirties in 2014–2015, when their incomes were measured. It identifies a systemic pattern of economic reproduction that disadvantages African Americans and American Indians relative to whites and Asian Americans. This pattern reveals that blacks and whites who are born to parents in the same economic location can be expected to end up as adults in different economic locations, with blacks on average significantly worse off than whites. One aspect of the pattern is that blacks are more likely than whites to experience downward mobility—to be relatively worse off as adults than their parents. Hispanic Americans are in between because even though they "are moving up significantly in the income distribution across generations," they start from relatively low incomes in the parental generation. This finding aligns with the discussion in past chapters, although Chetty and his group are unable to factor mixed family origins into the analysis.

Because of the range of information that the Chetty team has incorporated into their files linking census and income tax return data, they are able to test some commonly offered explanations for black-white inequalities, thereby narrowing the range of meaningful policy options. First, they note that intergenerational racial inequalities are much greater at the household level than at the individual level. This implies that racial differences in marriage are important to the story; since blacks are less likely to marry than whites are, white households benefit from two incomes more often than black households do. Second, they observe the critical importance of gender for differences at the individual level, where black-white inequality becomes mainly a story about the racial disadvantage borne by black men. The similarity of economic mobility between black and white women also rules out the possibility, so long a prominent theme of racist thinking, that racial differences in intelligence explain inequalities.

These findings partly reflect the very negative ramifications of the high levels of penalty and stigma imposed by the criminal justice system on black men. Much more commonly than white men, black men have been convicted of felonies or spent time in prison. As Michelle Alexander demonstrates in her illuminating book *The New Jim Crow* (2010), the racial discrepancies in these respects cannot be understood as a simple result of differences between whites and blacks in actual criminal behavior.[40] Instead, they stem from racial biases lodged throughout the criminal justice system, especially since the inauguration of the "war on drugs" during the Nixon administration in the early 1970s. Once black men are branded by felony conviction or by time spent in prison, they are severely handicapped in the labor market and may even be stripped of many ordinary citizens' rights, such as the right to vote.[41] These missing (through incarceration) and/or handicapped men are poor candidates for marriage, and the large number of incarcerated black men contributes substantially to low marriage rates among African Americans.

The Chetty team finds that differences associated with childhood neighborhood are crucial in explaining the inequalities between white and black men. They reach this conclusion after ruling out some other potential explanations, most notably, growing up in a single-parent family and parental wealth. These factors do affect racial inequalities, but only modestly, according to their results. By contrast, the extensive residential segregation of the races is crucial. More concretely, the analysis identifies a particular kind of neighborhood that promotes greater equality between adult black and white men. A "good" neighborhood is one with a low-poverty environment and other positive aggregate characteristics, such as residents' relatively high educational attainment and many two-parent families. Growing up in such a good neighborhood has positive effects on adult black men's incomes, but it does not close the gap with whites from the same neighborhoods because the latter still enjoy an advantage.

Two other features that are not blind to color are required to close the gap. One is the presence of many black fathers. The analysis finds that this neighborhood characteristic is helpful even for black youth whose own father is missing. The finding suggests that black fathers provide a key modeling of successful adult male roles that matters for boys, even when the fathers are in neighboring families rather than their own.[42] The second feature is low white bias, which is measured for larger geographical units than the neighborhood—the smallest measured is the county. Given the still high degree of neighborhood segregation between whites and blacks, assessments of white bias are probably not best measured in the relations between whites and blacks who live in the same neighborhood. The white bias measured on the larger geographic scale is still meaningful for outcomes because it can be reflected in the relationships between black children and white adults in key institutional contexts such as schools. Indeed, other research finds that areas of low white bias show lower racial disparities in disciplinary actions at school.[43] School discipline, such as suspension or expulsion, can manifest institutionalized racial bias that places black children, especially boys, on a distinct educational trajectory toward poor outcomes, such as secondary school dropout, and exposes them to much greater risk of criminal behavior and incarceration.

THINKING ABOUT POLICY

If we combine the findings of the Chetty team with ideas about reparations, we can make headway, I believe, in thinking about what it will take to really reduce racial inequality in this country. Reparations to African Americans for slavery and for the institutionalized racism that has continued to oppress them since emancipation—Jim Crow, de facto segregation, mass incarceration—have moved toward the center stage of public discussion in recent years.[44] The argument for reparations is potent on a moral plane, but it also rests on strong policy claims. The economist William Darity Jr. has been a forceful academic advocate.

The main point of departure for the proposals advanced by Darity and others is the huge wealth gap between whites and blacks: on average, blacks have 7 cents of wealth for every dollar possessed by whites. The implication of this enormous difference is that a large percentage of African Americans have no, or even negative, wealth.[45] Wealth is much more unequally distributed than income and is highly consequential because it can be deployed to create income streams, through business investment or the enhancement of human capital with additional education.[46] Darity and his colleagues argue that conventional strategies that have been touted for narrowing wealth inequality focus too often on improving the efforts and characteristics of individual African Americans and are not helpful because they leave intact the system that translates these improvements into economic outcomes. For example, one frequently recommended remedy is increasing black educational credentials, especially the achievement of the baccalaureate and more advanced degrees. However, African Americans with college degrees have much less wealth than comparable whites; in fact, blacks with baccalaureates (but not advanced degrees) have less wealth on average than whites without high school diplomas.

When we take into account that wealth is directly transmitted intergenerationally within families to an important extent—through investments made in children by parents and grandparents (who, for example, fund educational expenses) as well as through their gifts and bequests—these findings about the futility of individualistic strategies make sense. Black families have little wealth to pass on, and throughout post-emancipation history they have been repeatedly blocked by white racism from acquiring wealth. Consider, for instance, one of the pivotal racial injustices of mid-twentieth-century America: social policies that gave opportunities to white families to accumulate housing wealth while denying them to black families. Such were the policies of the Federal Housing Authority, created in 1934, during the depth of the Depression. By insuring home mortgages and setting standards for them, the FHA brought homeownership within the reach of many more white families, but its underwriting standards, by including so-called redlining of minority neighborhoods, prevented the vast majority of black families from also obtaining federally insured mortgages. VA home loans, which after World War II assisted many returning service men and women to purchase homes, operated on the same principles.[47] The wealth acquired by many white families in this period, partly in the equity built up through homeownership, has contributed mightily to the racial wealth gap.

But what about the finding of the Chetty team that wealth differences play only a modest role in explaining racial income inequalities? Limitations of their analysis indicate that we should weigh this finding with caution in considering strategies of amelioration. To begin with, there are limits to their measures of wealth: parental homeownership, self-reported home value, and number of vehicles used by the household, all variables that come from the census. Most obviously, these measures omit forms of wealth other than real property, such as bank accounts and stock ownership. Second, these measures fail to account for wealth in other parts of the family network, especially wealth held by grandparents, that can be consequential for the young generation.[48] Even so, the Chetty team's analysis shows that parental wealth, even in this limited form, is relevant to racial inequality in the economic position of children when they grow up, if not strongly so.

In fact, there is one compelling reason to think that the analysis by Chetty's team underestimates the role of parental wealth: blacks confront more serious issues with debt than whites (and Asians) do. Blacks are more likely to be victims of what Louise Seamster and Raphaël Charron-Chénier call "predatory inclusion—a process wherein lenders and financial actors offer needed services to black households but on exploitative terms that limit or eliminate their long-term benefits."[49] Predatory inclusion is evident in the subprime mortgages that many black (and Hispanic) borrowers have been offered to finance home purchases, even when whites in similar economic circumstances have been able to obtain conventional mortgages. Subprime mortgages, because of their unfavorable terms, became albatrosses during the financial crisis and led to numerous foreclosures and great investment losses.[50] Once again in American history, the disparate treatment of African Americans by institutions stymied their attempts to build wealth.

Debt problems also hamper black students at the college and postgraduate levels. According to a 2019 report of the American Council on Education, black college students "graduated with the greatest student loan debt of any group." Black undergraduates are also more likely to drop out before graduation, and financial problems are an important reason why they do.[51] For many white students, family wealth, from both parents and grandparents, provides assistance in paying for their education, assistance that is missing for the great majority of black students.[52] In short, wealth inequalities are implicated in the educational inequalities between the races.

Reparations have become discussable as policy precisely because of the widening recognition of the crucial importance of racial wealth differences, along with increasing acceptance of the view that these differences have emerged from a history of institutional discrimination that extends all the way from emancipation to the present. The case for reparations was introduced to a wide audience by Ta-Nehisi Coates in a 2014 essay in the *Atlantic*. The flesh of policy detail was added to the moral and political skeleton of the reparations argument by the economists William Darity Jr. and Darrick Hamilton, along with other social scientists.[53] Yet public support for reparations, as measured in polls, remains quite low. A 2018 poll found that only one-quarter of Americans are in favor of reparations; a larger fraction of them are strongly opposed.[54] Such thin support indicates that, at least for the present and near future, reparations are likely to remain out of reach in the political sphere. But the discussion of them has been far from futile. It has elicited proposals for elements of an inequality amelioration program that are eminently practical and can be separately pursued.

My reading of the reparations discussion suggests an overall strategy that can operate independently on several planes, as I will sketch here. I use the word "sketch" advisedly: many policy proposals die when they descend into too many details, which are always debatable. Safe to say, a range of specifics would be consistent with the three main strategic elements described in the remainder of this section.

1. Policies that give African Americans more financial resources than they now have: The examination of the impacts of wealth inequalities indicates that most African Americans are held back by meager economic resources, a consequence of systemic institutional forces that since emancipation have discriminated against them and prevented the kind of intergenerational asset accumulation that whites have taken for granted.

Policies to address this need can be implemented in different ways. Darity and Dania Francis point out some of the possible forms.[55] One is payment—in a lump sum or installments—to individuals. (Darity and Francis argue, however, that to avoid moral hazard the individuals who receive reparations payments must be able to demonstrate descent from enslaved ancestors.) Another form is a collective endowment to which individuals make application for grants to enable wealth-building activities, such as the completion of advanced education or entrepreneurial investment.

So-called baby bonds, invented by Hamilton and Darity, also have gotten a lot of attention. Baby bonds are accounts established by the federal government when children are born and funded by it through childhood. This is intended to be a universal program, but the amount of the endowment to each account would depend on the financial circumstances of the child's family. In this way, the program would compensate to some degree for inequalities of wealth and concentrate its benefits on children from minority and poor families.[56] Once the children reach adulthood, the funds would become available for investments, such as obtaining more education or starting businesses.

2. Investments in African-American communities: The Chetty team's analysis underscores the importance of place-based amenities and resources, many of them institutional in nature. Their analysis not only identified a particular kind of neighborhood that promotes parity between whites and blacks who grow up there, but found that controlling for the disparate distributions of blacks and whites across neighborhoods substantially reduces the black-white income disparity.[57] This finding implies that residential segregation—in particular, the inability of many African Americans to reside in better neighborhoods—plays a central role in maintaining racial economic inequality. Though black-white segregation has been easing for decades, the rate of decline has been glacially slow. Relying on this decline to continue is not a solution.

The finding about the advantages for black boys in particular of growing up in neighborhoods of low white bias appears to allude to underlying institutional mechanisms. When gatekeepers such as schoolteachers and administrators are more biased, black youth, especially boys, are more likely to suffer harsh disciplinary measures that exclude them from the normal classroom educational experience and set them on trajectories toward bad outcomes. This mechanism is undoubtedly enhanced by the inferiority of many of the schools that black students attend, which extends to the qualifications and experience of school personnel.[58]

It is no surprise, then, that one imperative form of investment is improving schools to ensure that minority and poor children receive an education appropriate to their needs, since they often come from families and communities that are not able to equip them with the same school-related skills that are usually developed by middle-class white children without much conscious effort. Communal investment could also take the form of improvements in the quality and affordability of housing and in the municipal services, such as sanitation, delivered to minority neighborhoods.

3. Mitigation, if not elimination, of the "mass incarceration" features of the criminal justice system: As long as a highly disproportionate fraction of black men can expect to be convicted of crimes or spend time in prison, it will remain impossible to substantially remedy black-white economic inequalities. The current criminal justice realities feed into white racial bias, condemn a large fraction of black men to lives that are impoverished economically and in other ways, and wreak havoc on black family life and on the next generation of young men.[59]

I am not going to pretend to be an expert on criminal justice reforms, but any attempt to reduce the immense burdens of the system for African Americans must begin with its front end—policing—and not just concern itself with incarceration. Police presence and activity in poor communities of color are intense and produce disproportionate arrests for minor crimes, from selling single cigarettes ("loosies") on the street (which led to the 2014 homicide in police hands of Eric Garner in New York City) to the vague misdemeanor of disorderly conduct. Misdemeanor arrests outnumber felony arrests by four-to-one.[60] Arrests of African Americans are also disproportionate for drug-related crimes of possession and sale, crimes that whites, as shown by research, commit with the same frequency as blacks.[61]

Once arrested, even for misdemeanors, black men are in the grip of a system that will not easily let them loose again and set on a pathway that leads all too often to criminal conviction and possible incarceration. Even if he avoids incarceration, conviction on a misdemeanor charge makes it much more difficult for a black man than for a white man to find or hold employment. In a brilliant analysis of the institutional processing of individuals arrested for misdemeanors in New York City, Issa Kohler-Hausmann shows that this processing follows a "managerial model."[62] Initial conviction rates are low. According to Kohler-Hausmann, the court system, which encompasses also the prosecuting and defense attorneys, is agnostic about guilt. Instead, it marks arrested individuals for further tracking, subjects them to procedural hassles, such as additional court dates, and establishes a series of performance tests for them to meet, such as completion of a treatment program. The point of such a system is social control: the management of the risk of further offending. Given the disorderly lives of many poor black men, a substantial percentage of those arrested find it impossible to make it through the gauntlet set up by the judicial system, and they eventually receive a conviction of some sort. Once convicted, they are publicly marked.

The final element of the reparations program advocated by Ta-Nehisi Coates and others is a moral one that is extremely challenging because it involves hearts and minds and cannot be controlled by policy. It is a call for whites to acknowledge that they have benefited from systemic racism, which has deprived African Americans collectively of the opportunities that most whites take for granted. Without this acknowledgment, white bias could increase if public policy sets the goal of reducing black-white inequalities. (Neither should we ignore the attitudes of other nonwhites, Asians and Latines, who could also react to a national program of reparations for slavery.) Blacks could be seen by many whites as having politically obtained benefits they have not earned. This possibility is consequential because, no matter how one reads the demographic trends, whites will remain by far the most powerful ethno-racial group for decades to come.

In his essay on reparations, Coates talks in terms of a national reconciliation and renewal that could be brought about by reparations.

> And so we must imagine a new country. Reparations—by which I mean the full acceptance of our collective biography and its consequences—is the price we must pay to see ourselves squarely. . . . What I'm talking about is more than recompense for past injustices—more than a handout, a payoff, hush money, or a reluctant bribe. What I'm talking about is a national reckoning that would lead to spiritual renewal.[63]

As a nation we are a long way from this point. For many whites, black oppression stopped with emancipation and the end of the Civil War; these whites have little understanding that soon afterwards African Americans were placed in another institutional vise that held them back, to be followed by another, and so on. Many whites also have little comprehension how much they collectively and individually have benefited from systemic racism, nor that the arrival of their own immigrant ancestors after emancipation does not obviate these benefits.

Fixing Defective Legal Status

The final major societal issue that must be confronted to widen access to the mainstream is the massively defective legal status of many contemporary immigrants, especially those from Latin America.

Jeffrey Passel of the Pew Research Center has regularly produced the most credible data on the size and characteristics of the undocumented population, and according to his estimates, its size in 2016 stood at 10.7 million, down from a high of 12.2 million just before the Great Recession of 2008.[64] As US policies have increased the difficulty and cost of crossing the southern border, the characteristics of the undocumented have changed. For one, the undocumented increasingly are longtime residents: two-thirds have been living in the United States for at least ten years. For another, the families of many unauthorized immigrants have reassembled in the United States, and 5 million US-born children—all of them US citizens—live with unauthorized parents. (Other children of unauthorized parents were brought to the US after birth; they are counted among the unauthorized.) Counting the unauthorized together with their legally resident family members produces an astonishing figure: 6 percent of the US population in 2016 was living in the shadows, their daily lives circumscribed by the extreme legal vulnerability of one or more family members.[65]

To this group can be added another, smaller one: the immigrant families that depend on temporary protected status (TPS), a time-limited, uncertain protection granted to immigrants who, because of conditions in their home countries (such as civil war or natural disaster), are unable to return home safely. As of early 2019, more than 300,000 immigrants, mostly from Latin America, held this status, and many of them had resided in the United States for more than a decade. The Trump administration has been attempting to terminate TPS for immigrants from numerous countries, but court decisions have blocked these terminations for the time being. If terminations are allowed, then any immigrants who cannot claim an alternative legal status will become unauthorized and subject to deportation.[66]

The exclusion of so many members of the society—members in the sense that they are workers, students, and parents raising citizen children—from many basic rights that legal residents and citizens take for granted is an immense problem for a democratic society. And the problems associated with defective or absent legal status are not fully extinguished in the US-born generation, who are citizens by virtue of the Fourteenth Amendment to the Constitution. We know from convincing research that the US-born children of the undocumented are handicapped by their parents' lack of status: for example, they have lower educational levels than children of low-wage immigrants who have legal status.[67] Their families of origin are held back by the lower earnings of the undocumented and by the limitations imposed on where the families can reside, given their need to avoid scrutiny by those who might betray their lack of papers.[68]

Ways of resolving the issue of the undocumented have been openly discussed for more than a decade, and there is no secret to the key element: granting some form of eventually permanent legal status to most of them. There are moral and political objections to doing so, and they should not be dismissed out of hand. But these objections can be met with compelling counterarguments. I accept the fundamental validity of the "moral hazard" objection: giving permanent legal status to the undocumented might encourage others to immigrate and settle without legal status, in the expectation that it will eventually be granted. And there is merit to the objection of unfairness: granting legal status to the undocumented will allow them to push themselves ahead of people in the immigration queue who have been waiting patiently for decades in their home countries for entry.

However, the experience of the long-term undocumented of living in constant fear of exposure and deportation reduces considerably, if it does not cancel, the moral hazard. And indeed, many have been deported, and some have suffered extremely harsh consequences of deportation to a "home" country that is no longer home. These are risks that not everyone will want to run. In the event, migration from the country that has been supplying by far the largest number of the undocumented, Mexico, seems to have run its course, owing in part to changes in Mexican demography, especially a smaller cohort of young adults, the most likely migrants. This, too, reduces the moral hazard.

Any sense of unfairness about bestowing legal status on the undocumented or objection to rewarding illegal behavior needs to be weighed in the same moral scale with the individuals and companies in the United States that have instigated the migration of the undocumented in order to exploit their labor. The punitiveness often shown in the conservative judgment of the undocumented as lawbreakers is not matched by any equivalent judgment of the American citizens who profit from their exploitation, such as the entrepreneur who is occupying the White House as I write these words. The reality, of course, is that the US economy needs low-wage workers; and immigrants, both legal and not, are filling this need.[69] Most undocumented immigration occurs because citizens of nearby Latin American countries know that they can find employment if they succeed in reaching the United States, and the legal portals of immigration are not wide enough to accommodate them or the need for the labor they supply.

When it comes to legalization, there are degrees of moral justification. At the apex are the "Dreamers," the undocumented who were brought to the United States as children and have grown up and attended school here. Granting them permanent legal status has a powerful moral justification. Dreamers are socially and culturally American, and it is immensely cruel to subject them to the risk of deportation to a "home" country they may not remember and whose language they may speak only a childish version of. Not everyone who came to the United States before the age of eighteen, however, deserves to be treated as a Dreamer. Some immigrants came as teenagers on their own to work and never attended school here; their situation is not in principle different from that of adult migrants. The Dreamers deserve the status of permanent legal resident, with its pathway to citizenship. The uncertain DACA (Deferred Action for Childhood Arrivals) status that some of them currently enjoy is not a reasonable basis for planning a life in the United States.

The undocumented parents of US-born children also have a strong case because their lack of legal status negatively affects the well-being of the US citizens they are raising. (Some conservatives would address this problem by restricting the unqualified birthright citizenship guaranteed by the Fourteenth Amendment. Such a change would be, in my view, a moral disaster for the United States: it would return us to something like the situation that prevailed during slavery, when the legal nonpersonhood of enslaved parents was inherited by their children.) The parents of US citizens need to be legalized. So do those undocumented who have been settled in the United States for a decade or more. This is effectively their home, and it would be unduly harsh to force them to return and reestablish their lives in their country of origin. I realize that in both of these cases there will be debate as to whether legalization should involve a pathway to citizenship, and some Americans will regard the granting of citizenship in these cases as an undeserved reward. Yet democratic principles insist that we give political voice to those who are settled here for the long term.

Those undocumented who have been here for a short period of time—I am being deliberately vague because the length of that period is obviously debatable—have a much more limited claim. Unless we as a nation are willing to open our borders and accept anyone who manages to arrive in the United States, we must be prepared to reject some migrants. Perhaps some of the short-term undocumented deserve temporary work visas, depending on their role in the workforce. But others, if caught, will be deported.

The argument for open borders has gained some traction. Its thrust is essentially moral: it seems grossly unjust that a relatively few humans enjoy access to abundant material goods and to better health and long life spans simply because they happened to be born in a wealthy country or because they were accepted there as immigrants while many others were rejected.[70] I agree that such vagaries of birth and fate seem to contravene our sense of basic fairness. But accepting all comers is not the way to make our border policy more just. The political hazards of an open borders policy should be apparent by now. Everywhere in the West, xenophobic and nationalist parties and politicians, taking advantage of native-majority anxieties about the ethno-racial changes wrought by immigration, are gaining a share of political power, if not outright rule. And frequently these forces pose a danger to democratic institutions, which do not seem capable of containing their grasp for increasing power. These ominous political developments are occurring even in some countries with very restrictive immigration policies.

More massive immigration flows would be likely to stimulate more extreme political reaction and potentially threaten the foundations of democracy.

Conclusion

Mainstream assimilation today is considerably smaller in magnitude than it was during the quarter-century following World War II. The salience of the ethnic and religious distinctions among whites faded rapidly during that period, to the point that formerly demeaned ethnic labels, like "Italian," became "ethnic options," in the well-known formulation of the sociologist Mary Waters. The educational attainment of young Italians, a group then near the bottom of the ethnic hierarchy among whites, climbed rapidly to attain parity with other white peers (and today is superior to the overall white average), while their intermarriage rate soared. Although that rate was never very low, about two-thirds of the second- and third-generation cohorts who came to maturity after the war married out.[71]

The Mexican immigrants of the last third of the twentieth century and their children, today's young-adult second generation, stand as a rough equivalent to Italians in the first half of that century. Although a lack of legal status troubles the adjustment of many Mexican immigrant families to American contexts—a situation with no equivalent among the Italians—most of the late-twentieth-century immigrants who were the parents of US-born young adults in the early twenty-first century did probably succeed in coming out of the shadows, helped by the large-scale legalizations in the early 1990s resulting from the 1986 Immigration Reform and Control Act. But the second generation, though far exceeding the immigrant parents in education, has come nowhere near parity with average white American education levels. And the intermarriage rate of this generation is quite modest. Indeed, even the intermarriage rate of the third generation is far below that of the post–World War II Italian Americans.[72]

Today's macro-economic conditions are much less favorable to the social mobility that is especially necessary for groups like pre–World War II Italians and the present-day Mexicans if they are to approach the mainstream. Economic growth in the 1950s and 1960s, as measured by annual GDP change, was not infrequently at 6 percent or higher; in recent years, it has struggled to reach 3 percent. And the very high levels of income and wealth inequality imply that what economic growth there is has not provided much of a boost at the bottom of the class structure. In the earlier period, states invested in education, creating or expanding public universities that, by 1970, were providing higher education to much larger percentages of American youth than ever before. Today states are mostly disinvesting in these same institutions. The United States, once the world's leader in mass education, has fallen behind many other countries.[73]

Yet mainstream assimilation today is far from negligible, as this book has shown. However, it is much more selective than in the past, favoring especially individuals and groups capable of achieving high levels of education and other forms of status advance. Public policy can once again make a big difference, especially by removing or lowering barriers to mainstream entry. These barriers have been raised by extremely high levels of inequality, which prevent many who start in the lower tiers of the income distribution from moving very far upwards; severe and persistent racism directed against African-descent and other dark-skinned Americans; and the handicaps imposed by lack of legal status on many immigrant parents and their children.

The question, of course, is whether the political will exists to make any of the legal and policy changes required to lower these barriers. As I write, the political opposition to positive change has been greatly reinforced by a newly robust white nationalism that was unimaginable just a few decades ago. White nationalism draws strength in turn from the distorted perceptions of the American future associated with the majority-minority narrative. Will replacing this narrative with a more accurate, less polarizing, and more inclusive narrative make a difference? We will find out only if we are willing to try.

9

Toward a New Understanding of American Possibilities

> The voice of civilization speaks an unmistakable language against the isolation of families, nations and races, and pleads for composite nationality as essential to her triumphs.
>
> —FREDERICK DOUGLASS, "COMPOSITE NATION"

There can be no question about the growing diversity of American society. Immigration during the last half-century has made the United States a very different place from the largely black-and-white nation of 1970, when whites were more than four-fifths of the population and blacks were by far the largest minority. And there is no end in sight to immigration (even if a conservative administration succeeds in imposing more restrictive policies that endure beyond it). Yet despite the decline in the white share of the population in the last fifty years, the narrative of the majority-minority society, imminent and inevitable, is profoundly misleading as a way of understanding the ethno-racial changes now taking place in the United States and the future they are likely to produce. It is the great demographic illusion.

The majority-minority conception is anchored in three core premises: (1) the society is split between two ethno-racial blocs, one white (and non-Hispanic) and the other minority (nonwhite or Hispanic); (2) the numerical dominance of the white bloc is declining rapidly, and the minority bloc will overtake it in size within a few decades; and (3) the processes producing this change are demographic in nature and inexorable. The belief that a so-called majority-minority nation lies inevitably in our near future can be encountered everywhere, from the pronouncements of white supremacists to the reporting of mainstream media like the *New York Times* to the predictions of progressive multiculturalists.

The politicized form of this idea—that whites will soon be outnumbered by minorities at the national level, with a concomitant loss of societal power—is open to the objection that it ignores internal diversity and assumes far too much coherence on the part of the minority bloc. The groups in that bloc—of African American, black immigrant, Asian, and Latin American origins—are themselves too diverse in their histories, experiences, and social situations for anyone to assume that they could act politically in a unified way. The recent history of California, a state where whites have in fact become a minority of the population, does not suggest an upheaval in the established ethno-racial order, though it is certainly true that an increasingly diverse set of Californians now occupy positions of prominence.[1]

A common misconception associated with the majority-minority idea is that whites will soon be a minority of voters, or even citizens. *New York Times* columnist Charles Blow, for instance, declared in a 2018 op-ed on "white extinction anxiety" that "white people have been the majority of people considered United States citizens since this country was founded, but that period is rapidly drawing to a close."[2] He cites census data and projections, but in fact that evidence does *not* support his conclusion *about citizens*. The census numbers in principle include all residents of the United States. That includes many foreign-born noncitizens, such as legal permanent residents, even some who reside temporarily in the United States (but not tourists and others whose presence is transient). And it appears that many undocumented residents fill out the census form, as government agencies encourage them to do. The Census Bureau population projections indicating whites as a numerical minority by midcentury also show a rising percentage of foreign-born US residents—about 17 percent by then. But today many of the foreign-born are not citizens.[3] Unless this situation changes, whites, even by the narrow and exclusive definition typically used in demographic data, will still be the majority of citizens at midcentury. And since nonwhite citizens tend to be younger than whites and hence more concentrated among children, nationally whites will be the majority of voters past 2050, even if Census Bureau population projections turn out to be exactly right.

Perhaps worse, the majority-minority idea and the demographic data on which it rests obscure and distort a new social reality that is potentially transformative. The mixing in families and the surge of young people from mixed minority-white family backgrounds are the developments on which the majority-minority nation founders. For one thing, they show that the view of American society as cleaved into two discrete blocs by race is too simplistic to describe the likely future of the country. As previous chapters have demonstrated, the rapidly growing group of mixed young people is, for the most part, positioned in between these blocs, though many in this group are well integrated with whites and are evidently functioning in the mainstream of the society.

Mixing represents a new phenomenon in the early twenty-first century because of the social recognition it receives, owing in part to the nation's demographic data system. The introduction of multiple-race reporting in the 2000 Census has validated mixed identities and generated data that bring mixed race into public discourse. At the same time, mixing ultimately undermines the binary, zero-sum understanding of ethno-racial change associated with the majority-minority conception of the American future. The fluidity of the identities of individuals from mixed family backgrounds reveals the essential falsity of the view that minority population gains are synchronized with white losses. When the same individuals can appear at different moments as mixed, as minority, or as white, we cannot in a straightforward way extrapolate, or project, from current data into the future: the children who today are represented as having mixed origins in census data could turn up as white in future data, or as minority. We cannot predict the outcome on a collective scale with confidence.

The social locations of mixed individuals have been described as "liminal," or permanently in between established states of ethno-racial membership.[4] However accurate today, that characterization seems too strong, since identities evolve and integration into one or another of the ancestry groups may increase across generations. But beyond their liminality, the social locations, attachments, and identities of mixed individuals are ultimately *indeterminate*, and hence so are the ethno-racial configurations in the American future. Bear in mind that the number of mixed minority-white individuals who will be born between today and the middle of the century, when population projections indicate a majority-minority society, could exceed the number of such individuals now alive. How these individuals-to-be identify and affiliate themselves will be determined in part by the future behavior of other Americans, white, minority, and mixed. Currently, there is considerable mixing across the major ethno-racial boundaries. This requires a willingness to cross these lines in intimate relationships on the part of many Americans. And the characteristics of the offspring of mixed unions reveal a new willingness on the part of many white Americans to accept partly minority individuals into kin and other close relationships; even those who are partly black, who encounter the most difficulties, are not inevitably excluded. The willingness to mix could continue to increase, or it could recede.[5] Such changes, if they occur, will shape the future in ways that we cannot predict today.

This is the final way in which the majority-minority conception misleads us about the future. It assumes that our ethno-racial future is demographically determined, strictly a product of the demographic components of change: fertility, mortality, migration. This simply is not so. Our ethno-racial future will also be powerfully shaped by social and economic forces and by social policies that will influence the opportunities for nonwhites to advance socially and economically as well as the character of relations across ethno-racial boundaries. More particularly, such forces will determine the social status, experiences, social affiliations, and identities of the individuals who are situated by family background in between the major ethno-racial blocs of American society, thereby molding who they become and how they present themselves.

Upgrading the Demographic Data System for the Twenty-First Century

Data are the screen through which we can perceive large-scale social realities. That screen can be more or less transparent, but often it seems akin to the screens of Javanese puppet theaters: events taking place behind them cast only shadows that are visible to the audience. But we have no choice for without data, our conclusions about social processes are largely guesswork. If data seem to be failing us, we have to seek improvements in our data.

We need a demographic data system that does full justice to the mixing across ethno-racial lines and allows Americans to better grasp its magnitude and significance for the society. In speaking again of a "demographic data system," I remind the reader that I am referring to something broader than the Census Bureau alone. As described in chapter 4, the Census Bureau is not a wholly free actor; it is a government agency, constrained by bureaucratic, legal, and political considerations. The requirements imposed by the Office of Management and Budget on the collection and management of ethno-racial data have crucially shaped Americans' perceptions of societal change.

This system moved in the right direction with the multiple-race innovation in the 2000 Census.[6] However, this innovation has not been enough. As we have seen, census data still do not allow us to identify the sizable group of Americans who are partly Hispanic and partly something else. Even more consequential are the standard ethno-racial classifications for the most widely disseminated data. They place mixed individuals in a separate category regardless of the components of their family backgrounds. This leads directly to formulations that they are not white and should be counted as minorities, even though many of them have a white parent.

That a large number of the mixed group are still children compounds this problem. They are described in census data by their parents, who often want to acknowledge both sides of their children's parentage. Consequently, the great majority of mixed children are counted by the census as "minority" (chapter 4). This distortion exaggerates the decline of the white population. For example, it obviously affects data about the ethno-racial composition of children, leading to false reports about the majority of infants, and of young children more generally, being "babies of color," a one-sided depiction that fails to acknowledge the white parentage of the majority.

This distortion is also a by-product of an assumption common to demographic classifications: that they should be mutually exclusive and exhaustive. In other words, every person should fit in one and only one category. There is a quantitative neatness to this assumption because it means that percentages add up across categories to 100. For ethno-racial groupings, this system worked well through the twentieth century—helped along, it must be pointed out, by the "one-drop" rule that consigned the many Americans with mixed white and black ancestry to the black category.

But this system no longer works. It has led to public presentations of demographic data that are no longer faithful to social realities and that mislead Americans about ethno-racial change. A few improvements would make a substantial difference.

First and foremost, our demographic data system needs to respect the growing complexity of ethno-racial backgrounds. Treating Americans as members of only a single ethno-racial category no longer makes sense when a large and growing number claim multiple family origins and these claims are socially meaningful. Individuals who assert a background in multiple groups should be classified in multiple categories. The Census Bureau already generates the appropriate tabulations, but they are not the ones that it calls the public's attention to.

Classifying mixed individuals in multiple categories will help Americans see that the apparently steep decline in the white population is partly, and ironically, a consequence of whites' mixing in families with minority partners. That is, as whites and minorities have children together, their children, as we have seen, tend to be classified as nonwhites in publicly disseminated demographic data. The more whites mix, the more children there will be who are categorized outside the white group. There is something perverse about a demographic data system that converts some whites' willingness to cross major ethno-racial boundaries in choosing a partner into data that alarm other whites about minorities becoming a population majority. Surely we can do better than this.

As a corollary, *demographic data need to be able to distinguish between Hispanics from mixed families—very often, the mixing is with white Americans—and other Hispanics.* This is a huge blind spot, given the overall importance of Hispanics to family mixing (as shown in chapter 4). This blindness results from the current two-question format used by the Census Bureau and many other organizations to collect data about ethno-racial origins. Because one of the two questions, on race, is not meaningful to many Hispanics, who see their social identity as exclusively Hispanic or as Latin American in national origin, their responses are not informative. This is especially true when their response is "white" because that is often seen as normative. (Or to put matters another way, we cannot know when this response is informative, as opposed to a choice forced by the question.)

The Census Bureau has developed a superior way of collecting these data: a single question that includes "Hispanic" as an option along with the standard races and allows multiple responses. Large-scale tests have shown that many Latines choose only the Hispanic option, but that it is meaningful when they choose another option as well, such as "white," the most frequent additional choice, claimed by about 15 percent. This question is not being used, however, because the Office of Management and Budget has not approved it. *The integrated question for collecting ethnic-racial origins data needs to be implemented in our demographic data system at the earliest possible opportunity.*

Other changes could be made to demographic data that would help Americans understand the social changes ensuing from immigration. Many demographers have pleaded for data on parental nativity that will allow the identification of the second generation, the children of immigrants, and also then a distinction between it and the third and later generations.[7] Since changes from the immigrant generation to the third are usually large, profiling these three generational groups is an important step in understanding the nature of those changes and the degree of eventual integration into the mainstream they imply. The necessary questions about mother's and father's birthplaces were included in earlier censuses but dropped after 1970 in favor of an ancestry question, because the second generation from earlier immigrations was declining. The questions are already part of one Census Bureau survey, the Current Population Survey, but the CPS is not large enough to permit rigorous analysis of anything but the largest immigrant-descent groups. Including parental nativity questions on the American Community Survey, a large-sample annual survey conducted by the Census Bureau, would answer this need.

Another major improvement to the role of demographic data in the public sphere would be *calling a halt—at least temporarily—to the Census Bureau's production of population projections by race and ethnicity*. Population projections can be extremely insightful about the implications of current demographic patterns, and projections of future population size or age distribution have indisputable value. However, the projections of the ethno-racial composition of the population are inevitably problematic and potentially inflammatory. (Consider: Extreme right-wing groups exploit the projections and the anxieties they stir up for some whites as recruiting tools. The home page of the website for *The Daily Stormer*, named after a rabidly anti-Semitic publication in circulation during the Third Reich, has featured a "Demographic Countdown" of white decline in the United States, apparently adapted directly from the published projections of the Census Bureau.)

The problems with population projections by race and ethnicity begin with the assumption of fixed ethno-racial identity, or group membership. That this assumption does not hold over time for individuals from mixed family backgrounds is powerfully demonstrated by the shifts between censuses revealed by the research of Carolyn Liebler and her colleagues (discussed in chapter 5).[8] Equally problematic is that identities are fixed for the projections when individuals are first encountered. Since the projections depend on data for mixed Americans who mainly are either still children or not even born yet, the identities involved are those given on their behalf by parents (or projected in this way). A priori we cannot know how these individuals will identify themselves when they are adults. These problems and the rapid growth of the mixed population undermine the credibility of the Census Bureau's population projections.

Our recitation of problems with ethno-racial projections exposes a huge lacuna in our knowledge about the ethno-racial identities of mixed Americans. We do not have a grasp of how these identities and their possible mutations emerge from complex family backgrounds. This is not the place for an inventory of all the important questions, and many of them are self-evident in any event: for instance, what leads some individuals of mixed background to report themselves in a single ethno-racial category in demographic data, and how do they choose it? And to state the obvious, phenotype has a poorly understood importance. How much difference, for instance, does it make for someone with Asian-white ancestry to resemble the Asian parent rather than the white one?

An investigation into the ethno-racial identities of mixed Americans and their manifestation in our demographic data system will require a concerted effort by the social-science community and involve qualitative and quantitative approaches. This is not an endeavor that the Census Bureau can tackle by itself. Needed is a series of studies like the one conducted by Hephzibah Strmic-Pawl, involving in-depth interviews with mixed Americans to discern the meanings they attach to the different components of their backgrounds and how these figure into the identities they present to others.[9] But as long as such qualitative studies depend on the willingness of mixed Americans to come forward and present themselves as mixed to the researcher, they run the risk of studying samples biased by unknown degrees of selectivity. Hence, the investigation also requires large-scale random-sample surveys—the Pew studies are a model—that can collect complete data about family backgrounds, both maternal and paternal, as well as about identity tendencies.[10] Such surveys can identify the size and social characteristics of mixed Americans. By collating the findings from multiple studies of different methodological types, we can achieve a sound grasp of the linkage between the growing complexity of family backgrounds and our demographic data.

Understanding Ethno-Racial Change and Persistent Inequality

Even more important is the issue of how we should think about the societal significance of the contemporary ethno-racial changes occurring for some members of the US population and not for others. To begin with, it must be recognized that we cannot hope to understand the evolution of the ethno-racial contours of American society in the current era of mass immigration with a single conceptual system. As I observed in chapter 6, two sets of ideas, race and assimilation theories, have been deployed to explain the array of research observations. Typically, these theories are drawn upon by different groups of researchers, who see themselves as working within distinct scholarly traditions that are at battle with each other for supremacy. The struggle to command the academic hill impedes a comprehensive vision of the societal terrain.

Race theory is currently the dominant approach, at least in the academy, and it is quite compatible with the view of ethno-racial change widely seen as emerging from the demographic data. Race theory, which provides valid perspectives on many aspects of American society, tends to see the society as cleaved between the dominant white group and everyone else (minorities). It depicts the white majority as exerting its dominance through the array of social institutions, from education to the polity, where it has the power to fabricate rules that appear neutral on their face but tacitly favor the dominant group. However, as the demographic situation tilts toward minority numerical predominance, white domination comes into question and maintaining it becomes more of a struggle.

Assimilation theory deserves more attention in our effort to grasp what is going on. The very idea of assimilation can provoke controversy, but this is largely because it has been distorted over time and no longer corresponds with the experiences in the American past that it is supposed to represent. Assimilation is too often misunderstood as requiring that minorities surrender their distinctiveness and seek complete absorption into the white majority. This conception is furthered by the notion, popularized by historians of whiteness, that the predominant problem faced before the middle of the twentieth century by groups such as the Irish, Italians, and eastern European Jews was attaining whiteness. Once they accomplished that, in part by distancing themselves resolutely from African Americans, other invidious distinctions separating them from white Protestants soon faded.

Certainly, these groups were once viewed by the white Christian majority as inferiors, but mostly as inferior whites. The whiteness approach loses sight of the fact that this inferiority was rooted in religious and ethnic dimensions of difference at least as much as in anything that can be understood as racial. And these dimensions of difference did not disappear with assimilation, though they changed in ways that muted them and made the valuations attached to them by the mainstream culture more positive.

Rather than seeing the ethnics as becoming white, it is more insightful to regard them as entering and eventually becoming full participants in the mainstream portion of American society. As this happened, they retained their religious distinctions from the former white Protestant majority, and they sometimes asserted ethnic distinctions by the use of hyphenated identities. But entry into the mainstream meant—by definition—the lessening of the impact of their ethno-racial and religious origins on their lives in such domains as the work they did and their chances for advancement, where they lived, and whom they married. More accurately, this impact receded when we compare them to other whites, and particularly to the native white Protestants who previously constituted the mainstream. In comparison with nonwhites, the impact of their ethno-racial origins remained strong and perhaps was enhanced, because they were now part of a new majority group. Within the mainstream, they were largely, and increasingly, "decategorized," to use the term I introduced in chapter 6. The receding influence of ethno-racial origins on interpersonal relationships within the mainstream was evident in the growing extent of intermarriage, which initially extended to whites of different ethnic origins who shared a common religion but eventually swept over religious barriers as well. Intermarriage became "normal," as whites increasingly mixed in amicable relationships and viewed the ethnic and religious differences among them as modest and not a bar to intimate relations and the formation of families. The consequence is that most young whites today have ancestors who came from multiple European countries.

The ethnics were greatly aided in their inclusion in the mainstream by America's paramount economic status in the decades immediately following the end of World War II, which allowed an enormous expansion of the opportunity for mobility, both socioeconomic and spatial (such as the movement to suburbia). And their full inclusion in America's fighting forces during the war, in contrast to the segregation of nonwhites, was the foundation for the metaphor of the combat unit as a melting pot, which became the prevalent image of the war experience during the war and afterwards. This image elevated the ethnics to moral equality with Protestant white natives.

Their inclusion also affected the mainstream culture in large and small ways. Most critically, the identity of the mainstream transmuted from white Christian (post-Reformation implied) to white Judeo-Christian. In tandem with this remaking came a change in emphasis in the canonical national historical narrative, insightfully described by Matthew Frye Jacobson as a shift from Plymouth Rock to Ellis Island. Intellectuals from ethnic backgrounds, such as Nathan Glazer and Daniel Patrick Moynihan, insisted that the stories associated with their origins be elevated into the American national narrative.[11] In doing so, they were undoubtedly resisting, in their own eyes, a one-way assimilation that would require them to take on the cultural garb of their WASP contemporaries.

In sum, in the mid-twentieth-century, the mainstream greatly expanded. Today it appears to be expanding again, though not as extensively as in the earlier period. The evidence assembled in chapters 5 and 7 indicates that individuals with minority-white family backgrounds mostly are becoming part of the mainstream; those with black-white backgrounds are the major, but only partial, exception. The story begins with childhood because mixed families are more educated and more affluent on average than families with the corresponding minority-only origins, and they locate their households in better neighborhoods than the latter. Consequently, their children grow up with diverse playmates, including whites. Presumably, they therefore feel more comfortable with whites than do others who have grown up in heavily minority, poorer areas. Further, the educational attainment of mixed minority-white young adults often resembles that of their white-only peers. Most mixed adults feel accepted by whites and count them among their friends, according to the evidence. They frequently live where they have many white neighbors, and they have high rates of marriage with whites. These statements about social environments are less true of black-white adults, though they partner with whites much more often than black-only individuals do.

However, this high level of integration with whites has not made mixed Americans white, partly because many mixed individuals encounter ethno-racial boundaries in their daily lives in their interactions with whites. This is the frictional aspect of mainstream entry, which was also part of the experience of many ethnic Catholics and Jews during the mid-twentieth-century mainstream expansion. Anyone who is addressed with an ethnic slur, or who feels denied an opportunity at school or work because of their background, is reminded of not having been fully incorporated into social milieus still dominated by the majority. The most extreme form that this friction takes is harassment or worse at the hands of the police, an experience that makes many black-white individuals feel the strength of their kinship with African Americans. These boundary experiences highlight the importance of physical appearance, a factor largely hidden in survey data. Some mixed individuals are largely white in appearance, while others have visible minority origins. The risks of encountering boundaries obviously depend on one's appearance.

Nor are the identities of mixed individuals consistent with exclusive whiteness. These identities have been shown to be far more fluid than the identities of individuals of undivided ethno-racial parentage. Individuals who come from mixed backgrounds can present themselves as mixed or as leaning toward one or the other side, white or minority. We do not have the knowledge at this point to say how and why they vary in this lean—that is, why, for some, identity gravitates mainly between mixed and white, while others lean toward the minority side. Yet this identity flexibility (within limits) shares some aspects with the identity assertions of the white ethnics in the second half of the last century. These assertions made hyphenated identities acceptable in the mainstream, in contrast to the exclusively American identities that dominated in the century's first half. Yet the intensity of these hyphenated identities and their social salience were highly variable, as both Mary Waters and I have shown.[12] The ethno-racial identities of young mixed Americans may or may not be different today; we do not have enough evidence to know. Another likely difference concerns the correspondence between identity and physical appearance, which is almost certainly stronger today than it was then. (But neither was it negligible during the earlier period, a time when white Americans made more social distinctions according to such physical differences as nose shape and size and hair color and degree of curliness.)

Mainstream entry today is not limited to individuals from mixed minority-white backgrounds; it is simply more evident for them. Of course, there are varying degrees of participation in the mainstream society. The minority parents of these individuals also participate in it, though perhaps not always as fully as their mixed children. Nevertheless, they are married to whites, and they tend to live in neighborhoods with many whites. They tend also to be relatively highly educated, and as such, those who work are likely to work in mainstream settings that require peer relationships that span ethno-racial boundaries. Insofar as minority individuals function, for part of their lives, in such institutional settings, they can be thought of as at least partial participants in the mainstream, having mastered a cultural code that allows relatively smooth interactions among individuals of diverse origins, even if the rest of their lives are spent apart from integrated contexts.

Yet the expanding mainstream is not a panacea to solve all the problems of ethno-racial exclusion and inequality. We must not forget that the mainstream expansion of today is not nearly as sweeping as that in the middle of the twentieth century, when large groups—in particular ethnic Catholics, one-quarter of the population—were ushered in. That expansion benefited from the flourishing of mobility opportunities during a period of great prosperity and limited inequality, epitomized by the fivefold expansion of higher education in a few decades. The present regime of non-zero-sum mobility, which depends far more on demographic shift than on a favorable economic climate, is much more selective and fosters the inclusion of minority groups in only modest proportions. Many minorities and some very poor whites are left behind and remain on the outside looking in. As described in the last chapter, there are barriers keeping many from approaching the mainstream—especially the institutionalized and individual racism that impedes broad African American advance, and the lack of legal status of one-quarter of the immigrant population, which impacts the life chances of their children, even their citizen children born in the United States. Understanding the mechanisms involved in these barriers is the province of race theory.

A New Majority?

Mainstream expansion suggests the possibility that we could be witnessing the emergence of a new majority, like a chrysalis struggling to free itself from its shell. Such a majority would be a grouplike social formation in the sense that its members would be socially integrated with one another and share cultural codes, which vary to be sure by social class, region of the country, and other variables. Such a new majority does seem to be emerging, but not everywhere in the country. In that respect, it is no different from the mainstream expansion of the past. As happened then, the process today is most advanced in the places that have experienced diversity for decades and where the mobility of new generations of minorities, especially those from immigrant backgrounds, has promoted numerous peer contacts between individuals with different ethno-racial origins. If the current expansion follows the same path as the earlier one, it will gradually spread outwards, assisted by the increasing "normality" of mixed families and of mixed and minority Americans in positions of prominence.

The emergence of a new majority that includes whites, most mixed minority-white individuals, and some others of exclusively minority origins would be the most powerful refutation of the basic understanding of the majority-minority society. Instead of a society riven along ethno-racial lines, between whites and nonwhites, we could see a society divided between an increasingly multi-hued majority and others whose lives are more determined by their minority status.

The potential political implications of a new majority are of supreme importance for grasping the long-run significance of contemporary ethno-racial changes. Integration into social contexts that are internally diverse—a hallmark of the expanding mainstream—tends to dampen intense attitudinal conflicts along lines of social origins and to encourage tolerance of moderate difference. During the earlier mainstream expansion, many of the ethnics, especially those from Catholic backgrounds, tended to take on the political colorations of their new surroundings. Middle-class ethnics who had moved to the suburbs, for instance, often became Republicans, though they retained Democratic family memories. We don't know yet whether a similar process will hold during the new mainstream expansion and how it will reshape the political inclinations of whites and others. Changes in political inclinations may turn out to be limited to the extent that family ties divided between mainstream individuals and minorities generate cross-cutting political loyalties.[13] Still, it seems a safe bet that conflict, especially as expressed in the political domain, ultimately will not follow the precise lines of the majority-minority script. This of course also means that the hopes of some that the current white majority will be dethroned by a new majority forged by minority status are likely to be disappointed.

Another stage in the development of this formation would be the emergence of a name. Groups need names and identities to cohere.

The majority that emerged from the mid-twentieth-century expansion had a label readily available: Judeo-Christian white, with the emphasis initially on the first part and later on the second. What will a new majority call itself if it emerges? A label that covers its diversity does not seem readily at hand, in the way that was true earlier (although we should keep in mind that "Judeo-Christian" was a wartime invention). One possibility, suggested by Eric Kaufmann in his book *Whiteshift*, is that a new majority could continue to define itself as white and to draw mainly on myths and symbols from the European cultural heritage.[14] That possibility cannot be excluded outright at this early juncture, but it does seem unlikely, given the evident ethno-racial diversity of the new majority, which, moreover, will probably only increase over time given current demographic dynamics. In any event, the United States has a different sort of tradition to draw on: the melting pot. I am not suggesting that "melting pot" is a suitable name; it has a specific historical resonance, associated with white ethnics, that would seem to rule it out. My point, rather, is that American culture already contains a set of references to a society forged by mixing. It is one with a long history extending back to the colonial period and celebrated in the 1782 book *Letters from an American Farmer* by Hector St. John de Crèvecouer. That tradition was invoked by Frederick Douglass in his luminous 1869 speech on the "Composite Nation," the source of the epigram at the head of this chapter. Creative individuals could draw on it to invent a new name, suitable for the twenty-first century, that continues in this tradition. All this being said, we cannot be sure that a self-conscious new majority will in fact emerge.

Final Thoughts: A New Narrative

The goal of this book has been to present a new way of understanding the ethno-racial changes under way in American society and their implications for the next several decades, as well as to suggest a new narrative to help Americans understand the direction in which their society is moving and its continuity with—not radical break from—the country's past. The idea of an expanding and more diverse mainstream can form the basis for a new narrative that emphasizes the openness of the majority to Americans from different ethno-racial backgrounds. Such a narrative idea would promote a sense of cohesion that convinces Americans of different origins that "we are all in it together," to borrow a phrase from the historian David Hollinger.[15]

This way of thinking about mainstream inclusion need not diminish the sense of urgency about social policies to enhance it. The new narrative can open space in public discourse for the argument that some groups are unfairly blocked from equitable access to the mainstream portion of society by poverty, systemic racism, or defective legal status. In the context of a narrative that highlights the similarity of contemporary processes of mainstream inclusion to those of the past, such an argument could have a more positive resonance for the white majority than it has today.

The current dominant narrative, that of the majority-minority society, is deeply problematic, and not just on grounds of accuracy. It is inherently divisive because it highlights a societal fracture line. To many whites it seems to augur a zero-sum future for them, one that couples minority ascent with their decline. That picture has helped to fuel an intense political polarization and ignite a flare-up of white nationalism. Social psychologists have demonstrated that the anxious reactions of many whites to the notion of the majority-minority society in the impending future arise from status threat, a phenomenon associated with hierarchy regardless of who is on top. As long as the majority-minority vision of the future remains dominant, there is no reason to expect a different reaction, even though minority population gains will not alter fundamentally the racial hierarchy anytime soon, at least not at the national level. Whites will remain the political majority past midcentury and the most powerful group for the foreseeable future. In this light, current political divisions do not bode well.

These divisions are not limited to the United States. In many other immigration societies, similar polarizations have arisen, produced by surges in extreme nationalist reactions by many in the majority to immigration and the growing ethno-racial diversity it spawns.

In France, right-wing intellectual circles have promoted so-called replacement theory, which envisions the eclipse of Western civilization as the current white majority is eventually replaced by a new majority composed of individuals descended from the post-1950 immigration from former colonies and other countries outside of Europe. The idea has been widely influential both in and outside of Europe and has been cited in the self-justifications for murderous assaults at such distant points on the globe as Oslo, Norway; Christchurch, New Zealand; and El Paso, Texas.

As long as we think about the current changes and their implications for the societal configuration of the future primarily in terms of ethno-racial divisions, we are not likely to overcome polarization and the political blockages it engenders. Yet Western societies need immigration to retain their demographic, economic, and cultural vitality, and they will necessarily become more diverse as a consequence. At the moment, many of these societies appear to be at a political impasse over immigration.

Assimilation into an expanding and increasingly inclusive mainstream offers a superior way of understanding some consequential contemporary ethno-racial changes in the United States. It is my hope that it can do the same for other Western immigration societies. Preliminary research suggests, for instance, that mixed minority-white family backgrounds are linked to mainstream inclusion in Canada, implying a mainstream expansion like that in the United States.[16] In all Western societies, moreover, there is a demographic transition to diversity that is likely to create non-zero-sum mobility for many descendants of immigrants, as it is doing in the United States.[17] As chapter 7 argued, this is one of the key levers for opening up the pathways leading to the mainstream.

Mainstream expansion and diversification offer a way to envision a new kind of "us" that crosses ethno-racial divisions. The minorities in the mainstream are sufficiently like the members of the native majority for comfortable interactions to occur between them, yet they have not been forced to surrender all sense of distinctiveness in the process of gaining entry. For the United States and the other immigration societies of the West, which are deeply divided politically over immigration and the societal changes it has unleashed, the idea of the mainstream as a part of the society where ethno-racial decategorization takes place provides a possible conceptual pathway to relaxing the taut tension between national cohesion and ethno-racial diversity. The idea of an expanded mainstream is consistent in this way with the historian Jill Lepore's call for a "new Americanism," and with other attempts to reclaim nationalism for progressive purposes.[18] The societies of North America and western Europe cannot prosper without immigration, yet many in their majorities seem stricken by the prospect of the rising demographic and eventually political and cultural strength of immigrant minorities. They need to see that many of the immigrants and their descendants are willing to assimilate and join the societal mainstream. In the United States, this calls up echoes of the canonical experience of assimilation—the inclusion of the second and third generations of white ethnics after World War II.

A vibrant, expanding, and inclusive mainstream—as fact and as narrative—constitutes the most realistic antidote available in the near future to the toxic white nationalism that proclaims, in the words of Iowa Republican congressman Steven King, "We can't restore our civilization with somebody else's babies," or in the words of the Dutch politician-provocateur Geert Wilders, "If we do not stop Islamification now, Eurabia and Netherabia will be just a matter of time."

This new narrative can allow members of the native majority to imagine that "somebody else's babies" are just like their own, or like their grandchildren, and to understand that the contemporary alterations to the mainstream are not a revolution but an evolution, consistent in the case of the United States with the common understanding of the country's past.

Chapter 1. Introduction: The Narrative of the Majority-Minority Society

1. Blow 2018.
2. Wazwaz 2015.
3. Public Religion Research Institute 2018, p. 25.
4. Higham 1970.
5. Alba and Nee 2003.
6. Roediger 2005; Staples 2019.
7. Waters and Kasinitz 2014.
8. Glazer 1992; Jung 2009.
9. Alba 1985, 1990, 2009; Waters 1990.

Chapter 2. The Enigma of November 2016

1. Waldman 2016.
2. Cohn 2017.
3. Huang et al. 2016.
4. Sides 2017.
5. Ibid., pp. 5–6.
6. Bureau of Labor Statistics 2017; Donovan and Bradley 2018.
7. Gest 2016.
8. Ibid., p. 84.
9. Wikipedia, 2020a.
10. Mutz 2018, p. 1.
11. Sides 2017.
12. Sides, Tesler, and Vavreck 2018, pp. 170–72, fig. 8.6.
13. Schaffner, Macwilliams, and Nteta 2018.
14. Lopez 2017; KQED News 2018; Stirewalt 2019.
15. Germane here is so-called group position theory, which originated with Herbert Blumer's famous 1958 article and has been reinvigorated by Lawrence Bobo (1999).
16. Lopez 2017.
17. Fowler, Medenica, and Cohen 2017.

18. Valentino, Neuner, and Vandenbroek 2018, p. 768.
19. Sides, Tesler, and Vavreck 2018, p. 3.
20. Jardina 2019; Jiménez 2017.
21. Sides, Tesler, and Vavreck 2018, p. 177.
22. Pew Research Center 2019.
23. Gonyea 2017.
24. Craig and Richeson 2014; Craig, Rucker, and Richeson 2018.
25. Wetts and Willer 2018.
26. Abascal 2015, p. 805.
27. Craig and Richeson 2014.
28. Wetts and Willer 2018, p. 816.
29. Levy and Myers 2018, p. 8; see also Myers and Levy 2018.
30. Lewis quoted in Alba and Foner 2015, p. 2; see also Kaufmann 2019a.
31. Bump 2017; see also Cherlin 2019.
32. Porter 2016.
33. See also Judis 2018a, 2018b.
34. Case and Deaton 2017, p. 397.
35. Cherlin 2014; Murray 2012.
36. Monnat and Brown 2017, pp. 228–29.
37. Sides, Tesler, and Vavreck 2018.
38. Media Matters 2013.
39. Hochschild 2016, chap. 9.
40. Jardina 2019.

Chapter 3. The Power of the Demographic Imagination

1. Frey 2018a.
2. National Academies of Sciences 2015; Reimers 1992; Zolberg 2006.
3. Passel and Cohn 2018.
4. The equation in demographic analysis between the foreign-born and immigrants is not perfect. At any single point in time, a significant fraction of the foreign-born counted in demographic data are individuals present in the United States on temporary visas, many of whom will depart when their visas expire. See National Academies of Sciences 2015, fig. 3.1.
5. Massey 2018; National Academies of Sciences 2015, chap. 1.
6. Tran 2018.
7. Sáenz and Johnson 2018.
8. Myers and Levy 2018. On the need to stratify the population by ethnicity and race for population projections, see Day 1993. I am grateful to Lauren Medina of the Census Bureau for digging up this report for me.
9. Roberts 2008.
10. US Census Bureau 2012b.
11. Cooper 2012.
12. Yen 2012a, 2012b, 2012c, 2012d.

13. Colby and Ortman 2015, p. 1.

14. US Census Bureau 2018a.

15. Frey 2018b.

16. Cohn 2016.

17. Yoshinaga 2016; Morello and Melinik 2012; Cauchon and Overberg 2012.

18. Wazwaz 2015.

19. Frey 2018c.

20. Anglin 2015.

21. Media Matters 2018; Serwer 2018.

22. Blow 2018. For Buchanan's views, see Buchanan 2001.

23. See Kaufmann 2019a.

24. Gitlin 2018.

25. Blow 2018.

26. Klein 2018.

27. Ibid.

28. Hsu 2009.

29. Hsu 2016.

30. Hsu 2009.

31. Brubaker 2016; Morning 2017.

32. Hsu 2009.

33. Ibid.

34. Frey 2018a, chap. 3; see also Marrow 2011; Singer 2015; Zuñiga and Hernández-León 2006.

35. Logan and Stults 2011; Vertovec 2007.

36. Zhang and Logan 2016. The data cited in the text come from my calculations using the supplementary online materials for the article. See also Logan and Zhang 2010.

37. Hall and Crowder 2015.

38. Newman and Velez 2014.

39. Alba, Rumbaut, and Marotz 2005; Wong 2007. For a German example of this connection, see Semyonov et al. 2004.

40. Alba, Rumbaut, and Marotz 2005; Blumer 1958; Bobo 1999. Also relevant is Robert Putnam's (2007) well-known claim that diversity produces a "hunkering down."

41. Enos 2014.

42. Allport 1954.

43. Pettigrew and Tropp 2006, 2008; see also Brown 1995.

44. My discussion shortchanges the importance of the local political response to immigrants' arrival. For insightful essays, see Mollenkopf and Pastor 2016; Lichter, Parisi, and Taquino 2016.

45. Jiménez 2017; Anderson 2011; see also Hall, Iceland, and Yi 2019; Tropp et al. 2018.

46. Livingston 2017.

47. Grant 1916.

48. Stoddard 1920; Higham 1970, pp. 270–77.
49. Fitzgerald 1925, p. 13.
50. Norris 2018.
51. Jones et al. 2018.
52. Wills 1998, p. 67.

Chapter 4. The Demographic Data System and the Surge of Young Americans from Mixed Family Backgrounds

1. Lind 1998.
2. Sáenz and Johnson 2016.
3. Frey 2018c.
4. Prewitt 2013.
5. Gordon 1964; Spickard 1989; Alba and Nee 2003.
6. Treitler 2013; Liebler 2018.
7. Perlmann and Waters 2002; Prewitt 2013.
8. Pew Research Center 2015. See also Anderson and Fienberg 1999, chap. 8. On the antebellum history of the race question, see Anderson 2002; Prewitt 2013, chaps. 4 and 5. Valuable also is a Census Bureau mapping of historical categories onto present ones; see Pratt, Hixson, and Jones 2015.
9. The story is well told by Mora 2014.
10. Cohn 2010.
11. DaCosta 2007; see also Perlmann and Waters, "Introduction," in Perlmann and Waters 2002; Prewitt 2013, chap. 8.
12. US Census Bureau 2018b.
13. Liebler et al. 2017.
14. Later in this chapter, in the analysis of the birth certificate data, I include the Native Hawaiian and other Pacific Islanders in the Asian category in order to arrive at a complete count of mixed versus unmixed family backgrounds. However, when analyzing the characteristics of the Asian and Asian-white categories in the next chapter, I exclude them. The reader should bear in mind that the Hawaiians and Pacific Islanders represent a small part of the population, 0.4 percent in 2010. See Hixson, Kepler, and Kim (2012) for a description of their characteristics in census data.
15. Dowling 2014; Roth 2012. For an empirical demonstration of the frequent disparity between skin color and reported race among Hispanics, see Golash-Boza and Darity 2008.
16. Prewitt 2013, p. 172.
17. For OMB standards, see Office of Civil Rights 1997.
18. Office of Management and Budget 2000.
19. US Census Bureau 2017.
20. Cohn 2017.
21. Wang 2018.
22. On the potential for intermarriage to remake race in the United States, see Hochschild, Weaver, and Burch 2012; Lee and Bean 2010. For the relevant history, see Spickard 1989.

23. Livingston and Brown 2017.

24. Ibid. For additional confirmation of the connection between minority education level and intermarriage, see McManus and Apgar 2019. The absence of a similar connection among whites echoes a very long-standing hypothesis about the exchange of social advantages and disadvantages in intermarriage; see Merton 1941.

25. Wang 2012; see also Goldstein 1999; Hochschild, Weaver, and Burch 2012, chap 3.

26. Livingston 2017; see also Frey 2018a, chap. 10.

27. Alba 1990; Waters 1990.

28. Mothers' ethno-racial data were missing in fewer than 1 percent of births. By contrast with the birth certificates, data for a parent are missing for about one-quarter of infants in American Community Survey public-use data files.

29. The distinction comes from Morning and Saperstein 2018.

30. Unlike census data, which are collected by a federal agency, birth certificates are generated by states, which do not uniformly adopt changing standards, thus playing havoc with over-time comparisons. I am grateful to Aliya Saperstein of Stanford University and Larry Sink of the Census Bureau for bringing this issue to my attention.

31. As in figure 4.5, I must rely on census data here because birth certificates do not provide the necessary data in that year. This also means that my calculations are limited to infants in households where both parents are present.

32. Bean, Brown, and Bachmeier 2015. The relevant literature on Mexican Americans is huge. See Jiménez 2010; Telles and Ortiz 2008; Telles and Sue 2019; Vasquez 2011. On relations between Mexicans and Anglos after conquest, see Montejano 1986.

33. The birth certificate data do not indicate the father's nativity. Incidentally, all of these calculations include infants with no data about fathers; they are counted as unmixed.

34. Lichter and Qian 2018.

35. In census documentation of the projections, this is described as the KidLink procedure; see US Census Bureau 2018c.

36. The construction of figure 4.6 requires some analysis at a very detailed level of the projections. The Census Bureau makes available a file that, for each year of the projection and each year of age, shows breakdowns for specific combinations of sex, Hispanicity, and race. Thus, to find the specific figures by year and age for non-Hispanics of mixed white and some other race, one must subtract the number for non-Hispanics with only white race from the number for non-Hispanics with any white race.

This procedure implies that, in analyzing the projections, I am including second- and later-generation white mixtures in the mixed group. At any rate, it is not possible in the projections data to separate first-generation white mixes (one parent is exclusively non-Hispanic and white) from others. Moreover, since the number of mixed minority-white infants is projected to increase sharply, it is obvious that many of the mixed of the present will be among the future parents. Hence, including later-generation mixes is appropriate.

37. Another way of arriving at an estimate is as follows: The 2015 National Content Test shows that about 15 percent of Hispanics also declared meaningfully that they were "white." If this percentage is applied to the total percentage of Hispanics in the 2016 population data, 17.8 percent (table 4.1), then it seems that 2.7 percent of the population would have reported mixed Anglo and Hispanic ancestry if they could. This is of the same order of magnitude as the percentage who were non-Hispanic and reported two or more races, 2.1 percent (table 4.1), the great majority of whom (nearly 90 percent) were part white. The fact that the percentage who were part Hispanic is larger suggests that the assumption of equality is likely to be conservative. See also the discussion in Alba 2018.

Chapter 5. What We Know about Americans from Mixed Minority-White Families

1. For data from the Census Bureau, I rely on the data sets provided by a unique source, IPUMS, based at the University of Minnesota and directed by the demographer Steven Ruggles (see Ruggles et al. 2019). IPUMS does not simply serve as a repository for census data sets, but it has also reconfigured some to make them more useful to researchers. I make use in particular of versions of these files that attach data for parents to the records for children. It deserves note here that the identification of children's parents in some complex households requires inferential steps that may introduce error. Nevertheless, I accept that the IPUMS procedures are the best we can expect to do with the limited information available, and I am grateful to the IPUMS staff for their work.

2. Lopez, Gonzalez-Barrera, and López 2017; Parker et al. 2015.

3. The most important of the in-depth interview studies for my purposes is Strmic-Pawl 2016. See also Lee and Bean 2010; Rockquemore and Brunsma 2008.

4. Liebler et al. 2017; Harris and Sim 2002.

5. Duncan and Trejo 2018.

6. Telles and Ortiz 2008.

7. Chetty et al. 2018; Corak 2013.

8. Cherlin 2014, chap. 6.

9. Because California apparently did not report marital status on its birth certificates in 2017, the data in this section come from the 2016 birth certificates.

10. Iceland 2009; Logan and Stults 2011; Krysan and Crowder 2017.

11. On segregation, see Reardon and Owens 2014. On school inequalities, see, for example, Hochschild and Scovronick 2003; Kasinitz et al. 2008, chap. 5.

12. Logan and Stults 2011; Iceland 2009; Alba et al. 2014.

13. I rely here on geographical divisions of residential space that have been developed by IPUMS based on Public Use Microdata Area (PUMA) designations in public use data samples. PUMAs are fairly large areas, with a minimum of 100,000 inhabitants, and sometimes cross important political boundaries—for example, between cities and inner suburbs (described in the IPUMS as "central/principal city status unknown"). To arrive at the category of city edge/suburban homeowners,

I combined homeownership with the geographical categories of "outside central/ principal city" and "central/principal city status unknown." For the category of urban/inner suburban renter, we have combined renter status with "central city" with "central/principal city status unknown." The broad-gauge classification of residential space in the text is a reasonable approximation and the best we can do.

14. Gabriel and Spring 2019.

15. Strmic-Pawl 2016.

16. Ibid., chap. 5; Lee and Bean 2010.

17. Kao, Joyner, and Balistreri 2019, pp. 55–57.

18. Ibid., p. 59; Quillian and Campbell 2003.

19. The analysis reported here is mine. I am grateful to Nathaniel Kang of UCLA's HERI for sharing with me the parental data, which is not available in the online survey file.

20. For this comparison, students born outside the United States should be excluded, but this is not possible with these data. I have made a reasonably effective substitute by restricting the comparison to US-citizen students. Insofar as immigrant students are included, they work against the hypothesis of an advantage for Hispanic-white students because they are likely to be counted in the Hispanic-only category of the freshman data.

21. See, for example, Telles and Ortiz 2008; also Portes and Rumbaut 2001.

22. Duncan and Trejo 2018; Duncan et al. 2020; Alba and Islam 2009; Emeka and Vallejo 2011.

23. Duncan et al. 2020.

24. Tilly 1998.

25. Strmic-Pawl 2016, p. 53.

26. Parker et al. 2015, p. 8.

27. I calculated the Anglo-Hispanic figures from Pew in this paragraph and later from the Pew database for its multiracial survey.

28. Parker et al. 2015, p. 131.

29. Strmic-Pawl 2016, chap. 4

30. Names play a major role in distinguishing light-skinned Latines, and hence individuals of mixed Latine-white background, from non-Latine whites. See Vasquez 2011.

31. I do not discuss some more complex mixtures involving partly black ancestry—for example, American Indian, black, and white—that are included in the Pew survey. In general, the patterns of contact with relatives appear to be governed by the black part of an individual's family heritage, indicating that those of visibly African descent are treated as black, even when they also have white and other ancestries.

32. Childs 2005.

33. Miyawaki 2015.

34. Telles and Ortiz 2008.

35. I am grateful to Mark Hugo Lopez of the Pew Research Center for these tabulations.

36. Le Gall and Meintel 2015; Song 2017.

37. Quoted in Jardina 2019, p. 55.

38. Gans 1979; Vasquez-Tokos 2017. For two empirical studies that appeared simultaneously and bear out Gans's conception, see Alba 1990 and Waters 1990.

39. This was noticed in the early studies, such as those in Root 1996.

40. Liebler et al. 2017.

41. Duncan and Trejo 2017.

42. This figure is not available in the published paper. I am grateful to Brian Duncan for producing a special tabulation for me.

43. Fernández et al. 2018.

44. Alba and Islam 2009; Emeka and Vallejo 2011.

45. Parker et al. 2015, p. 40.

46. Davenport 2016.

47. Strmic-Pawl 2016, p. 96.

48. Ibid., pp. 102, 125.

49. Ibid., p. 69.

50. For a description of the complex methodology involved, which requires merging two different samples, see Lopez, Gonzalez-Barrera, and López 2017, pp. 23–29.

51. Ibid., pp. 4, 6, 18.

52. Special tabulations provided by Mark Hugo Lopez.

53. Telles and Ortiz 2008, p. 281.

54. Alba, Jiménez, and Marrow 2014.

55. Alba and Islam 2009.

56. Jardina 2019.

57. For evidence that the ethno-racial composition of the neighborhood during childhood is related to intermarriage, see Zhang and Sassler 2019.

58. Germane to this finding is the fact that Strmic-Pawl's research is sited in Chicago and New York, two places where the memories and influences of the ethnic communities established by waves of European immigration are very strong.

59. Song 2019.

Chapter 6. Some Ideas and History for Understanding Today's Ethno-Racial Mixing

1. Some major texts on race theory include Omi and Winant 2015; Bonilla-Silva 2018; Feagin 2014; López [1996] 2006; Bobo, Kluegel, and Smith 1997.

2. Du Bois 1903, p. 9; see also Winant 2002.

3. Frederickson 2003; see also Mills 1997.

4. Painter 2010.

5. Orfield et al. 2019.

6. Bonilla-Silva 1997; Bobo 1999; Ray 2019.

7. Massey and Denton 1993; Wilson 1996.

8. Alexander 2010.

9. Shannon et al. 2017; Pager 2007.

10. Western and Wildeman 2009; Wilson 1987.

11. Tilly 1998.

12. Feagin 2014, p. 8.

13. Bonilla-Silva 2004.

14. Perlmann and Waldinger 1997; Foner 2000.

15. Weber 1968, p. 389.

16. These ideas were introduced by Zolberg and Long 1999. They have been extended by Alba 2005 and Wimmer 2008.

17. Park and Burgess [1921] 1969, p. 735.

18. Gordon 1964.

19. Alba and Nee 2003.

20. Ibid., p. 11.

21. My concept of "decategorization" is a generalization of Gans's (2012) idea of "deracialization."

22. Jiménez 2017; cf. Anderson 2011.

23. Alba and Duyvendak 2019, pp. 110–11.

24. Alba and Nee 2003, p. 282.

25. Jiménez 2017.

26. Dobbin 2009; Stainback and Tomaskovic-Devey 2012; see also Skrentny 2009. On "workhood" integration (the degree to which members of different groups work in the same neighborhoods), see Hall, Iceland, and Yi 2019.

27. Massey et al. 2003; Warikoo 2016.

28. Ashkenas, Park, and Pearce 2017.

29. Schuman, Steeh, and Bobo 1985. Many dispute the ability of classical polling of racial attitudes to capture whites' attitudes toward blacks; see Jardina 2019, chap. 1.

30. Alba 2005.

31. Lieberson 1961, 1980; Blauner 1972; Ogbu 1978; Jung 2009.

32. Portes and Zhou 1993, p. 82; Portes and Rumbaut 2001.

33. Golash Boza 2006; Portes and Rumbaut 2001; Zhou and Gonzales 2019.

34. See the debate between Haller et al. 2011 and Alba et al. 2011; see also Kasinitz et al. 2008; Perlmann 2011; and National Academies of Science 2015.

35. Valdez and Golash-Boza 2017.

36. Treitler 2013, p. 172; cf. Rockquemore and Brunsma 2008, pp. 105–8.

37. Bonilla-Silva 2004.

38. Covello 1972; Gans 1982; Alba 1985; Steinberg 1989; Perlmann 2005.

39. Steinberg 1989; Silberman 1985; Waldinger 1996; Karabel 2005.

40. Fishman 2004.

41. For the whiteness narrative, see Roediger 1991, 2005; Ignatiev 1995; Brodkin 1998; Jacobson 1998; López [1996] 2006.

42. Katznelson 2005; Roediger 2005.

43. Oliver and Shapiro 2006.

44. Guglielmo 2003; Perlmann 2018.

45. Higham 1970; McGreevey 2003.

46. Putnam 2007, p. 160. For the data on parochial school attendance, see Greeley and Rossi 1966, p. 33; see also Lopez 2008; Steinfels 2003.

47. Goldstein 1969.

48. Kennedy 1944.

49. There is evidence of such Asian American disadvantage: see Alba 2009, chap. 4; also Tran, Lee, and Huang 2019.

50. Pettigrew and Tropp 2006.

51. Maddison 2007.

52. Trow 1961.

53. Gans 1967, pp. 23–24.

54. Jackson 1985, p. 241.

55. Gary Gerstle (2001, pp. 236–37) makes the same point with a different set of references.

56. Wikipedia 2020c.

57. See, for example, Maraniss 2019.

58. Wikipedia 2020b.

59. President's Commission on Law Enforcement and Administration of Justice 1967, p. 7. See also the rather sensationalized account by Donald Cressey (1969), a famous criminologist.

60. Hofstadter 1965; Schrag 2010.

61. Geraldine Ferraro and Mario Cuomo come readily to mind. In both cases, the suspicions were mobilized when these politicians sought national office but not before.

62. Dinnerstein 1994; Gerstle 2001; Karabel 2005.

63. Treitler 2013.

64. The events surrounding the murder of Yusef Hawkins in Bensonhurst, Brooklyn, in 1989, which included the racist jeering of civil rights marchers afterwards, are a painful illustration.

65. Gans 1999; Lee and Bean 2010. Evidence that black-white inequalities are unusually resilient can be found in Iceland 2017.

66. Lieberson 1980.

67. Ray et al. 2017.

68. Hirschman and Kraly 1990.

69. See US Census Bureau 2012a.

70. Stainback, Robinson, and Tomaskovic-Devey 2005.

71. Gerstle 2001, p. 185.

72. Steinfels 2003.

73. Herberg 1960.

74. Moore 2004.

75. Gerstle 2001.

76. See, for example, Greeley 1971; Novak 1972. More recently, the idea of an ethnic revival was embraced by Jacobson 2006.

77. Freedman 1996.

78. Hollinger 1996.

Chapter 7. Assimilation in the Early Twenty-First Century

1. Chetty et al. 2016; Corak 2013; Zucman 2019.

2. Coleman 2006.

3. The potential role of this demographic shift for minority mobility is the core subject of my 2009 book; see also Myers 2007. On the educational achievements of baby boomers, see Fischer and Hout 2006.

4. Alba and Yrizar Barbosa 2016. I am grateful to Brenden Beck for calculating the figures in table 7.1 for 2015.

5. Ibid., p. 924; see also National Academies of Sciences 2015, chap. 6.

6. Alba and Yrizar Barbosa 2016.

7. For evidence that minority supervisors make a difference, see Tomaskovic-Devey, Hällsten, and Avent-Holt 2015.

8. Lee and Zhou 2015.

9. Murnane 2013.

10. Espinosa et al. 2019, p. xiii.

11. National Center for Educational Statistics 2017.

12. Espinosa et al. 2019, p. 138.

13. The statistically minded reader may note that the representation of Anglo-Hispanic young adults in table 7.2 is much smaller than we should expect based on the proportion of mixed Anglo-Hispanic to unmixed Hispanic infants, not only recently but in the past. What I have called the "expanded" definition of the mixed Hispanic-white group in the ACS clearly "underperforms." It does not capture all of the individuals with this mixed background. That does not mean that the conclusion about the relative educational position of Anglo-Hispanics in table 7.2 is wrong. The CIRP freshman data, discussed in chapter 5, describe the cohorts entering college in the very early 2000s and are near in time to the cohorts represented by the twenty-five- to twenty-six-year-olds of 2000 in the table. The educational advantages of the mixed group are quite consistent between the two data sets. Since the same pattern of inequality holds for this age group in 2017, the conclusion that it represents substantial advantage for the mixed group is supported by the consistency over time in the table.

14. Ashkenas, Park, and Pearce 2017. The headline of their article, incidentally, is quite misleading because of a flawed trend analysis.

15. Massey et al. 2007.

16. Espinosa et al. 2019, pp. xiv, 88.

17. Tran, Lee, and Huang 2019.

18. Massey and Denton 1993; Iceland 2009; Logan and Stults 2011; Lichter, Parisi, and Taquino 2015.

19. Sharkey 2014; cf. Krivo, Peterson, and Kuhl 2009.

20. Parisi, Lichter, and Taquino 2019; Crowder, Hall, and Tolnay 2011.

21. Hall, Tach, and Lee 2016; see also Friedman 2008.

22. Hamilton 2019.

23. Logan and Stults 2011.

24. Alba et al. 2014.

25. Brown 2007; South, Crowder, and Pais 2008; Iceland 2009; Massey and Tannen 2018; Crowell and Fossett 2018.

26. Li 2009.

27. Logan and Stults 2011.

28. Ibid.; Sharkey 2013.

29. Sharkey 2014, p. 932; see also South, Crowder, and Pais 2011.

30. Parisi, Lichter, and Taquino 2015.

31. Logan and Stults 2011. In both 2000 and 2010, 80 percent of whites were found in metropolitan regions. This stability suggests that few whites were fleeing metropolitan regions in the early 2000s to escape diversity.

32. *Newsday* 2018.

33. Hunt et al. 2018, p. 4.

34. Ibid., p. 21.

35. Ibid., pp. 3, 5.

36. Smith et al. 2019.

37. Zweigenhaft and Domhoff 2018.

38. Alba 2006.

39. Jacobson 2006.

40. Gans 2012; Twine and Gallagher 2008; Kaufmann 2019a.

41. Jiménez 2010.

42. Lichter, Parisi, and Taquino 2016.

43. Alba and Foner 2017.

44. Kaufmann 2019b.

45. Kasinitz et al. 2008.

46. Kao and Tienda 1995; White and Glick 2009.

47. Parisi, Lichter, and Taquino 2015.

48. Imoagene 2017; cf. Emeka 2019.

49. Macartney, Bishaw, and Fontenot 2013.

50. Telles and Ortiz 2008; cf. Telles and Sue 2019.

51. Bean, Brown, and Bachmeier 2015.

52. Lee, Ramakrishnan, and Wong 2018.

53. Jiménez 2010.

54. Freedman 1996.

55. Alba 1985.

56. Ramakrishnan and Ahmad 2014.

57. Huang et al. 2016.

58. Enten 2016; Pedraza and Wilcox-Archuleta 2017.

59. Alba 1985.

Chapter 8. Social Policies to Broaden Mainstream Assimilation

1. See Corak 2013, pp. 80–81.

2. Ibid., p. 82.

3. Ibid., p. 83.

4. Chetty et al. 2016, fig. 1.

5. Ibid., p. 15.

6. Ibid., fig. S5.

7. Judis 2018a.

8. Thomas Piketty, Emmanuel Saez, and Gabriel Zucman (2018) estimate that the top 10 percent took in 55 percent of national income growth between 1979 and 2014. But there is dispute about the precise degree to which those at the top of the income distribution monopolize the fruits of economic growth; see Rose 2018.

9. Duncan and Murnane 2011.

10. *New York Times* 2019.

11. Corak 2013, pp. 87–89.

12. Chetty et al. 2017, table III. The claim that college graduation has an equalizing effect originates with Michael Hout (1988).

13. Ibid., p. 2.

14. Ibid., pp. 2–3.

15. On CUNY, see Lavin, Attewell, and Domina 2009.

16. Chetty et al. 2017, p. 5.

17. Piketty and Saez 2003; Saez and Zucman 2016.

18. Piketty, Saez, and Zucman 2018.

19. Desilver 2018.

20. Tax Policy Center 2019.

21. Saez and Zucman 2019.

22. Fox 2018.

23. Edmond 2017.

24. National Academies of Sciences 2019.

25. Amadeo 2019.

26. National Academies of Sciences 2019.

27. Reardon 2011; Garcia and Weiss 2017; see also Alba and Holdaway 2013.

28. See Hochschild and Scovronick 2003; Alba, Sloan and Sperling 2011. On income segregation, see Reardon and Bischoff 2011.

29. Alba and Holdaway 2013.

30. Organization for Economic Cooperation and Development 2016.

31. Goldin and Katz 2008, chap. 9.

32. Morgan and Amerikaner 2019.

33. See US Department of Education 2005.

34. Alba 2009.

35. Mortenson 2012; Mitchell et al. 2018.

36. Alba 2009.

37. Sentencing Project, n.d.

38. On Nigerians, see Imoagene 2017; Emeka 2019.

39. Chetty et al. 2018.

40. Alexander 2010, pp. 98–99.

41. Pager 2007.

42. This idea has been emphasized in the writings of William Julius Wilson (for example, Wilson 1996).

43. Riddle and Sinclair 2019.

44. Coates 2014; Brooks 2019.

45. Darity et al. 2018; see also Oliver and Shapiro 2006.

46. Pfeffer and Killewald 2018.

47. Katznelson 2005; Oliver and Shapiro 2006.

48. Pfeffer and Killewald 2018.

49. Seamster and Charron-Chénier 2017, p.199.

50. Rugh, Albright, and Massey 2015.

51. Espinosa et al. 2019, p. xiv; Darity et al. 2018, p. 7.

52. Pfeffer and Killewald 2018.

53. Coates 2014; Feagin 2014, chap. 9; Darity et al. 2018.

54. Bacon 2019.

55. Darity and Francis 2003.

56. Collins et al. 2019.

57. Chetty et al. 2018, p. 30.

58. Kozol 1991; Hochschild and Scovronick 2003.

59. Haskins 2014.

60. Beck 2019.

61. Alexander 2010.

62. Kohler-Hausmann 2018.

63. Coates 2014.

64. Passel and Cohn 2018.

65. Ibid.; Gonzales 2015.

66. Miroff 2018.

67. Bean, Brown, and Bachmeier 2015.

68. Alba et al. 2014.

69. Bean et al. 2012.

70. Manjoo 2019.

71. Waters 1990; Alba 1985.

72. National Academies of Sciences 2015; Lichter, Carmalt, and Qian 2011.

73. Goldin and Katz 2008.

Chapter 9. Toward a New Understanding of American Possibilities

1. Pastor 2018.

2. Blow 2018.

3. National Academies of Sciences 2015; Bloemraad 2006.

4. Strmic-Pawl 2016.

5. Lamont 2018.

6. Prewitt 2013; see also Hochschild, Weaver, and Burch 2012, chap. 1.

7. National Academies of Sciences 2015; Massey 2018.

8. Liebler et al. 2017.

9. Strmic-Pawl 2016.

10. Parker et al. 2015; Lopez, Gonzalez-Barrera, and López 2017.
11. Jacobson 2006; Glazer and Moynihan 1963.
12. Alba 1990; Waters 1990.
13. Jiménez 2010.
14. Kaufmann 2019a.
15. Hollinger 2006.
16. Alba and Reitz 2019.
17. Alba and Foner 2015; Drouhot and Nee 2019.
18. Lepore 2019; see also Judis 2018a.

BIBLIOGRAPHY

Abascal, Maria. 2015. "Us and Them: Black-White Relations in the Wake of His-panic Population Growth." *American Sociological Review* 80: 789–813.

Alba, Richard. 1985. *Italian Americans: Into the Twilight of Ethnicity*. Englewood Cliffs, NJ: Prentice-Hall.

———. 1990. *Ethnic Identity: The Transformation of White America*. New Haven, CT: Yale University Press.

———. 2005. "Bright vs. Blurred Boundaries: Second-Generation Assimilation and Exclusion in France, Germany, and the United States." *Ethnic and Racial Studies* 28: 20–49.

———. 2006. "Diversity's Blind Spot: Catholic Ethnics on the Faculties of Elite American Universities." *Ethnicities* 6: 562–79.

———. 2009. *Blurring the Color Line: The New Chance for a More Integrated America*. Cambridge, MA: Harvard University Press.

———. 2018. "What Majority-Minority Society? A Critical Analysis of the Census Bureau's Population Projections." *Socius* 4 (August). https://doi.org/10.1177/2378023118796932.

Alba, Richard, Brenden Beck, and Duygu Basaran Sahin. 2018. "The US Main-stream Expands—Again." *Journal of Ethnic and Migration Studies* 44: 99–117.

Alba, Richard, Glenn Deane, Nancy Denton, Ilir Disha, Brian McKenzie, and Jef-frey Napierala. 2014. "The Role of Immigrant Enclaves for Latino Residential Inequalities." *Journal of Ethnic and Migration Studies* 40: 1–20.

Alba, Richard, and Jan Willem Duyvendak. 2019. "What about the Mainstream? Assimilation in Super-Diverse Times." *Ethnic and Racial Studies* 42: 105–24.

Alba, Richard, and Nancy Foner. 2015. *Strangers No More: Immigration and the Challenges of Integration in North America and Western Europe*. Princeton, NJ: Princeton University Press.

———. 2017. "Immigration and the Geography of Polarization." *City and Community* 16: 239–43.

Alba, Richard, and Jennifer Holdaway, eds. 2013. *The Children of Immigrants at School: A Comparative Look at Integration in the United States and Western Europe*. New York: New York University Press.

Alba, Richard, and Tariqul Islam. 2009. "The Case of the Disappearing Mexican Americans: An Ethnic-Identity Mystery." *Population Research and Policy Review* 28: 109–21.

Alba, Richard, Tomás Jiménez, and Helen Marrow. 2014. "Mexican Americans as a Paradigm for Contemporary Intergroup Heterogeneity." *Ethnic and Racial Studies* 37: 446–66.

Alba, Richard, Philip Kasinitz, and Mary Waters. 2011. "The Children Are (Mostly) Alright: Second-Generation Assimilation: Comments on Haller, Portes, and Lynch." *Social Forces* 89: 763–73.

Alba, Richard, and Victor Nee. 2003. *Remaking the American Mainstream: Assimilation and Contemporary Immigration*. Cambridge, MA: Harvard University Press.

Alba, Richard, and Jeffrey Reitz. 2019. "The Significance of Mixed Family Backgrounds for Mainstream Integration in Canada." *Journal of Ethnic and Migration Studies* (October 30). https://doi.org/10.1080/1369183X.2019.1654162.

Alba, Richard, Rubén Rumbaut, and Karen Marotz. 2005. "A Distorted Nation: Perceptions of Racial/Ethnic Group Sizes and Attitudes toward Immigrants and Other Minorities." *Social Forces* 84: 901–20.

Alba, Richard, Jennifer Sloan and Jessica Sperling. 2011. "The Integration Imperative: The Children of Low-Status Immigrants in the Schools of Wealthy Societies." *Annual Review of Sociology* 37: 395–416.

Alba, Richard, and Guillermo Yrizar Barbosa. 2016. "Room at the Top? Minority Mobility and the Transition to Demographic Diversity in the US." *Ethnic and Racial Studies* 39: 917–38.

Alexander, Michelle. 2010. *The New Jim Crow: Mass Incarceration in an Age of Colorblindness*. New York: New Press.

Allport, Gordon. 1954. *The Nature of Prejudice*. Garden City, NY: Doubleday.

Amadeo, Kimberly. 2019. "US Military Budget, Its Components, Challenges, and Growth." *The Balance* (April 22). https://www.thebalance.com/u-s-military-budget-components-challenges-growth-3306320.

Anderson, Elijah. 2011. *The Cosmopolitan Canopy: Race and Civility in Everyday Life*. New Haven, CT: Yale University Press.

Anderson, Margo. 2002. "Counting by Race: The Antebellum Legacy." In *The New Race Question: How the Census Counts Multiracial Individuals*, edited by Joel Perlmann and Mary C. Waters. New York: Russell Sage Foundation.

Anderson, Margo, and Stephen Fienberg. 1999. *Who Counts? The Politics of Census-Taking in Contemporary America*. New York: Russell Sage Foundation.

Anglin, Andrew. 2015. "Jew Explains That Coming White Minority Doesn't Matter Because Non-Whites 'Look White to Me.'" *The Daily Stormer* (June 15), https://dailystormer.name/jew-explains-that-coming-white-minority-doesnt-matter-because-non-whites-looks-white-to-me/ (webpage no longer available).

Ashkenas, Jeremy, Haeyoun Park, and Adam Pearce. 2017. "Even with Affirmative Action, Blacks and Hispanics Are More Underrepresented at Top Colleges than 35 Years Ago." *New York Times* (August 24).

Bacon, Perry, Jr. 2019. "What Americans Think about Reparations and Other Race-Related Questions." *FiveThirtyEight* (February 28).

Bean, Frank, Susan Brown, and James Bachmeier. 2015. *Parents without Papers: The Progress and Pitfalls of Mexican American Integration*. New York: Russell Sage Foundation.

Bean, Frank, Susan Brown, James Bachmeier, Zoya Gubernskaya, and Christopher
    Smith. 2012. "Luxury, Necessity, and Anachronistic Workers: Does the United
    States Need Unskilled Immigrant Labor?" *American Behavioral Scientist* 56:
    1008–28.

Beck, Brenden. 2019. "The Decline of Broken Windows Policing." Working paper.
    Gainesville: University of Florida, Department of Sociology and Criminology
    and Law.

Blauner, Robert. 1972. *Racial Oppression in America*. New York: Harper & Row.

Bloemraad, Irene. 2006. *Becoming a Citizen: Incorporating Immigrants and Refu-
    gees in the United States and Canada*. Berkeley: University of California Press.

Blow, Charles. 2018. "White Extinction Anxiety." *New York Times* (June 24).

Blumer, Herbert. 1958. "Race Prejudice as a Sense of Group Position." *Pacific Socio-
    logical Review* 1: 3–7.

Bobo, Lawrence. 1999. "Prejudice as Group Position: Microfoundations of a Socio-
    logical Approach to Racism and Race Relations." *Journal of Social Issues* 55:
    445–72.

Bobo, Lawrence, James Kluegel, and Ryan Smith. 1997. "Laissez-Faire Racism:
    The Crystallization of a Kinder, Gentler, Antiblack Racism." In *Racial Attitudes
    in the 1990s: Continuity and Change*, edited by Steven Touch and Jack Martin.
    Westport, CT: Praeger.

Bonilla-Silva, Eduardo. 1997. "Rethinking Racism: Toward a Structural Interpreta-
    tion." *American Sociological Review* 62: 465–80.

———. 2004. "From Bi-racial to Tri-racial: Towards a New System of Racial Strati-
    fication in the USA." *Ethnic and Racial Studies* 27: 931–50.

———. 2018. *Racism without Racists: Color-Blind Racism and the Persistence of
    Racial Inequality in America*. Lanham, MD: Rowman & Littlefield.

Brodkin, Karen. 1998. *How Jews Became White Folks and What That Says about
    Race in America*. New Brunswick, NJ: Rutgers University Press.

Brooks, David. 2019. "The Case for Reparations: A Slow Convert to the Cause."
    New York Times (March 7).

Brown, Rupert. 1995. *Prejudice: Its Social Psychology*. Malden, MA: Wiley/
    Blackwell.

Brown, Susan. 2007. "Delayed Spatial Assimilation: Multi-Generational Incorpora-
    tion of the Mexican-Origin Population in Los Angeles." *City and Community*
    6: 193–209.

Brubaker, Rogers. 2016. "The Dolezal Affair: Race, Gender, and the Micropolitics
    of Identity." *Ethnic and Racial Studies* 39: 414–48.

Buchanan, Patrick. 2001. *The Death of the West: How Dying Populations and Immi-
    grant Invasions Imperil Our Culture and Civilization*. New York: St. Martin's Press.

Bump, Philip. 2017. "Places That Backed Trump Skewed Poor; Voters Who Backed
    Trump Skewed Wealthier." *Washington Post* (December 29).

Bureau of Labor Statistics. 2017. "Estimating the US Labor Share." *Monthly Labor
    Review* (February).

Case, Anne, and Angus Deaton. 2017. "Mortality and Morbidity in the 21st Century."
    Brookings Papers on Economic Activity (Spring).

Cauchon, Dennis, and Paul Overberg. 2012. "Minorities Are Now a Majority of Births; Census Shows How Fast the Nation Is Changing." *USA Today* (May 17).

Cherlin, Andrew. 2014. *Labor's Love Lost: The Rise and Fall of the Working-Class Family in America*. New York: Russell Sage Foundation.

———. 2019. "In the Shadow of Sparrows Point: Racialized Labor in the White and Black Working Classes." New York: Russell Sage Foundation (October 22). https://www.russellsage.org/sites/default/files/In%20the%20Shadow%20of%20Sparrows%20Point.pdf.

Chetty, Raj, John Friedman, Emmanuel Saez, Nicholas Turner, and Danny Yagan. 2017. "Mobility Report Cards: The Role of Colleges in Intergenerational Mobility." Working Paper 23618. Cambridge, MA: National Bureau of Economic Research (July).

Chetty, Raj, David Grusky, Maximilian Hell, Nathan Hendren, Robert Manduca, and Jimmy Narang. 2016. "The Fading American Dream: Trends in Absolute Income Mobility since 1940." Working Paper 22910. Cambridge, MA: National Bureau of Economic Research (December).

Chetty, Raj, Nathaniel Herndon, Maggie Jones, and Sonja Porter. 2018. "Race and Economic Opportunity in the United States: An Intergenerational Perspective." Working Paper 24441 Cambridge, MA: National Bureau of Economic Research (March).

Childs, Erica Chito. 2005. *Navigating Interracial Borders: Black-White Couples and Their Social Worlds*. New Brunswick, NJ: Rutgers University Press.

Coates, Ta-Nehisi. 2014. "The Case for Reparations." *Atlantic* (June).

Cohn, D'Vera. 2010. "Census History: Counting Hispanics." Washington, DC: Pew Research Center (March 3).

———. 2016. "It's Official: Minority Babies Are the Majority among the Nation's Infants, but Only Just." Washington, DC: Pew Research Center (June 23).

_____. 2017. "Seeking Better Data on Hispanics, Census Bureau May Change How It Asks about Race." Washington, DC: Pew Research Center (April 20).

Cohn, Nate. 2017. "A 2016 Review: Turnout Wasn't the Driver of Clinton's Defeat." *New York Times* (March 28).

Colby, Sandra, and Jennifer Ortman. 2015. "Projections of the Size and Composition of the US Population: 2014 to 2060." *Current Population Reports* P25–1143 (March). Washington, DC: US Census Bureau.

Coleman, David. 2006. "Immigration and Ethnic Change in Low-Fertility Countries: A Third Demographic Transition." *Population and Development Review* 32: 401–46.

Collins, Chuck, Darrick Hamilton, Dedrick Asante-Muhammad, and Josh Hoxie. 2019. "Ten Solutions to Bridge the Racial Wealth Divide." Washington, DC: Institute for Policy Studies (April).

Cooper, Michael. 2012. "Census Officials, Citing Increasing Diversity, Say US Will Be a 'Plurality Nation.'" *New York Times* (December 12).

Corak, Miles. 2013. "Income Inequality, Equality of Opportunity, and Intergenerational Mobility." *Journal of Economic Perspectives* 27: 79–102.

Covello, Leonard. 1972. *The Social Background of the Italo-American School Child*. Totowa, NJ: Rowman & Littlefield.

Craig, Maureen, and Jennifer Richeson. 2014. "On the Precipice of a 'Majority-Minority' America: Perceived Status Threat from the Racial Demographic Shift Affects White Americans' Political Ideology." *Psychological Science* 25: 1189–97.

Craig, Maureen, Julian Rucker, and Jennifer Richeson. 2018. "Racial and Political Dynamics of an Approaching 'Majority-Minority' United States." *Annals of the American Academy of Political and Social Science* 677: 204–14.

Cressey, Donald. 1969. *Theft of the Nation: The Structure and Operations of Organized Crime in America*. New York: Harper & Row.

Crowder, Kyle, Matthew Hall, and Stewart Tolnay. 2011. "Neighborhood Immigration and Native Out-migration." *American Sociological Review* 76: 25–47.

Crowell, Amber, and Mark Fossett. 2018. "White and Latino Locational Attainments: Assessing the Role of Race and Resources in US Metropolitan Residential Segregation." *Sociology of Race and Ethnicity* 4: 491–507.

DaCosta, Kimberley McClain. 2007. *Making Multiracials: State, Family, and Market in the Redrawing of the Color Line*. Stanford, CA: Stanford University Press.

Darity, William, Jr., and Dania Francis. 2003. "The Economics of Reparations." *American Economic Review* 93: 326–29.

Darity, William, Jr., Darrick Hamilton, Mark Paul, Alan Aja, Anne Price, Antonio Moore, and Caterina Chiopris. 2018. "What We Get Wrong about Closing the Racial Wealth Gap." Durham, NC: Duke University, Samuel DuBois Cook Center on Social Equity (April).

Davenport, Lauren. 2016. "The Role of Gender, Class, and Religion in Biracial Americans' Racial Labeling Decisions." *American Sociological Review* 81: 57–84.

Day, Jennifer Cheeseman. 1993. "Population Projections of the United States, by Age, Sex, Race, and Hispanic Origin: 1993 to 2050." *Current Population Reports* P25–1104. Washington, DC: US Bureau of the Census.

Desilver, Drew. 2018. "For Most US Workers, Real Wages Have Barely Budged in Decades." Washington, DC: Pew Research Center (August 7).

Dinnerstein, Leonard. 1994. *Antisemitism in America*. New York: Oxford University Press.

Dobbin, Frank. 2009. *Inventing Equal Opportunity*. Princeton, NJ: Princeton University Press.

Donovan, Sarah, and David Bradley. 2018. "Real Wage Trends, 1979 to 2017." Washington, DC: Congressional Research Service (March 15). https://fas.org/sgp/crs/misc/R45090.pdf.

Dowling, Julie. 2014. *Mexican Americans and the Question of Race*. Austin: University of Texas Press.

Drouhot, Lucas, and Victor Nee. 2019. "Assimilation and the Second Generation in Europe and America: Blending and Segregating Dynamics between Immigrants and Natives." *Annual Review of Sociology* 45: 177–99.

Du Bois, W. E. B. 1903. *The Souls of Black Folk*. New York: New American Library.

Duncan, Brian, Jeffrey Grogger, Ana Sofia Leon, and Stephen Trejo. 2020. "New Evidence of Generational Progress for Mexican Americans." *Labour Economics* 62. https://doi.org/10.1016/j.labeco.2019.101771.

Duncan, Brian and Stephen Trejo. 2017. "The Complexity of Immigrant Generations: Implications for Assessing the Socioeconomic Integration of Hispanics and Asians," *ILR Review* 70 : 1146–75.

———. 2018. "Identifying the Later-Generation Descendants of US Immigrants: Issues Arising from Selective Ethnic Attrition." *Annals of the American Academy of Political and Social Science* 677: 131–38.

Duncan, Greg, and Richard Murnane. 2011. "Enrichment Expenditures on Children, 1972–2006." In *Whither Opportunity: Rising Inequality, Schools, and Children's Life Chances*, edited by Greg Duncan and Richard Murnane. New York: Russell Sage Foundation.

Duyvendak, Jan Willem. 2011. *The Politics of Home: Nostalgia and Belonging in Western Europe and the United States*. Basingstoke, UK: Palgrave Macmillan.

Edmond, Charlotte. 2017. "These Rich Countries Have High Levels of Child Poverty." Cologny-Geneva, Switzerland: World Economic Forum (June 28).

Emeka, Amon. 2019. "'Just Black' or Not 'Just Black'? Ethnic Attrition in the Nigerian-American Second Generation." *Ethnic and Racial Studies* 42: 272–90.

Emeka, Amon, and Jody Agius Vallejo. 2011. "Non-Hispanics with Latin American Ancestry: Assimilation, Race, and Identity among Latin American Descendants in the US." *Social Science Research* 40: 1547–63.

Enos, Ryan. 2014. "Causal Effect of Intergroup Contact on Exclusionary Attitudes." *Proceedings of the National Academy of Sciences* (February 19).

Enten, Harry. 2016. "Trump Probably Did Better with Latino Voters than Romney Did." *FiveThirtyEight* (November 18).

Espinosa, Lorelle, Jonathan Turk, Morgan Taylor, and Hollie Chessman. 2019. *Race and Ethnicity in Higher Education: A Status Report*. Washington, DC: American Council on Education.

Feagin, Joe. 2014. *Racist America: Roots, Current Realities, and Future Reparations*, 3rd ed. New York: Routledge.

Fernández, Leticia, Sonya Porter, Sharon Ennis, and Renuka Bhaskar. 2018. "Factors That Influence Change in Hispanic Identification: Evidence from Linked Decennial Census and American Community Survey Data." Report CES 18–45 (October). Washington, DC: US Census Bureau.

Fischer, Claude, and Michael Hout. 2006. *Century of Difference: How America Changed in the Last One Hundred Years*. New York: Russell Sage Foundation.

Fishman, Sylvia Barack. 2004. *Double or Nothing? Jewish Families and Mixed Marriage*. Hanover, NH: Brandeis University Press.

Fitzgerald, F. Scott. 1925. *The Great Gatsby*. New York: Charles Scribner's Sons.

Foner, Nancy. 2000. *From Ellis Island to JFK: New York's Two Great Waves of Immigration*. New Haven, CT: Yale University Press.

Fowler, Matthew, Vladimir Medenica, and Cathy Cohen. 2017. "Why 41 Percent of White Millennials Voted for Trump." "The Monkey Cage," *Washington Post* (December 15).

Fox, Liana. 2018. "The Supplemental Poverty Measure: 2017." Report P60–265 (September 12). Washington, DC: US Census Bureau.

Frederickson, George. 2003. *Racism: A Short History*. Princeton, NJ: Princeton University Press.

Freedman, Samuel. 1996. *The Inheritance: How Three Families and America Moved from Roosevelt to Reagan and Beyond*. New York: Simon & Schuster.

Frey, William. 2018a. *Diversity Explosion: How New Racial Demographics Are Remaking America*. Washington, DC: Brookings Institution.

———. 2018b. "The US Will Become 'Minority White' in 2045, Census Projects." Washington, DC: Brookings Institution (March 14).

———. 2018c. "US White Population Declines and Generation 'Z-Plus' Is Minority White, Census Shows." Washington, DC: Brookings Institution (June 22).

Friedman, Samantha. 2008. "Do Declines in Residential Segregation Mean Stable Neighborhood Racial Integration in Metropolitan America? A Research Note." *Social Science Research* 37: 920–33.

Gabriel, Ryan, and Amy Spring. 2019. "Neighborhood Diversity, Neighborhood Affluence: An Analysis of Neighborhood Destination Choices of Mixed-Race Couples with Children." *Demography* 56: 1051–73.

Gans, Herbert. 1967. *The Levittowners: Ways of Life and Politics in a New Suburban Community*. New York: Pantheon.

———. 1979. "Symbolic Ethnicity: The Future of Ethnic Groups and Cultures in America." *Ethnic and Racial Studies* 2: 1–20.

———. 1982. *The Urban Villagers: Group and Class in the Life of Italian-Americans*. New York: Free Press.

———. 1999. "The Possibility of a New Racial Hierarchy in the Twenty-First Century United States." In *The Cultural Territories of Race: Black and White Boundaries,* edited by Michèle Lamont. Chicago and New York: University of Chicago Press and Russell Sage Foundation.

———. 2012. "'Whitening' and the Changing American Racial Hierarchy." *Du Bois Review* 9: 267–79.

Garcia, Emma, and Elaine Weiss. 2017. "Educational Inequalities at the School Starting Gate." Washington, DC: Economic Policy Institute (September 27).

Gerstle, Gary. 2001. *American Crucible: Race and Nation in the Twentieth Century*. Princeton, NJ: Princeton University Press.

Gest, Justin. 2016. *The New Minority: White Working Class Politics in an Age of Immigration and Inequality*. New York: Oxford University Press.

Gibson, Campbell, and Kay Jung. 2005. "Historical Census Statistics on Population Totals by Race, 1790 to 1990, and by Hispanic Origin, 1970 to 1990 for Large Cities and Other Urban Places in the United States." Working Paper 76. Washington, DC: US Census Bureau, Population Division.

Gitlin, Todd. 2018. "The Great Race Panic." *Dissent* (November 16). https://www.dissentmagazine.org/blog/the-great-race-panic.

Glazer, Nathan. 1992. "Is Assimilation Dead?" *Annals of the American Academy of Political and Social Science* 530(1): 122–36.

Glazer, Nathan, and Daniel Patrick Moynihan. 1963. *Beyond the Melting Pot: The Negroes, Puerto Ricans, Jews, Italians, and Irish of New York City.* Cambridge, MA: MIT Press.

Golash-Boza, Tanya. 2006. "Dropping the Hyphen? Becoming Latino(a) American through Racialized Assimilation." *Social Forces* 85: 27–55.

Golash-Boza, Tanya, and William Darity Jr. 2006. "Latino Racial Choices: The Effects of Skin Colour and Discrimination on Latinos' and Latinas' Racial Self-Identifications." *Ethnic and Racial Studies* 31: 899–934.

Goldin, Claudia, and Lawrence Katz. 2008. *The Race between Education and Technology.* Cambridge, MA: Harvard University Press.

Goldstein, Joshua. 1999. "Kinship Networks That Cross Racial Lines: The Exception or the Rule?" *Demography* 36: 399–407.

Goldstein, Sidney. 1969. "Socioeconomic Differentials among Religious Groups in the United States." *American Journal of Sociology* 74: 712–31.

Gonyea, Don. 2017. "Majority of White Americans Say They Believe Whites Face Discrimination." National Public Radio (October 24).

Gonzales, Roberto. 2015. *Lives in Limbo: Undocumented and Coming of Age in America.* Berkeley: University of California Press.

Gordon, Milton. 1964. *Assimilation in American Life.* New York: Oxford University Press.

Grant, Madison. 1916. *The Passing of the Great Race; Or, The Racial Basis of European History.* New York: Charles Scribner's Sons.

Gratton, Brian, and Myron Gutmann. 2006. "Hispanic Population." In *Historical Statistics of the United States,* millennial edition. New York: Cambridge University Press.

Greeley, Andrew. 1971. *Why Can't They Be Like Us? America's White Ethnic Groups.* New York: E. P. Dutton.

Greeley, Andrew, and Peter Rossi. 1966. *The Education of Catholic Americans.* Chicago: Aldine.

Guglielmo, Thomas. 2003. *White on Arrival: Italians, Race, Color, and Power in Chicago, 1890–1945.* New York: Oxford University Press.

Hall, Matthew, and Kyle Crowder. 2015. "Native Out-Migration and Neighborhood Immigration in New Destinations." *Demography* 51: 2179–2202.

Hall, Matthew, John Iceland, and Youngmin Yi. 2019. "Racial Separation at Home and Work: Segregation in Residential and Workplace Settings." *Population Research and Policy Review* 38: 671–94.

Hall, Matthew, Laura Tach, and Barrett Lee. 2016. "Trajectories of Ethnoracial Diversity in American Communities, 1980–2010." *Population and Development Review* 42: 271–97.

Haller, William, Alejandro Portes, and Scott Lynch. 2011. "Dreams Fulfilled and Shattered: Determinants of Segmented Assimilation in the Second Generation." *Social Forces* 89: 733–62.

Hamilton, Tod. 2019. *Immigration and the Remaking of Black America*. New York: Russell Sage Foundation.

Harris, David, and Jeremiah Joseph Sim. 2002. "Who Is Multiracial? Assessing the Complexity of Lived Race." *American Sociological Review* 67: 614–27.

Haskins, Anna. 2014. "Unintended Consequences: Effects of Parental Incarceration on Child School Readiness and Later Special Education Placement." *Sociological Science* 1: 141–58.

Herberg, Will. 1960. *Protestant-Catholic-Jew*. New York: Anchor.

Higham, John. 1970. *Strangers in the Land: Patterns of American Nativism, 1860–1925*. New York: Atheneum.

Hirschman, Charles, and Ellen Kraly. 1990. "Racial and Ethnic Inequality in the United States, 1940 and 1950: The Impact of Geographic Location and Human Capital." *International Migration Review* 24: 4–33.

Hixson, Lindsay, Bradford Hepler, and Myoung Ouk Kim. 2012. "The Native Hawaiian and Other Pacific Islander Population: 2010." *Census Briefs* (May). Washington, DC: US Census Bureau.

Hochschild, Arlie. 2016. *Strangers in Their Own Land: Anger and Mourning on the American Right*. New York: New Press.

Hochschild, Jennifer, and Nathan Scovronick. 2003. *The American Dream and the Public Schools*. New York: Oxford University Press.

Hochschild, Jennifer, Vesla Weaver, and Traci Burch. 2012. *Creating a New Racial Order: How Immigration, Multiracialism, Genomics, and the Young Can Remake Race in America*. Princeton, NJ: Princeton University Press.

Hofstadter, Richard. 1965. *The Paranoid Style in American Politics*. New York: Alfred A. Knopf.

Hollinger, David. 1996. "Jewish Intellectuals and the De-Christianization of American Public Culture in the Twentieth Century." In *Science, Jews, and Secular Culture: Studies in Mid-Twentieth-Century Intellectual History*. Princeton, NJ: Princeton University Press.

———. 2006. *Postethnic America: Beyond Multiculturalism*. New York: Basic Books.

Hout, Michael. 1988. "More Universalism, Less Structural Mobility: The American Occupational Structure in the 1980s." *American Sociological Review* 93: 1358–1400.

Hsu, Hua. 2009. "The End of White America?" *Atlantic* (January/February).

———. 2016. "White Plight?" *New Yorker* (July 25).

Huang, Jon, Samuel Jacoby, Michael Strickland, and K. K. Rebecca Lai. 2016. "Election 2016: Exit Polls." *New York Times* (November 8). https://www.nytimes.com/interactive/2016/11/08/us/politics/election-exit-polls.html.

Humes, Karen, Nicholas Jones, and Roberto Ramirez. 2011. "Overview of Race and Hispanic Origin: 2010." *2010 Census Briefs* (March). Washington, DC: US Census Bureau.

Hunt, Darnell, Ana-Christina Ramón, Michael Tran, Amberia Sargent, and Debanjan Roychoudhury. 2018. *Hollywood Diversity Report 2018: Five Years of Progress and Missed Opportunities*. Los Angeles: UCLA College of Social Sciences.

Iceland, John. 2009. *Where We Live Now: Immigration and Race in the United States*. Berkeley, CA: University of California Press.

———. 2017. *Race and Ethnicity in America*. Oakland: University of California Press.

Ignatiev, Noel. 1995. *How the Irish Became White*. New York: Routledge.

Imoagene, Onoso. 2017. *Beyond Expectations: Second-Generation Nigerians in the United States and Britain*. Berkeley: University of California Press.

Jackson, Kenneth. 1985. *Crabgrass Frontier: The Suburbanization of the United States*. New York: Oxford University Press.

Jacobson, Matthew Frye. 1998. *Whiteness of a Different Color: European Immigrants and the Alchemy of Race*. Cambridge, MA: Harvard University Press.

———. 2006. *Roots, Too: White Ethnic Revival in Post–Civil Rights America*. Cambridge, MA: Harvard University Press.

Jardina, Ashley. 2019. *White Identity Politics*. Cambridge: Cambridge University Press.

Jiménez, Tomás. 2010. *Replenished Ethnicity: Mexican Americans, Immigration, and Ethnicity*. Berkeley: University of California Press.

———. 2017. *The Other Side of Assimilation: How Immigrants Are Changing American Life*. Oakland: University of California Press.

Jones, Robert, Daniel Cox, Rob Griffin, Maxine Najle, Molly Fisch-Friedman, and Alex Vandermass-Peeler. 2018. "Partisan Polarization Dominates Trump Era: Findings from the 2018 American Values Survey." Washington, DC: Public Religion Research Institute (October 29).

Judis, John. 2018a. *The Nationalist Revival: Trade, Immigration, and the Revolt against Globalization*. New York: Columbia Global Reports.

———. 2018b. "It's the Economies, Stupid." *Washington Post* (November 29).

Jung, Moon-Kie. 2009. "The Racial Unconscious of Assimilation Theory." *Du Bois Review* 6: 375–95.

Kao, Grace, Kara Joyner, and Kelly Balistreri. 2019. *Interracial Friendships and Romantic Relationships from Adolescence to Adulthood*. New York: Russell Sage Foundation.

Kao, Grace, and Marta Tienda. 1995. "Optimism and Achievement: The Educational Performance of Immigrant Youth." *Social Science Quarterly* 76: 1–19.

Karabel, Jerome. 2005. *The Chosen: The Hidden History of Admission and Exclusion at Harvard, Yale, and Princeton*. New York: Houghton Mifflin Harcourt.

Kasinitz, Philip, John Mollenkopf, Mary Waters, and Jennifer Holdaway. 2008. *Inheriting the City: The Children of Immigrants Come of Age*. New York and Cambridge, MA: Russell Sage Foundation and Harvard University Press.

Katznelson, Ira. 2005. *When Affirmative Action Was White: An Untold History of Racial Inequality in Twentieth-Century America*. New York: W. W. Norton.

Kaufmann, Eric. 2019a. *Whiteshift: Populism, Immigration, and the Future of White Majorities*. New York: Abrams.

———. 2019b. "Americans Are Divided by Their Views on Race, Not Race Itself." *New York Times* (March 18).

Kennedy, Ruby Jo Reeves. 1944. "Single or Triple Melting Pot? Intermarriage Trends in New Haven, 1870–1940." *American Journal of Sociology* 49: 331–39.

Klein, Ezra. 2018. "White Threat in a Browning America," *Vox* (July 30).

Kohler-Hausmann, Issa. 2018. *Misdemeanorland: Criminal Courts and Social Control in an Age of Broken Windows Policing.* Princeton, NJ: Princeton University Press.

Kozol, Jonathan. 1991. *Savage Inequalities: Children in America's Schools.* New York: Crown.

KQED News. 2018. "Racial Resentment and White Cultural Anxiety Fuel Support of President Trump, Studies Find," hosted by Mina Kim (July 13).

Krivo, Lauren, Ruth Peterson, and Danielle Kuhl. 2009. "Segregation, Racial Structure, and Neighborhood Violent Crime." *American Journal of Sociology* 114: 1765–1802.

Krysan, Maria, and Kyle Crowder. 2017. *Cycle of Segregation: Social Processes and Residential Segregation.* New York: Russell Sage Foundation.

Lamont, Michèle. 2018. "Addressing Recognition Gaps: Destigmatization and the Reduction of Inequality." *American Sociological Review* 83: 419–44.

Lavin, David, Paul Attewell, and Thurston Domina. 2009. *Passing the Torch: Does Higher Education for the Disadvantaged Pay Off across the Generations?* New York: Russell Sage Foundation.

Lee, Jennifer, and Frank Bean. 2010. *The Diversity Paradox: Immigration and the Color Line in Twenty-First Century America.* New York: Russell Sage Foundation.

Lee, Jennifer, Karthick Ramakrishnan, and Janelle Wong. 2018. "Accurately Counting Asian Americans Is a Civil Rights Issue." *Annals of the American Academy of Political and Social Science* 677: 191–202.

Lee, Jennifer, and Min Zhou. 2015. *The Asian-American Achievement Paradox.* New York: Russell Sage Foundation.

Le Gall, Josiane, and Deirdre Meintel. 2015. "Normalizing Plural Identities as a Path to Social Integration." *Annals of the American Academy of Political and Social Science* 662: 112–28.

Lepore, Jill. 2019. *This America: The Case for the Nation.* New York: Liveright Publishing.

Levy, Morris, and Dowell Myers. 2018. "Forecasts and Frames: Narratives about Rising Racial Diversity and the Political Attitudes of US Whites." Los Angeles: University of Southern California (May 1). https://dornsife.usc.edu/assets /sites/741/docs/forecasts_and_frames_wp_5-1-18.pdf.

Li, Wei. 2009. *Ethnoburb: The New Ethnic Community in Urban America.* Honolulu: University of Hawai'i Press.

Lichter, Daniel, Julie Carmalt, and Zhenchao Qian. 2011. "Immigration and Intermarriage among Hispanics: Crossing Racial and Generational Boundaries." *Sociological Forum* 26: 241–64.

Lichter, Daniel, Domenico Parisi, and Michael Taquino. 2015. "Toward a New Macro-Segregation? Decomposing Segregation Within and Between Metropolitan Cities and Suburbs." *American Sociological Review* 80: 843–73.

———. 2016. "Emerging Patterns of Hispanic Residential Segregation: Lessons from Rural and Small-Town America." *Rural Sociology* 81: 483–518.

Lichter, Daniel, and Zhenchao Qian. 2018. "Boundary Blurring? Racial Identification among the Children of Interracial Couples." *Annals of the American Academy of Political and Social Science* 677: 81–94.

Lieberson, Stanley. 1961. "A Societal Theory of Race and Ethnic Relations." *American Sociological Review* 26: 902–10.

———. 1980. *A Piece of the Pie: Blacks and White Immigrants since 1880*. Berkeley: University of California Press.

Liebler, Carolyn. 2018. "Counting America's First Peoples." *Annals of the American Academy of Political and Social Science* 677: 180–90.

Liebler, Carolyn, Sonya Porter, Leticia Fernandez, James Noon, and Sharon Ennis. 2017. "America's Churning Races: Race and Ethnicity Response Changes between Census 2000 and the 2010 Census." *Demography* 54: 259–84.

Lind, Michael. 1998. "The Beige and the Black." *New York Times Magazine* (August 16).

Livingston, Gretchen. 2017. "In US Metro Areas, Huge Variation in Intermarriage Rates." Washington, DC: Pew Research Center (May 18).

Livingston, Gretchen, and Anna Brown. 2017. "Intermarriage in the US 50 Years after *Loving v. Virginia*." Washington, DC: Pew Research Center (May 18).

Logan, John, and Brian Stults. 2011. "The Persistence of Segregation in the Metropolis: New Findings from the 2010 Census." Report of the US2010 Project (March 24). https://s4.ad.brown.edu/Projects/Diversity/Data/Report/report2.pdf.

Logan, John, and Charles Zhang. 2010. "Global Neighborhoods: New Pathways to Diversity and Separation." *American Journal of Sociology* 115: 1069–1109.

Lopez, David. 2008. "Whither the Flock? The Catholic Church and the Success of Mexicans in America." In *Immigration and Religion in America: Comparative and Historical Perspectives*, edited by Richard Alba, Albert Raboteau, and Josh DeWind. New York: New York University Press.

Lopez, German. 2017. "The Past Year of Research Has Made It Very Clear: Trump Won Because of Racial Resentment." *Vox* (December 15).

López, Ian Haney. [1996] 2006. *White by Law: The Legal Construction of Race*, revised and updated. New York: NYU Press.

Lopez, Mark Hugo, Ana Gonzalez-Barrera, and Gustavo López. 2017. "Latino Identity Fades across Generations as Immigrant Connections Fall Away." Washington, DC: Pew Research Center (December 20).

Macartney, Suzanne, Alemayehu Bishaw, and Kayla Fontenot. 2013. "Poverty Rates for Selected Detailed Race and Hispanic Groups by State and Place: 2007–2011." *American Community Survey Briefs* (February). Washington, DC: US Census Bureau.

Maddison, Angus. 2007. *Contours of the World Economy*. Oxford: Oxford University Press.

Manjoo, Farhad. 2019. "There's Nothing Wrong with Open Borders." *New York Times* (January 16).

Maraniss, David. 2019. *A Good American Family: The Red Scare and My Father*. New York: Simon & Schuster.

Marrow, Helen. 2011. *New Destination Dreaming: Immigration, Race, and Legal Status in the Rural American South*. Stanford, CA: Stanford University Press.

Massey, Douglas. 2018. "Finding the Lost Generation: Identifying Second-Generation Immigrants in Federal Statistics." *Annals of the American Academy of Political and Social Science* 677: 96–104.

Massey, Douglas, Camille Charles, Garvey Lundy, and Mary Fischer. 2003. *Source of the River: The Social Origins of Freshmen at America's Selective Colleges and Universities*. Princeton, NJ: Princeton University Press.

Massey, Douglas, and Nancy Denton. 1993. *American Apartheid: Segregation and the Making of the Underclass*. Cambridge, MA: Harvard University Press.

Massey, Douglas, Margarita Mooney, Kimberly Torres, and Camille Charles. 2007. "Black Immigrants and Black Natives Attending Selective Colleges and Universities in the United States." *American Journal of Education* 113: 243–71.

Massey, Douglas, and Jonathan Tannen. 2018. "Suburbanization and Segregation in the United States: 1970–2010." *Ethnic and Racial Studies* 41: 1594–1611.

McGreevey, John. 2003. *Catholicism and American Freedom: A History*. New York: W. W. Norton.

McManus, Patricia, and Lauren Apgar. 2019. "Parental Origins, Mixed Unions, and the Labor Supply of Second-Generation Women in the United States." *Demography* 56: 49–73.

Media Matters. 2013. "The 20 Most Racist Things Rush Limbaugh Has Ever Said." *AlterNet* (January 21). https://www.alternet.org/2013/01/20-most-racist-things-rush-limbaugh-has-ever-said/.

———. 2018. "Laura Ingraham: 'Massive Demographic Changes Have Been Foisted upon the American People, and They Are Changes That None of Us Ever Voted For, and Most of Us Don't Like.'" *Media Matters* (August 8).

Merton, Robert. 1941. "Intermarriage and Social Structure: Fact and Theory." *Psychiatry* 4: 361–74.

Mills, Charles. 1997. *The Racial Contract*. Ithaca, NY: Cornell University Press.

Miroff, Nick. 2018. "What Is TPS, and What Will Happen to the 200,000 Salvadorans Whose Status Is Revoked?" *Washington Post* (January 9).

Mitchell, Michael, Michael Leachman, Kathleen Masterson, and Samantha Waxman. 2018. "Unkept Promises: State Cuts to Higher Education Threaten Access and Equity." Washington, DC: Center on Budget and Policy Priorities (October 4).

Miyawaki, Michael. 2015. "Expanding Boundaries of Whiteness? A Look at the Marital Patterns of Part-White Multiracial Groups." *Sociological Forum* 30: 995–1016.

Mollenkopf, John, and Manuel Pastor. 2016. *Unsettled Americans: Metropolitan Context and Civic Leadership for Immigrant Integration*. Ithaca, NY: Cornell University Press.

Monnat, Shannon, and Warren Brown. 2017. "More than a Rural Revolt: Landscapes of Despair and the 2016 Presidential Election." *Journal of Rural Studies* 55: 227–36.

Montejano, David. 1986. *Anglos and Mexicans in the Making of Texas*. Austin: University of Texas Press.

Moore, Deborah Dash. 2004. *GI Jews: How World War II Changed a Generation*. Cambridge, MA: Harvard University Press.

Mora, G. Cristina. 2014. *Making Hispanics: How Activists, Bureaucrats, and Media Constructed a New American*. Chicago: University of Chicago Press.

Morello, Carol and Ted Melinik. 2012. "Census: Minority Babies Are Now Majority in the United States." *Washington Post* (May 17).

Morgan, Ivy, and Ary Amerikaner. 2018. "Funding Gaps 2018." Washington, DC: Education Trust (February 27).

Morning, Ann. 2017. "Race and Rachel Dolezal: An Interview." *Contexts* (Spring,).

Morning, Ann, and Aliya Saperstein. 2018. "The Generational Locus of Multiraciality and Its Implications for Racial Self-Identification." *Annals of the American Academy of Political and Social Science* 677: 57–68.

Mortenson, Thomas. 2012. "State Funding: A Race to the Bottom." Washington, DC: American Council on Education (Winter).

Murnane, Richard. 2013. "US High School Graduation Rates." *Journal of Economic Literature* 51: 370–422.

Murray, Charles. 2012. *Coming Apart: The State of White America, 1960–2010*. New York: Crown Forum.

Mutz, Diana. 2018. "Status Threat, Not Economic Hardship, Explains the 2016 Presidential Vote." *Proceedings of the National Academy of Sciences* (May 8).

Myers, Dowell. 2007. *Immigrants and Boomers: Forging a New Social Contract for the Future of America*. New York: Russell Sage Foundation.

Myers, Dowell, and Morris Levy. 2018. "Racial Population Projections and Reactions to Alternative News Accounts of Growing Diversity." *Annals of the American Academy of Political and Social Science* 677: 215–28.

National Academies of Sciences, Engineering, and Medicine. 2015. *The Integration of Immigrants into American Society*, edited by Mary C. Waters and Marisa Pineau. Washington, DC: National Academies Press.

———. 2019. *A Roadmap to Reducing Child Poverty*, edited by Greg Duncan and Suzanne Le Menestrel. Washington, DC: National Academies Press.

National Center for Educational Statistics. 2017. "Certificates and Degrees Conferred by Race/Ethnicity." In *The Condition of Education 2017*, edited by Joel McFarland et al. NCES 2017–144. Washington, DC: US Department of Education, NCES. https://nces.ed.gov/programs/coe/pdf/coe_svc.pdf.

Newman, Benjamin, and Yamil Velez. 2014. "Group Size versus Change? Assessing Americans' Perception of Local Immigration." *Political Research Quarterly* 67: 293–303.

Newsday. 2018. "The Biggest Box Office Hits of All Time." *Newsday* (August 24).

New York Times. 2019. "College Admissions Scandal: Your Questions Answered." *New York Times* (March 14).

Norris, Michele. 2018. "The Rising Anxiety of White America." *National Geographic* 233 (April).

Novak, Michael. 1972. *The Rise of the Unmeltable Ethnics*. New York: Macmillan.

Office of Civil Rights. 1997. "Standards for Maintaining, Collecting, and Presenting Federal Data on Race and Ethnicity." Washington, DC: US Department of the Interior (October 30). https://www.doi.gov/pmb/eeo/Data-Standards.

Office of Immigration Statistics. Various years. *Yearbook of Immigration Statistics*. Washington, DC: US Department of Homeland Security.

Office of Management and Budget. 1997. "Revision to the Standards for the Classification of Federal Data on Race and Ethnicity." *Federal Register Notice* (October 30). Washington, DC: OMB. https://www.whitehouse.gov/wp-content/uploads/2017/11/Revisions-to-the-Standards-for-the-Classification-of-Federal-Data-on-Race-and-Ethnicity-October30-1997.pdf.

———. 2000. "Guidance on Aggregation and Allocation of Data on Race for Use in Civil Rights Monitoring and Enforcement." *Bulletin* 00–02 (March 9). Washington, DC: The White House. https://obamawhitehouse.archives.gov/omb/bulletins_b00-02/.

Ogbu, John. 1978. *Minority Education and Caste: The American System in Cross-Cultural Perspective*. New York: Academic Press.

Oliver, Melvin, and Thomas Shapiro. 2006. *Black Wealth/White Wealth: A New Perspective on Racial Inequality*, 2nd ed. New York: Routledge.

Omi, Michael, and Howard Winant. 2015. *Racial Formation in the United States: From the 1960s to the 1990s*, 3rd ed. New York: Routledge & Kegan Paul.

Orfield, Gary, Erica Frankenberg, Jongyeon Ee, and Jennifer Ayscue. 2019. "Harming Our Common Future: America's Segregated Schools 65 Years after Brown." Los Angeles: UCLA, The Civil Rights Project (May 10). https://www.civilrightsproject.ucla.edu/research/k-12-education/integration-and-diversity/harming-our-common-future-americas-segregated-schools-65-years-after-brown/Brown-65-050919v4-final.pdf.

Organization for Economic Cooperation and Development. 2016. *PISA 2015 Results: Excellence and Equity in Education*, vol. 1. Paris: OECD Publishing.

Pager, Devah. 2007. *Marked: Race, Crime, and Finding Work in an Era of Mass Incarceration*. Chicago: University of Chicago Press.

Painter, Nell Irvin. 2010. *The History of White People*. New York: W. W. Norton.

Parisi, Domenico, Daniel Lichter, and Michael Taquino. 2015. "The Buffering Hypothesis: Growing Diversity and Declining Black-White Segregation in America's Cities, Suburbs, and Small Towns?" *Sociological Science* 2: 125–57.

———. 2019. "Remaking Metropolitan America? Residential Mobility and Racial Integration in the Suburbs." *Socius* 5: 1–18

Park, Robert Ezra, and Ernest W. Burgess. [1921] 1969. *Introduction to the Science of Sociology*. Chicago: University of Chicago Press.

Parker, Kim, Juliana Menasce Horowitz, Rich Morin, and Mark Hugo Lopez. 2015. *Multiracial in America: Proud, Diverse, and Growing in Numbers*. Washington, DC: Pew Research Center (June 11).

Passel, Jeffrey, and D'Vera Cohn. 2018. "US Unauthorized Immigrant Total Dips to Lowest Level in a Decade." Washington, DC: Pew Research Center (November 27).

Pastor, Manuel. 2018. *State of Resistance: What California's Dizzying Descent and Remarkable Resurgence Mean for America's Future.* New York: New Press.

Pedraza, Francisco, and Bryan Wilcox-Archuleta. 2017. "Did Latino Voters Actually Turn Out for Trump? Not Really." *Los Angeles Times* (January 11).

Perlmann, Joel. 2005. *Italians Then, Mexicans Now: Immigrant Origins and Second-Generation Progress, 1890–2000.* New York: Russell Sage Foundation.

———. 2011. "The Mexican American Second Generation in Census 2000: Education and Earnings." In Richard Alba and Mary C. Waters, *The Next Generation: Immigrant Youth in Comparative Perspective.* New York: New York University Press.

———. 2018. *America Classifies the Immigrants: From Ellis Island to the 2020 Census.* Cambridge, MA: Harvard University Press.

Perlmann, Joel, and Roger Waldinger. 1997. "Second Generation Decline? Children of Immigrants, Past and Present—A Reconsideration." *International Migration Review* 31: 893–922.

Perlmann, Joel, and Mary C. Waters, eds. 2002. *The New Race Question: How the Census Counts Multiracial Individuals.* New York: Russell Sage Foundation.

Pettigrew, Thomas, and Linda Tropp. 2006. "A Meta-Analytic Test of Intergroup Contact Theory." *Journal of Personality and Social Psychology* 90: 751–83.

———. 2008. "How Does Intergroup Contact Reduce Prejudice? Meta-Analytic Tests of Three Mediators." *European Journal of Social Psychology* 38: 922–34.

Pew Research Center. 2015. "What Census Calls Us: A Historical Timeline." Washington, DC: Pew Research Center (June 15).

———. 2019. "Sharp Rise in the Share of Americans Saying Jews Face Discrimination." Washington, DC: Pew Research Center (April 15).

Pfeffer, Fabian, and Alexandra Killewald. 2018. "Generations of Advantage: Multigenerational Correlations in Family Wealth." *Social Forces* 96: 1411–41.

Piketty, Thomas, and Emmanuel Saez. 2003. "Income Inequality in the United States, 1913–1998." *Quarterly Journal of Economics* 118: 1–38.

Piketty, Thomas, Emmanuel Saez, and Gabriel Zucman. 2018. "Distributional National Accounts: Methods and Estimates for the United States." *Quarterly Journal of Economics* 133: 553–609.

Porter, Eduardo. 2016. "Where Were Trump's Votes? Where the Jobs Weren't." *New York Times* (December 13).

Portes, Alejandro, and Rubén Rumbaut. 2001. *Legacies: The Story of the Immigrant Second Generation.* Berkeley: University of California Press.

Portes, Alejandro, and Min Zhou. 1993. "The New Second Generation: Segmented Assimilation and Its Variants." *Annals of the American Academy of Political and Social Science* 530: 74–96.

Pratt, Beverly, Lindsay Hixson, and Nicholas Jones. 2015. "Measuring Race and Ethnicity across the Decades: 1790–2010." Washington, DC: US Census Bureau. https://www.census.gov/data-tools/demo/race/MREAD_1790_2010.html.

President's Commission on Law Enforcement and Administration of Justice. 1967. *The Challenge of Crime in a Free Society: Task Force Report: Organized Crime.* Washington, DC: US Government Printing Office.

Prewitt, Kenneth. 2013. *What Is Your Race? The Census and Our Flawed Attempts to Classify Americans.* Princeton, NJ: Princeton University Press.

Public Religion Research Institute. 2018. "PRRI 2018 American Values Survey: September 17–October 1, 2018." Washington, DC: PRRI. https://www.prri.org/wp-content/uploads/2018/10/AVS-2018-Topline-COMBINED.pdf.

Putnam, Robert. 2007. "E Pluribus Unum: Diversity and Community in the Twenty-First Century." *Scandinavian Political Studies* 30: 137–74.

Quillian, Lincoln, and Mary Campbell. 2003. "Beyond Black and White: The Present and Future of Multiracial Friendship Segregation." *American Sociological Review* 68: 540–66.

Ramakrishnan, Karthick, and Farah Ahmad. 2014. "State of Asian Americans and Pacific Islanders Series: A Multifaceted Portrait of a Growing Population." Washington, DC: Center for American Progress (September).

Ray, Victor. 2019. "A Theory of Racialized Organizations." *American Sociological Review* 84: 26–53.

Ray, Victor Erik, Antonia Randolph, Megan Underhill, and David Luke. 2017. "Critical Race Theory, Afro-Pessimism, and Progress Narratives." *Sociology of Race and Ethnicity* 3: 147–58.

Reardon, Sean. 2011. "The Widening Achievement Gap between the Rich and the Poor: New Evidence and Possible Explanations." In *Whither Opportunity: Rising Inequality, Schools, and Children's Life Chances*, edited by Greg Duncan and Richard Murnane. New York: Russell Sage Foundation.

Reardon, Sean, and Kendra Bischoff. 2011. "Income Inequality and Income Segregation." *American Journal of Sociology* 116: 1092–1153.

Reardon, Sean, and Ann Owens. 2014. "60 Years after Brown: Trends and Consequences of School Segregation." *Annual Review of Sociology* 40: 199–218.

Reimers, David. 1992. *Still the Golden Door: The Third World Comes to America.* New York: Columbia University Press.

Riddle, Travis, and Stacey Sinclair. 2019. "Racial Disparities in School-Based Disciplinary Actions Are Associated with County-Level Rates of Racial Bias." *Proceedings of the National Academy of Sciences* (April 2).

Roberts, Sam. 2008. "In a Generation, Minorities May Be the US Majority." *New York Times* (August 13).

Rockquemore, Kerry Ann, and David L. Brunsma. 2008. *Beyond Black: Biracial Identity in America*, 2nd ed. Lanham, MD: Rowman & Littlefield.

Roediger, David. 1991. *The Wages of Whiteness: Race and the Making of the American Working Class.* New York: Verso.

———. 2005. *Working toward Whiteness: How America's Immigrants Became White; The Strange Journey from Ellis Island to the Suburbs.* New York: Basic Books.

Root, Maria. 1996. *The Multiracial Experience: Racial Borders as the New Frontier.* Thousand Oaks, CA: Sage Publications.

Rose, Stephen. 2018. "How Different Studies Measure Income Inequality in the US: Piketty and Company Are Not the Only Game in Town." Washington, DC: Urban Institute (December).

Roth, Wendy. 2012. *Race Migrations: Latinos and the Cultural Transformation of Race*. Stanford, CA: Stanford University Press.

Ruggles, Steven, Sarah Flood, Ronald Goeken, Josiah Grover, Erin Meyer, Jose Pacas, and Matthew Sobek. 2019. IPUMS USA: Version 9.0 (data set). Minneapolis, MN: IPUMS. https://doi.org/10.18128/D010.V9.0.

Rugh, Jacob, Len Albright, and Douglas Massey. 2015. "Race, Space, and Cumulative Disadvantage: A Case Study of the Subprime Lending Collapse." *Social Problems* 62: 186–218.

Sáenz, Rogelio, and Kenneth Johnson. 2016. "White Deaths Exceed Births in One-Third of US States." *Carsey Research National Issue Brief* 110 (Fall). Durham: University of New Hampshire, Casey School of Public Policy.

Saez, Emmanuel, and Gabriel Zucman. 2016. "Wealth Inequality since 1913: Evidence from Capitalized Income Tax Data." *Quarterly Journal of Economics* 131: 519–78.

———. 2019. "How Would a Progressive Wealth Tax Work? Evidence from the Economics Literature." Berkeley: University of California, Department of Economics (February 5). http://gabriel-zucman.eu/files/saez-zucman -wealthtaxobjections.pdf.

Scammon, Richard, and Ben Wattenberg. 1970. *The Real Majority: An Extraordinary Examination of the American Electorate*. New York: Coward-McCann.

Schaffner, Brian, Matthew Macwilliams, and Tatishe Nteta. 2018. "Understanding White Polarization in the 2016 Vote for President: The Sobering Role of Racism and Sexism." *Political Science Quarterly* 133: 9–34.

Schrag, Peter. 2010. *Not Fit for Our Society: Nativism and Immigration*. Berkeley: University of California Press.

Schuman, Howard, Charlotte Steeh, and Lawrence Bobo. 1985. *Racial Attitudes in America: Trends and Interpretations*. Cambridge, MA: Harvard University Press.

Seamster, Louise, and Raphaël Charron-Chénier. 2017. "Predatory Inclusion and Education Debt: Rethinking the Racial Wealth Gap." *Social Currents* 4: 199–207.

Semyonov, Moshe, Rebeca Raijman, Anat Yom Tov, and Peter Schmidt. 2004. "Population Size, Perceived Threat, and Exclusion: A Multiple-Indicators Analysis of Attitudes toward Foreigners in Germany." *Social Science Research* 33: 681–701.

Sentencing Project. N.d. "Criminal Justice Facts." https://www.sentencingproject .org/criminal-justice-facts/.

Serwer, Adam. 2018. "The White Nationalists Are Winning." *Atlantic* (August 10).

Shannon, Sarah, Christopher Uggen, Jason Schnittker, Melissa Thompson, Sara Wakefield, and Michael Massoglia. 2017. "The Growth, Scope, and Spatial Distribution of People with Felony Records in the United States, 1948–2010." *Demography* 54: 1795–1818.

Sharkey, Patrick. 2013. *Stuck in Place: Urban Neighborhoods and the End of Progress toward Racial Equality*. Chicago: University of Chicago Press.

———. 2014. "Spatial Segmentation and the Black Middle Class." *American Journal of Sociology* 119: 903–54.

Sides, John. 2017. "Race, Religion, and Immigration in 2016: How the Debate over American Identity Shaped the Election and What It Means for a Trump Presidency." Washington, DC: Democracy Fund, Voter Study Group (June). https://www.voterstudygroup.org/publication/race-religion-immigration-2016.

Sides, John, Michael Tesler, and Lynn Vavreck. 2018. *Identity Crisis: The 2016 Campaign and the Battle for the Meaning of America*. Princeton, NJ: Princeton University Press.

Silberman, Charles. 1985. *A Certain People: American Jews and Their Lives Today*. New York: Summit.

Singer, Audrey. 2015. "Metropolitan Immigrant Gateways Revisited, 2014." Washington, DC: Brookings Institution (December 1).

Skrentny, John. 2009. *The Minority Rights Revolution*. Cambridge, MA: Harvard University Press.

Smith, Stacy, Marc Choueiti, Katherine Pieper, Hannah Clark, Ariana Case, and Sylvia Villanueva. 2019. "Inclusion in the Recording Studio? Gender and Race/Ethnicity of Artists, Songwriters, and Producers across 700 Popular Songs from 2012–2018." Los Angeles: USC Annenberg Inclusion Initiative (February).

Song, Miri. 2017. *Multiracial Parents: Mixed Families, Generational Change, and the Future of Race*. New York: New York University Press.

———. 2019. "Is There Evidence of 'Whitening' for Asian/White Multiracial People in Britain?" *Journal of Ethnic and Migration Studies* (October 30). https://doi.org/10.1080/1369183X.2019.1654163.

South, Scott, Kyle Crowder, and Jeremy Pais. 2008. "Inter-Neighborhood Migration and Spatial Assimilation in a Multi-Ethnic World: Comparing Latinos, Blacks, and Anglos." *Social Forces* 87: 415–44.

———. 2011. "Metropolitan Structure and Neighborhood Attainment: Exploring Intermetropolitan Variation in Racial Residential Segregation." *Demography* 48: 1263–92.

Spickard, Paul. 1989. *Mixed Blood: Intermarriage and Ethnic Identity in Twentieth-Century America*. Madison: University of Wisconsin Press.

Stainback, Kevin, Corre Robinson, and Donald Tomaskovic-Devey. 2005. "Race and Workplace Integration: A Politically Mediated Process." *American Behavioral Scientist* 48: 1200–1228.

Stainback, Kevin, and Donald Tomaskovic-Devey. 2012. *Documenting Desegregation: Race and Gender Segregation in Private-Sector Employment since the Civil Rights Act*. New York: Russell Sage Foundation.

Staples, Brent. 2019. "How Italians Became 'White.'" *New York Times* (October 12).

Steinberg, Stephen. 1989. *The Ethnic Myth: Race, Ethnicity, and Class in America*. Boston: Beacon Press.

Steinfels, Peter. 2003. *A People Adrift: The Crisis of the Roman Catholic Church in America*. New York: Simon & Schuster.

Stirewalt, Chris. 2019. "Trump Stokes Racial Resentment to Hinder Biden's Rise." *Fox News Halftime Report* (May 28).

Stoddard, Lothrop. 1920. *The Rising Tide of Color against White World-Supremacy*. New York: Charles Scribner's Sons.

Strmic-Pawl, Hephzibah. 2016. *Multiracialism and Its Discontents: A Comparative Analysis of Asian-White and Black-White Multiracials*. Lanham, MD: Lexington Books.

Tax Policy Center. 2019. "Historical Highest Marginal Income Tax Rates." Washington, DC: Tax Policy Center (January 19). https://www.taxpolicycenter.org/statistics/historical-highest-marginal-income-tax-rates.

Telles, Edward, and Vilma Ortiz. 2008. *Generations of Exclusion: Mexican Americans, Assimilation, and Race*. New York: Russell Sage Foundation.

Telles, Edward, and Cristine Sue. 2019. *Durable Ethnicity: Mexican Americans and the Ethnic Core*. New York: Oxford University Press.

Tilly, Charles. 1998. *Durable Inequality*. Berkeley: University of California Press.

Tomaskovic-Devey, Donald, Martin Hällsten, and Dustin Avent-Holt. 2015. "Where Do Immigrants Fare Worse? Modeling Workplace Wage Gap Variation with Longitudinal Employer-Employee Data." *American Journal of Sociology* 120: 1095–1143.

Tran, Van. 2018. "Social Mobility across Immigrant Generations: Recent Evidence and Future Data Requirements." *Annals of the American Academy of Political and Social Science* 677: 105–18.

Tran, Van, Jennifer Lee, and Tiffany Huang. 2019. "Revisiting the Asian Second-Generation Advantage." *Ethnic and Racial Studies* 42: 2248–69.

Treitler, Vilna Bashi. 2013. *The Ethnic Project: Transforming Racial Fiction into Ethnic Factions*. Stanford, CA: Stanford University Press.

Tropp, Linda, Dina Okamoto, Helen Marrow, and Michael Jones-Correa. 2018. "How Contact Experiences Shape Welcoming: Perspectives from US-Born and Immigrant Groups." *Social Psychology Quarterly* 81: 23–47.

Trow, Martin. 1961. "The Second Transformation of American Secondary Education." *International Journal of Comparative Sociology* 2: 144–66.

Twine, France Windance, and Charles Gallagher. 2008. "The Future of Whiteness: A Map of the Third Wave." *Ethnic and Racial Studies* 31: 4–24.

US Census Bureau. 2012a. "The Great Migration, 1910–1970." Washington, DC: US Census Bureau (September 13). https://www.census.gov/dataviz/visualizations/020/.

———. 2012b. "US Census Bureau Projections Show a Slower Growing, Older, More Diverse Nation a Half Century from Now." Press release (December 12). https://www.census.gov/newsroom/releases/archives/population/cb12-243.html.

———. 2017. "2015 National Content Test: Race and Ethnicity Analysis Report: A New Design for the 21st Century." Washington, DC: US Census Bureau (February 28).

———. 2018a. "Older People Projected to Outnumber Children for First Time in US History." Press release (March 1; amended September 6).

———. 2018b. "2018 Census Test." Washington, DC: US Department of Commerce. https://www2.census.gov/programs-surveys/decennial/2020/program-management/memo-series/2020-memo-2018_02_questionnaire.pdf.

———. 2018c. "Methodology, Assumptions, Inputs for the 2017 Population Projections." Washington, DC: US Census Bureau (September).

US Department of Education. 2005. "10 Facts about K-12 Education Funding." Washington, DC: US Department of Education (June). https://www2.ed.gov /about/overview/fed/10facts/index.html?exp.

Valdez, Zulema, and Tanya Golash-Boza. 2017. "US Racial and Ethnic Relations in the Twenty-First Century." *Ethnic and Racial Studies* 40: 2181–209.

Valentino, Nicholas, Fabian Neuner, and L. Matthew Vandenbroek. 2018. "The Changing Norms of Racial Political Rhetoric and the End of Racial Priming." *Journal of Politics* 80: 757–71.

Vasquez, Jessica. 2011. *Mexican Americans across Generations: Immigrant Families, Racial Realities*. New York: New York University Press.

Vasquez-Tokos, Jessica. 2017. *Marriage Vows and Racial Choices*. New York: Russell Sage Foundation.

Vertovec, Steven. 2007. "Super-Diversity and Its Implications." *Ethnic and Racial Studies* 30: 1024–54.

Vespa, Jonathan, David Armstrong, and Lauren Medina. 2018. "Demographic Turning Points for the United States: Population Projections for 2020 to 2060." *Current Population Reports* P25–1144 (March). Washington, DC: US Bureau of the Census.

Waldinger, Roger. 1996. *Still the Promised City? African-Americans and New Immigrants in Postindustrial New York*. Cambridge, MA: Harvard University Press.

Waldman, Paul. 2016. "Why Did Trump Win? In Part Because Voter Turnout Plunged." *Washington Post* (November 10).

Wang, Hansi Lo. 2018. "2020 Census to Keep Racial, Ethnic Categories Used in 2010." National Public Radio (January 26).

Wang, Wanda. 2012. "The Rise of Intermarriage." Washington, DC: Pew Research Center (February 16).

Warikoo, Natasha. 2016. *The Diversity Bargain and Other Dilemmas of Race, Admissions, and Meritocracy at Elite Universities*. Chicago: University of Chicago Press.

Waters, Mary. 1990. *Ethnic Options: Choosing Identities in America*. Berkeley: University of California Press.

Waters, Mary, and Philip Kasinitz. 2014. "The War on Crime and the War on Immigrants: Racial and Legal Exclusion in the Twenty-First Century United States." In *Fear, Anxiety, and National Identity: Immigration and Belonging in North America and Western Europe*, edited by Nancy Foner and Patrick Simon. New York: Russell Sage Foundation.

Wazwaz, Noor. 2015. "It's Official: The US Is Becoming a Minority-Majority Nation." *US News & World Report* (July 6).

Weber, Max. 1968. *Economy and Society*. New York: Bedminster Press.

Western, Bruce, and Christopher Wildeman. 2009. "The Black Family and Mass Incarceration." *Annals of the American Academy of Political and Social Science* 621: 221–42.

Wetts, Rachel, and Robb Willer. 2018. "Privilege on the Precipice: Perceived Racial Status Threats Lead White Americans to Oppose Welfare Programs." *Social Forces* 97: 793–822.

White, Michael, and Jennifer Glick. 2009. *Achieving Anew: How New Immigrants Do in American Schools, Jobs, and Neighborhoods*. New York: Russell Sage Foundation.

Wikipedia. 2020a. "Racial Views of Donald Trump." Wikipedia (last updated February 7, 2020). https://en.wikipedia.org/wiki/Racial_views_of_Donald_Trump.

———. 2020b. "McCarthyism." Wikipedia (last updated February 5, 2020). http://en.wikipedia.org/wiki/McCarthyism.

———. 2020c. "Milton Berle." Wikipedia (last updated January 24, 2020). https://en.wikipedia.org/wiki/Milton_Berle.

Williams, Thomas Chatterton. 2019. "Shades of Meaning." *New York Times Magazine* (September 22).

Wills, Gary. 1998. "What Ever Happened to Politics? Washington Is Not Where It's At." *New York Times Magazine* (January 25).

Wilson, William Julius. 1987. *The Truly Disadvantaged: The Inner City, the Underclass, and Public Policy*. Chicago: University of Chicago Press.

———. 1996. *When Work Disappears: The New World of the Urban Poor*. New York: Alfred A. Knopf.

Wimmer, Andreas. 2008. "Elementary Strategies of Ethnic Boundary Making." *Ethnic and Racial Studies* 31: 1025–55.

Winant, Howard. 2002. *The World Is a Ghetto: Race and Democracy since World War II*. New York: Basic Books.

Wong, Cara. 2007. "'Little' and 'Big' Pictures in Our Heads: Race, Local Context, and Innumeracy about Racial Groups in the United States." *Public Opinion Quarterly* 71: 393–412.

Yen, Hope (Associated Press). 2012a. "Whites No Longer a Majority in US by 2043, Census Bureau Projects." *Pittsburgh Tribune Review* (December 12).

———. 2012b. "Census: Whites in Minority by 2043." *Pantagraph* (Bloomington, IL) (December 13).

———. 2012c. "Census: Whites No Longer a Majority in US by 2043." *Bismarck Tribune* (December 13).

———. 2012d. "Minorities Projected to Be Majority by 2043." *Charleston* (WV) *Daily Mail* (December 13, 2012).

Yoshinaga, Kendra. 2016. "Babies of Color Are Now the Majority, Census Says." National Public Radio (July 1).

Zhang, Charles, and John Logan. 2016. "Global Neighborhoods: Beyond the Multiethnic Metropolis." *Demography* 53: 1933–53.

Zhang, Xing, and Sharon Sassler. 2019. "*The Age of Independence*, Revisited: Parents and Interracial Union Formation across the Life Course." *Sociological Forum* 34: 361–85.

Zhou, Min, and Roberto Gonzales. 2019. "Divergent Destinies: Children of Immigrants Growing Up in the United States." *Annual Review of Sociology* 45: 383–99.

Zolberg, Aristide. 2006. *A Nation by Design: Immigration Policy in the Fashioning of America*. Cambridge, MA: Harvard University Press.

Zolberg, Aristide, and Long Litt Woon. 1999. "Why Islam Is Like Spanish: Cultural Incorporation in Europe and the United States." *Politics and Society* 27: 5–38.

Zucman, Gabriel. 2019. "Global Wealth Inequality." Working Paper 25462. Cambridge, MA: National Bureau of Economic Research (January).

Zuñiga, Victor, and Ruben Hernández-León. 2006. *New Destinations: Mexican Immigration in the United States.* New York: Russell Sage Foundation.

Zweigenhaft, Richard, and G. William Domhoff. 2018. *Diversity in the Power Elite: Ironies and Unfulfilled Promises.* Lanham, MD: Rowman & Littlefield.

INDEX

Note: Page numbers followed by "f" or "t" refer to figures and tables, respectively.

A NOTE ON THE TYPE

This book has been composed in Adobe Text and Gotham.
Adobe Text, designed by Robert Slimbach for Adobe,
bridges the gap between fifteenth- and sixteenth-century
calligraphic and eighteenth-century Modern styles.
Gotham, inspired by New York street signs, was designed
by Tobias Frere-Jones for Hoefler & Co.